ARTHURIAN STUDIES LII

KING ARTHUR IN MUSIC

ARTHURIAN STUDIES

ISSN 0261–9814

Previously published volumes in the series
are listed at the back of this book

KING ARTHUR IN MUSIC

Edited by Richard Barber

D. S. BREWER

First published 2002
D. S. Brewer, Cambridge

ISBN 0 85991 767 3

'Ernest Chausson's *Le Roi Arthur*', by Tony Hunt
was first published in *Arthurian Literature* IV,
1984, 127–54, and is reprinted here with corrections.

The music examples in Robert Adlington's essay
' "*Good lodging*": *Harrison Birtwistle's Reception of*
Sir Gawain and the Green Knight'
are © Copyright 1990 by Universal Edition (London) Ltd.,
London. Reproduced by permission.

D. S. Brewer is an imprint of Boydell & Brewer Ltd
PO Box 9, Woodbridge, Suffolk IP12 3DF, UK
and of Boydell & Brewer Inc.
PO Box 41026, Rochester, NY 14604–4126, USA
website: www.boydell.co.uk

A catalogue record for this book is available
from the British Library

Library of Congress Cataloging-in-Publication Data
King Arthur in music / edited by Richard Barber. – 1st ed.
    p. cm. – (Arthurian studies)
Includes bibliographical references and index.
    ISBN 0–85991–767–3 (hardback : alk. paper)
1. Arthur, King – Songs and music – History and criticism. 2. Music and
literature. I. Barber, Richard W. II. Series.
    ML3849 .K55 2003
    781.5'9 – dc21   2002012567

This publication is printed on acid-free paper

Typeset by Joshua Associates Ltd, Oxford
Printed in Great Britain by
Antony Rowe Ltd, Chippenham, Wiltshire

Contents

Notes on Contributors   vii

Introduction   1
  Richard Barber

Dryden and Purcell's *King Arthur*: Legend and Politics on the Restoration   9
Stage
  Robert Shay

Wagner *Tristan und Isolde* and *Parsifal*   23
  Derek Watson

Parry's *Guenever*: Trauma and Catharsis   35
  Jeremy Dibble

King Arthur and the Wagner Cult in Spain: Isaac Albéniz's Opera *Merlin*   51
  Walter A. Clark

Ernest Chausson's *Le Roi Arthus*   61
  Tony Hunt

Rutland Boughton's Arthurian Cycle   91
  Michael Hurd

An Exotic Tristan in Boston: the First Performance of Messiaen's   105
Turangalîla-Symphonie
  Nigel Simeone

'Good lodging': Harrison Birtwistle's Reception of *Sir Gawain and the*   127
Green Knight
  Robert Adlington

King Arthur in Popular Musical Theatre and Film   145
  William A. Everett

A Listing of Arthurian Music   161
  Jerome V. Reel

Index   189

Notes on contributors

Robert Adlington is Lecturer in Music at the University of Nottingham. He has written extensively on contemporary music in *The Musical Times* and *Tempo*, and his monograph on Harrison Birtwistle was published by Cambridge University Press in 2000. A study of Louis Andriessen's *De Staat* is to be published by Ashgate in 2004.

Walter Aaron Clark is a professor of musicology at the University of Kansas. He is the author of *Isaac Albeniz: A Guide to Research* (Garland, 1998), *Isaac Albeniz: Portrait of a Romantic* (Oxford, 1999/2002), and the editor of *From Tejano to Tango: Latin American Popular Music* (Routledge, 2002).

Jeremy Dibble is Reader in Music at the University of Durham. His interests in British music of the Victorian, Edwardian and Georgian eras are reflected by his two largescale studies of Hubert Parry and Charles Villiers Stanford for Oxford University Press. He has plans for a book on the work of John Stainer and a critical edition of Parry's Piano Trios to add to that of Parry's Violin Sonatas prepared for *Musica Britannica*.

William A. Everett teaches music history and musicology at University of Missouri–Kansas City Conservatory of Music. HIs principal areas of research include the American musical theatre and national identity in music. He is coeditor of and contributor to the *Cambridge Companion to the Musical*. His publications have appeared in *American Music*, *Opera Quarterly*, *International Review of the Aesthetics and Sociology of Music* and elsewhere.

Tony Hunt is Lecturer in Medieval French Literature at Oxford, and a Fellow of St Peter's College. His article combines two of his particular enthusiasms, Arthurian literature, on which he has published numerous items, and opera. His books include editions of Anglo-Norman texts and studies of Anglo-Norman medicine and teaching methods.

Michael Hurd was born in Gloucester (1928), read music at Oxford University, and studied composition with Sir Lennox Berkeley. A successful freelance composer, his music is published exclusively by Novello & Company. He is an authority on British music and has written pioneer biographies of Rutland Boughton and Ivor Gurney.

Jerome V. Reel, Jr. is Senior Vice Provost and Dean of Undergraduate Studies at Clemson University in South Carolina, USA. His Ph.D. is from Emory University in medieval British history. He has published an index to British lives and in institutional and music history. His bibliography of music inspired by Arthurian legends has been a major concern for the past ten years.

Robert Shay is Academic Dean and a member of the faculty at the Longy School of Music in Cambridge, Massachusetts. He is coauthor with Robert Thompson of *Purcell Manuscripts* (Cambridge, 2000), which received the Music Library Association's Vincent Duckles Award, has published several articles and reviews on the music of Restoration England.

Derek Watson, a freelance musician and writer living in the Scottish Borders, is the author of a biography of Richard Wagner, volumes on Liszt and Bruckner in the 'Master Musicians' series and has broadcast, lectured widely and written many articles on opera. He is currently writing a biography of Meyerbeer.

Introduction

RICHARD BARBER

The influence of the Arthurian legends on music is very different from its place in the visual arts. Arthurian art is plentiful in the middle ages, which, given that it is an ideal subject for lavishly illuminated manuscripts, is hardly surprising. By contrast, Arthurian music is marginal and obscure until the nineteenth century, when the roles are reversed and the greatest masterpieces are musical rather than visual.

As a result, the inspiration which composers have drawn from the story of Arthur has been relatively little studied, and this may fairly claim to be the first book devoted exclusively to the Arthurian legends in music.[1] It does not pretend to offer a comprehensive coverage, but rather looks at the major works in the field. This introduction aims to provide a context for the essays which follow, and to survey, if briefly, the history of Arthurian music.

The most striking aspect of the subject is its domination by the theme of Tristan and Iseult; from troubadour lyrics to Messiaen, this is the story above all others to which composers have been attracted. As archetypes of the star-crossed lovers, they afford the opportunity to write love-music on the most intimate or the grandest scale. The sparse Arthurian references in medieval music are largely centred on Tristan, beginning with the troubadours. The Provençal lyrics name Tristan and Isolde relatively frequently, though rarely together; but there are no poems which actually take their tragic story as the main theme. The poets use them as examples of love's pangs and sufferings. For songs which actually narrate Tristan's adventures, we have to look to the ballads of Italy and Scandinavia in the fourteenth and fifteenth centuries. More striking is the fourteenth century instrumental piece from Italy, the *Lamento di Tristano*, which is probably the first surviving composition to be inspired by the legends rather than simply setting verses narrating the story.

In the late fifteenth century, a number of songs survive within the text of the *Prose Tristan*, partly because the subject was an admirable context for such lyrics, and partly because Tristan, from his earliest appearance in romance in the twelfth century, was famous as a harpist. A late fifteenth century manuscript of the *Prose Tristan*, produced in England and once the property of Jacques, duc de Nemours, who may have commissioned it, goes one stage further, and becomes a kind of

---

[1] The only previous general survey that I have found is by Barry J. Ward in *The New Arthurian Encyclopedia*, ed. Norris J. Lacy (Chicago and London, 1991), pp. 334–9.

multi-media presentation of the story, complete with pictures and music: musical settings, 'at once simple and refined', of a number of songs are embedded in the text.[2] Three of the songs also appear with different music in a Parisian manuscript of the *Prose Tristan* from the late thirteenth century, so there was evidently a tradition of providing performing material of this kind within the romances.[3]

The Arthurian stories largely disappeared from view after the early printings of the romances between 1477 and 1527, but the Tristan theme survives in the work of Hans Sachs, the original of Wagner's chararacter in *Die Meistersinger von Nürnberg*. He was a prolific writer and composer, and besides a lengthy tragedy based on the story, he wrote half a dozen *meisterlieder* on episodes from the romance of Tristan. Wagner alludes to Sachs' interest in the story in *Die Meistersinger*; when it is suggested that Sachs himself – who is portrayed as a middle-aged widower – should compete in the song contest for Eva's hand, he turns down the idea, replying that he does not wish to share King Mark's fate. The real Sachs wrote so copiously that we cannot tell whether the songs, a mere handful against the nearly five thousand that he wrote in all, represent a continuing public interest in the legend or are simply a personal enthusiasm.

It is only at the end of the seventeenth century that we come to the first real masterpiece of Arthurian music, Henry Purcell's semi-opera to a libretto by John Dryden, which Robert Shay discusses in the first essay in this volume. The origins of the opera lay in the claim of the Stuart kings to be the heirs of Arthur, as proposed in the anagram 'Charles James Stuart claims Arthur's seat'. The piece was in preparation at the time of the Glorious Revolution of 1688, and had to be hurriedly adapted before its première in 1691 to take account of the change of régime. If the Stuart dynasty had continued in power, it is possible that other such Arthurian stage-pieces might have appeared, but the association with the fallen royal house deterred further explorations. In any case, *King Arthur* was medieval in name only, as were the Merlin-based musical plays of the early eighteenth century, in which Merlin was simply a common or garden wizard with only the faintest overtones of his legendary past.

It was only with the revival of scholarly interest in medieval literature that the Arthurian legends once more came to public attention. Just as the Pre-Raphaelite artists enthused over Malory's *Le Morte Darthur*, so German readers discovered their medieval poets, Gottfried von Strassburg and Wolfram von Eschenbach. Among those readers was Richard Wagner, who based two of his major operas on their work; Derek Watson discusses his medieval enthusiasms in his essay on *Tristan* and *Parsifal*. Wagner's explorations of medieval romance produced first *Tannhäuser*, based on the tales woven around the real thirteenth century poet of that name, and then the semi-Arthurian *Lohengrin*. In this Parzival's son Lohengrin is sent from the kingdom of the Grail to the rescue of the heiress of Brabant; he marries her on condition that she never asks his name, and her tragedy is that she cannot resist putting the question to him. Wagner's original was a thirteenth century romance, probably written in honour of the counts of

---

[2] It is now Österreichisches Nationalbibliothek, Vienna, MS 2542. See Tatiana Fotitch and Ruth Steiner, *Les lais du Roman de Tristan en prose d'après le manuscrit de Vienne 2542*, Münchener Romanistische Arbeiten XXXVIII (Munich, 1974). The quotation is on p. 137.

[3] *Ibid.*, 137. The manuscript is Bibliothèque Nationale, MS Fr. 776.

Brabant. This whetted his appetite for medieval themes, and he then turned to Gottfried von Strassburg; as always, he wrote the libretto for *Tristan und Isolde* himself. Although *Tristan* and *Parsifal* were completed twenty-three years apart, the two subjects were clearly connected in Wagner's mind, and many of the ideas for *Parsifal* date from the period of the composition of *Tristan*. *Tristan* nearly contained a highly original scene in the third act, in which Parsifal, in quest of the Grail, was to come to the castle where Tristan lay on his sickbed.

Wagner's immense influence on music, particularly opera, in the late nineteenth century makes it no surprise that the next three Arthurian operas that we encounter are all heavily indebted to him, but with very different results. Enthusiasm for Wagner's music was not confined to Germany; there were ardent Wagnerites in England, Spain and France, and the next three essays explore the results of this vogue. Hubert Parry heard the second complete performance of *Der Ring des Nibelungen* and, as Jeremy Dibble tells us, the effect was 'cataclysmic'. His attempt at an Arthurian opera on Wagnerian lines, *Guenever*, was bedevilled by the the breakdown of relations between composer and librettist. Wagner was regarded with deep suspicion by large sections of the musical establishment, and Carl Rosa, whose opera company dominated the London scene, rejected Parry's work. As a result it was never fully scored, though a concert version of Guenever's soliloquy from Act I was edited for a BBC performance in 1995. This was probably the high point of the score; since even the libretto has disappeared, the details of the plot only survive in outline.

If Parry fell out with his librettist, the opposite was true of Isaac Albéniz and Francis Burdett Money-Coutts. Money-Coutts had inherited a fortune from his family s ownership of Coutts Bank, and spent lavishly on his ambition to create a cycle of national operas, for which he was to be librettist. Parry was free to criticise the poor quality of his librettist's work; Albéniz, whom Money-Coutts supported for the best part of a decade while he composed *Merlin*, was in no such position to object, though there is no evidence that he was dissatisfied with his material. Perhaps a native English speaker would have been less happy with what can only be described as a gloriously banal text. *Merlin* was not performed in the composer's lifetime, and there was only a single amateur staging in 1950 before the enthusiasm of the Spanish conductor José Eusebio and the tenor Placido Domingo brought about a recording in 1998, which reveals a work of striking originality. Walter Clark explores the strange story of this neglected masterpiece; even if it is unlikely to enter the standard repertory, it is a rewarding and surprising musical experience.

Money-Coutts was much concerned when in 1895 the most spectacular of a number of attempts to stage the tragedy of Arthur was mounted at the Lyceum by Henry Irving; his company was at the height of its success. The author of the blank verse drama *King Arthur* was J. Comyns Carr, better known as a critic than as a writer, and Money-Coutts claimed that Comyns Carr had adopted some of his ideas for the treatment of the legend. Comyns Carr's play is not much of an improvement on Money-Coutts' libretto in literary terms; but Henry Irvine himself played Arthur, while Ellen Terry was Guinevere, and the sets were designed by Edward Burne-Jones. The music was by Sir Arthur Sullivan; the score was intended to provide not merely an overture, interludes and choruses, but also a background to some of the scenes. In effect it was nearer to a film score than to the traditional form of theatre music. The purely musical episodes were mostly choral, and the concert suite which was arranged by Sullivan's secretary after his death relies largely on these. It is sound, workmanlike stuff, with a rather foursquare feel to it, and none of the lightness of touch of the Savoy operettas – which would in any case have been inappropriate to the atmosphere of solemn grandeur to which the occasion aspired.

One of the few Arthurian operas to reach the stage at the turn of the nineteenth century was Ernest Chausson's *Le roi Arthus*, the subject of Tony Hunt's essay. *Le roi Artus* was staged at the Théâtre de la Monnaie in Brussels in 1903, four years after the composer's untimely death in a bicycling accident. Chausson had already written the striking tone-poem *Viviane*, on Merlin's love for Nimue, in 1882, before embarking on the opera three years later. He wrote the libretto himself, with considerable literary skill; the music is an impressive piece in post-Wagnerian style, and the plot owes something to *Tristan*. Again, a recent recording by Armin Jordan has made it possible to appreciate the power of this music, which would certainly stand a modern revival.

Arthurian tone-poems such as *Viviane* are surprisingly rare; indeed, the only major English composer to write a piece in this form was Arnold Bax, and even that is more a personal response to an Arthurian site than an evocation of part of the legend. Bax himself describes the subject of *Tintagel*, written in October 1917, vividly:

> Though detailing no definite programme, this work is intended to evoke a tone-picture of the castle-crowned cliff of Tintagel, and more particularly the wide distances of the Atlantic as seen from the cliffs of Cornwall on a sunny but not windless summer day. In the middle section of the piece it may be imagined that with the increasing tumult of the sea arise memories of the historical associations of the place, especially those connected with King Arthur, King Mark, and Tristram and Iseult.[4]

Tintagel was written at a time of emotional crisis for the composer, as he realised that he wanted to leave his wife for the pianist Harriet Cohen, with whom he had visited Cornwall during the summer of 1917. There is an echo of *Tristan* in the concluding section of the work which reflects these tensions. As a whole, it is a skilful piece of nature-painting, more akin to a Romantic watercolour of the castle than to the literary versions of the legend.

A full-scale Arthurian work from the pen of Edward Elgar would have been treasure indeed; he showed that he could create a musical picture of the medieval past in his overture *Froissart*, but his Arthurian music was for the theatre, and for restricted forces. Although his friend Laurence Binyon's *Arthur* was staged with a large cast at the Old Vic in 1923, the musical resources were little more than a chamber ensemble: three woodwind, two trombones, percussion, harp, strings and piano. The music served as interludes between the eight scenes, and was later reworked as a suite. The play deals with the final book of *Le Morte Darthur*, and centres on Lancelot, Elaine, Guinevere and Arthur. Elgar

---

[4] This note prefaces the printed editions of the score.

had written little since the death of his wife in 1920, and wrote to Binyon saying that he feared 'my music has vanished . . . it may be that I can furnish (quite inadequately) music for "Arthur" '.[5] The score reflects this hesitant mood, but is nonetheless vintage, if modest, Elgar, with a fine romantic touch in the portrayal of 'Elaine Asleep' in the second movement. The final vision of Arthur's departure for Avalon, which Elgar envisaged (in a letter to Binyon after the performances) as 'Arthur and *all* his train to march mistily past',[6] is set to the sound of tolling bells.

While Binyon's play was being performed to modest critical acclaim, a very different work was taking London by storm. Rutland Boughton's work was inspired by a curious mixture of socialist ideals in the vein of William Morris combined with an enthusiasm for Wagner. He had established a festival at Glastonbury in 1914, which drew on the contemporary vogue for all things Celtic – whether in art or in literature – and had written an opera using a libretto drawn from Irish myth. Despite the onset of war, an amateur production of *The Immortal Hour*, was organised and mounted in three weeks; it was an instant success. After the war, it was performed in Birmingham, finally reaching London in the autumn of 1922 with the young Gwen ffrangcon-Davies in the title role. It ran for 316 performances in 1922–3, and therefore overlapped with the production of *King Arthur*. The Glastonbury connection suggests that Boughton might have had interests in the Arthurian field, and he had already found the source for a potential Arthurian cycle on the grandest scale. However, his first Arthurian work was based on Thomas Hardy's play about Iseult; *The Queen of Cornwall* was produced at Glastonbury in 1924. The story of the composition of the larger cycle is told by Michael Hurd, who draws on his extensive knowledge of Boughton's life and work to explain why this apparently appealing idea, by a composer with a popular success to his name, is unlikely to appear on the stage.

If Boughton and Elgar, in very different ways, were sympathetic to the Arthurian story even when presented with relatively weak librettos, Benjamin Britten was much more critical. It was not that, despite his association with the avant-garde poets of the 1930s, he disliked Malory, whom he appears to have read: his literary taste was too discriminating to suffer fools gladly. His first commission for a score for a radio feature from the BBC, however, had relatively little literary merit. Bax had rejected the commission – though on what grounds is not clear – and the BBC turned to the younger composer instead. *King Arthur* was billed as a pageant, written by D.G. Bridson, and Britten initially noted that it was 'a good size job anyhow if not exactly to my taste'.[7] Later, composing the music of Galahad, he reiterated his discomfort: 'can't do much with that, tho' – subject doesn't interest me'. Even at the end, when the piece was well received, he still felt the same about it, calling his own music 'facile' and the script 'a pale pastiche of Malory'. Britten was almost certainly hyper-sensitive about the

---

[5] Edward Elgar, *Letters of a Lifetime*, ed. Jerrold Northrop Moore (Oxford, 1990), p. 370.

[6] *Ibid.* p. 371.

[7] The quotations from the diaries of Benjamin Britten are © copyright the Trustees of the Britten–Pears Foundation and may not be further reproduced without the written permission of the Trustees.

occasion, and his expression of dissatisfaction is belied by the fact that he drew on the music for *A Ballad of Heroes*, and for one of the movements of his Piano Concerto. A concert suite was adapted from the score by Paul Hindmarsh, and performed at Aldeburgh in 1995; as might be expected, it was not one of Britten's more memorable pieces.

In 1938, just as Britten left for Canada, he accepted another BBC commission, this time for a score to accompany the serialised version of T.H. White's *The Sword in the Stone*. This is of course the comic section of White's book, with a strong element of parody; and Britten echoes this in his music. He was a superb parodist – witness the rustics' play in *A Midsummer Night's Dream* – and the obvious target was Wagner, given his dominant position in music connected with Arthur. Some of the parody is actually based on direct quotation: the motif for the sword is that for Nothung, Siegfried's sword in the Ring cycle, and echoes of *Das Rheingold* appear in the music for Merlin. This is light-hearted music, matching the mood of T.H. White's book, and Britten entered into the spirit of the occasion, providing 'a highly amusing set of performing instructions' when he delivered the score.[8] Again, it was adapted by Oliver Knussen and Colin Matthews as a concert suite and performed at Aldeburgh in 1983.[9]

The Swiss composer Frank Martin was deeply interested by medieval literature; perhaps his best-known work on a medieval theme was a setting of six monologues from the morality play *Jedermann* (*Everyman*), which, despite a powerful recording by Dietrich Fischer-Dieskau, is relatively little known. His treatment of the legend of Tristan, *Le vin herbé* (*The spiced wine*), completed in 1941, goes back to the roots of the legend. In 1900, the French scholar Joseph Bédier recreated the early versions of the legend, none of which are complete, in a modern retelling which draws on both the Anglo-Norman poems by Béroul and Thomas and those by the German writers Eilhart von Oberge and Gottfried von Strassburg. It is a simple and powerful text, strikingly translated into English by Hilaire Belloc in 1904.

Martin set first of all four scenes (*tableaux*) which correspond to the first part of the poem, and later added a prologue, two longer parts (of twelve scenes) and an epilogue, which cover the entire romance. The work was commissioned by a madrigal ensemble, and the chorus tells most of the story, with parts for nine main soloists. Martin sets Bédier's text for each scene unchanged, so that the soloists take up the passages which are in direct speech in the original. He does however choose the great monologues in which the lovers and Mark express their feelings, particularly in the scene in the forest of Morois, where each of them has an extended recitative in which they meditate on their fate.

The musical language is spare but elegant, with a wide range of influences, from Bach to chromaticism to 12-tone rows; the instruments (strings and piano) act entirely as an accompaniment, and Martin specified that their role should be like the scenery in a play. The music is often highly pictorial: the visual elements of the drama are recreated in often minute detail: we hear Tristan's steps as he

---

[8] Philip Reed: programme notes for *The Sword in the Stone, Forty-third Aldeburgh Festival of Music and the Arts, 8–24 June 1990*, pp. 88–89.
[9] It was revived in 1990.

returns from the hunt, the flash of gold in Iseult's hair, the beating of the lovers' hearts in their first embrace. Martin is not afraid of simple effects: Iseult's declaration of love is a simple unaccompanied phrase, where one might expect a crescendo. Equally, the result has, despite its use of entirely modern resources, something of the feeling of a performance by minstrels, a direct and challenging presentation of the text. It was presented as an opera at the Salzburg Festival in 1948, but it is essentially a work for the concert hall, an original and rewarding, if little-known, addition to the repertory of Arthurian music, which co-exists without difficulty beside Wagner's towering presentation of the same story.

The most important Arthurian work by an English composer since Purcell's *King Arthur* is Harrison Birtwistle's *Sir Gawain and the Green Knight*, first performed at the Royal Opera House, Covent Garden, in 1991, and revised in 1994. Robert Adlington points out the many attractions of the medieval poem for Birtwistle, from its elaborate structure and metre to its mythical background. Conceived on an ambitious scale, the production was notable not only for the music, but also for the brilliant technical effects which allowed the decapitated head of the Green Knight to continue to sing after Gawain had struck the blow. The original version had an ambitious interlude representing the passing of the year's interval between the first challenge and Gawain's departure in search of the return blow. 'The Turning of the Seasons' was musically and stylistically of great interest, but in the theatre it failed, running to forty minutes of virtually static staging at the end of the first act. This section was much shortened in the revision; but there is an underlying problem in staging a work as tightly integrated as *Sir Gawain and the Green Knight*, whose structures are essentially non-dramatic, a tale told rather than a story enacted. Birtwistle, apart from this, succeeded remarkably well, thanks to a highly intelligent and polished libretto by David Harsent.

Not all Arthurian music aspires to the high seriousness of *Sir Gawain and the Green Knight*. William Everitt explores Arthur's adventures in the world of film and musicals: it is notable that film makers have tended to prefer comedy to tragedy, and have chosen Mark Twain or T.H. White in preference to Malory. Both *A Connecticut Yankee at King Arthur's Court* and *The Once and Future King* have appeared on both stage and screen. The shape of *Camelot*, the Lerner and Loewe musical based on the latter book, was influenced by the fact that Disney held the film rights in *The Sword in the Stone*: in effect, *Camelot* begins where *The Sword in the Stone* leaves off. It was hugely successful both as musical and as film; but it had a more lasting legacy. It was Lerner's line, 'one brief shining moment that was known as Camelot', that became the image of the brief presidency of John F. Kennedy, and created a new form of the Arthurian myth for the twentieth century.

But there is much Arthurian music still to be explored, and here we turn to Jerome V. Reel's listing of Arthurian musical items, a collection which ranges from the forgotten Merlin spectacles of eighteenth century England to the Arthurian discs of Rick Wakeman and other pop artists. If the list contains only a handful of masterpieces, discovered or perhaps undiscovered, there is evidence of the huge and vibrant influence of the Arthurian legend on music, of which the present volume can only explore a few facets.

Dryden and Purcell's King Arthur: Legend and Politics on the Restoration Stage

ROBERT SHAY

King Arthur; or, The British Worthy, written by John Dryden, with music by Henry Purcell, premiered in the spring of 1691 at London's Dorset Garden Theatre. The precise date of the first performance is unknown, but the *London Gazette* from 4 to 8 June 1691 advertised the availability of the published wordbook, suggesting that performances were recently underway.[1] Dryden had completed the text some seven years before, in all likelihood intending it to mark the twenty-fifth anniversary of the Restoration.[2] But the project was delayed when he decided to expand (probably from royal encouragement) his *Albion and Albanius* – originally planned as a sung prologue to *King Arthur* – into a three-act opera, with music by Louis Grabu, a Spaniard who had previously served as Charles II's Master of the Musick, and who was brought back to England in the winter of 1683–84 for the express purpose of composing opera.[3] *Albion* 'was often practis'd before [Charles II] at Whitehal' and was possibly read through at Windsor as early as May 1684, but Charles's death in February 1685 delayed the first public performances until June, when they failed miserably, unluckily coinciding with the Duke of Monmouth's rebellion.[4] Dryden then apparently put aside *Albion's* likely successor, *King Arthur*, with nothing of it set to music.

---

[1] [John] Dryden, *King Arthur: or, The British Worthy. A Dramatick Opera* (London: Jacob Tonson, 1691); for bibliographic discussion and an edition of the wordbook see H. Neville Davies, 'King Arthur; or, The British Worthy,' in *Henry Purcell's Operas: The Complete Texts*, ed. Michael Burden (Oxford: Oxford University Press, 2000), pp. 255–335. On the *London Gazette* advertisement see Michael Tilmouth, 'A Calendar of References to Music in Newspapers Published in London and the Provinces (1660–1719),' *Royal Musical Association Research Chronicle* 1 (1961); and Sybil Rosenfeld, 'Dramatic Advertisements in the Burney Newspapers, 1660–1700,' *Publications of the Modern Language Association* 51 (1936), p. 136.

[2] Margaret Laurie, ed., *The Works of Henry Purcell*, vol. 26, *King Arthur*, rev. edn (London: Novello, 1971), p. vii; Andrew Pinnock, 'King Arthur Expos'd: A Lesson in Anatomy,' in *Purcell Studies*, ed. Curtis Price (Cambridge: Cambridge University Press, 1995), pp. 245–6.

[3] Peter Holman, 'Louis Grabu,' in *A Biographical Dictionary of English Court Musicians, 1485–1714*, 2 vols., ed. Andrew Ashbee *et al.* (Aldershot: Ashgate, 1998), vol. I, p. 504.

[4] Quoted material is from Dryden's dedication to the published wordbook of *King Arthur*, p. [i]. On rehearsals of *Albion* see James Anderson Winn, *John Dryden and his World* (New Haven and London: Yale University Press, 1987), p. 394 and the sources cited in n. 35 on p. 608. On the premiere of *Albion and Albanius* see the contemporary account of the longtime London prompter John Downes, in his *Roscius Anglicanus*, ed. Judith Milhous and Robert D. Hume (London: Theatre Research, 1987), p. 84; and also Curtis A. Price, *Henry Purcell and the London Stage* (Cambridge: Cambridge University Press, 1984), pp. 266–7.

The circumstances behind the 1691 premiere, by comparison, seem to reflect concerns more professional (and personal) than political. Dryden's stock had fallen mightily since the accession of William and Mary. He had become both the poet laureate and a Catholic under James II, but by 1689, refusing to revert to Anglicanism, Dryden found himself displaced from the former position in favor of Thomas Shadwell, fearful for the safety of his family, and more than concerned about his professional well-being.[5] Henry Purcell's career, too, had changed considerably since William's arrival in England. Purcell effectively grew up at the court of Charles II, with its lively musical culture, and rightly viewed himself as a court composer until Charles's death. Purcell's royal activities surely waned during James's reign, but the more significant changes occurred under William, whose artistic views were grounded in Calvinist austerity. Purcell, in a real sense, had to reinvent himself in the late 1680s as a freelance musician.[6]

Meanwhile, the London theatre establishment – chiefly Thomas Betterton, the key figure in the production of English musical theatre throughout the Restoration period – was ready to try opera once again, having mounted no such works since *Albion and Albanius*. First came *The Prophetess; or, The History of Dioclesian*, premiering in late May 1690. The text was Betterton's adaptation of the play by John Fletcher and Philip Massinger, and the music was Purcell's. Unlike *Albion*, the work was not sung throughout but was in the form of a 'semiopera' or, as Dryden described the genre, 'dramatick opera,' with vocal and instrumental music interspersed amidst spoken passages.[7] John Downes reported that *Dioclesian* (as it is usually called) was 'set out with Coastly Scenes, Machines and Cloaths: The Vocal and Instrumental Musick, done by Mr. *Purcel*; and Dances by Mr. *Priest*; it gratify'd the Expectation of Court and City; and got the Author great Reputation.'[8] It was, in short, a hit, and not least because of the inspired music. Purcell further consolidated his reputation as a theatre composer by contributing songs and instrumental music to several more plays before the end of the year. Dryden had at least a small hand in *Dioclesian* (a work with close ties to *Albion*), penning the prologue (critical of William's foreign

---

[5] Bibliographical study of the first edition of the *King Arthur* wordbook has yielded some intriguing biographical information about Dryden; see Fredson Bowers, 'Dryden as Laureate: The Cancel Leaf in *King Arthur*,' *Times Literary Supplement* (10 April 1953); cited and discussed in Andrew Pinnock, ' "From Rosy Bowers": Coming to Purcell the Bibliographical Way,' in *Henry Purcell's Operas: The Complete Texts*, ed. Michael Burden (Oxford: Oxford University Press, 2000), pp. 62–5. See also Winn, *Dryden and his World*, p. 434 and *passim*.

[6] On Purcell's later career see Roger Savage, 'The Theatre Music,' in *The Purcell Companion*, ed. Michael Burden (London: Faber and Faber, 1994), pp. 318–23; and Robert Shay and Robert Thompson, *Purcell Manuscripts: The Principal Musical Sources* (Cambridge: Cambridge University Press, 2000), pp. 5–7.

[7] The term 'dramatick opera' was first used by Dryden on the title page of the *King Arthur* wordbook; 'semiopera' also comes from a contemporary observer, Roger North: 'Mr. Betterton . . . contrived a sort of plays, which were called operas but had bin more properly styled semioperas, for they consisted of half musick, and half drama; the cheif of these were Circe, The Fayery Queen, Dioclesian and King Arthur' (*Roger North's The Musicall Grammarian 1728*, ed. Mary Chan and Jamie C. Kassler [Cambridge: Cambridge University Press, 1990], p. 266).

[8] Downes, *Roscius Anglicanus*, ed. Milhous and Hume, p. 89. 'Mr. *Priest*' refers to Josias Priest, schoolmaster and the leading choreographer of the period, who created the dances for *King Arthur*.

wars and banned after opening night) and assisting Purcell with or possibly ghostwriting the preface to the published score.[9] Later in 1690, when the wordbook for Dryden's *Amphitryon* appeared (one of the plays for which Purcell provided music), Dryden was calling Purcell 'an *English-man*, equal with the best abroad,' quite a change from his remarks about Grabu in the preface to *Albion*: 'When any of our Country-men excel him, I shall be glad, for the sake of old *England*, to be shown my error.'[10] The old poet, it seems, now needed the young composer, and the two great figures of the age must have discovered the mutual benefits of collaboration. Dryden thus dusted off *King Arthur*, and he and Purcell prepared for a production.

Dramatick Opera in England

It would be difficult to approach a work like *King Arthur* – where, for example, none of the principal characters sing – without understanding something of the history and conventions (however unfocused) of dramatick opera in England. The sentiment expressed in *The Gentleman's Journal* from January 1692 is not an uncommon one: 'Other Nations bestow the name Opera only on such Plays whereof every word is sung . . . experience hath taught us that our English genius will not rellish that perpetual Singing.'[11] Thus the development of English opera during the last three decades of the seventeenth century stood largely on the idea that plays could be adapted and successfully augmented with songs, dances, and especially large, self-contained musical episodes or masques, with singing and dancing characters brought into the action, if necessary through some dramatic contrivance. Four works from the 1670s – *Macbeth* (1673), *The Tempest* (1674), *Psyche* (1675), and *Circe* (1677)[12] – comprise the early history of dramatick opera, and the composer Matthew Locke, who had a hand in the music for three of them, quickly recognized the significance of the achievement, publishing the music from *Psyche* as *The English Opera*.[13] A detour on the road to establishing dramatick opera during this time came in the 1680s, with the creation of a trio of all-sung works – *Venus and Adonis*, *Dido and Aeneas*, and *Albion and Albanius*[14] – probably all instigated by the Caroline court

---

[9] Winn, *Dryden and his World*, pp. 442–4; Price, *Purcell and the London Stage*, pp. 264–5.
[10] Earl Minor et al., eds., *The Works of John Dryden*, vol. 15, *Plays: Albion and Albanius, Don Sebastian, Amphitryon* (Berkeley: University of California Press, 1976), pp. 8 and 225.
[11] Cited in Richard Luckett, 'Exotick but Rational Entertainments: The English Dramatick Operas,' in *English Drama: Forms and Development*, ed. Marie Axton and Raymond Williams (Cambridge: Cambridge University Press, 1977), p. 133.
[12] The Shakespearean adaptations have a somewhat complex history: the 1673 *Macbeth* was given in William Davenant's version (of 1663–4) with new music by Locke; *The Tempest* of 1674, with music by Locke, Pelham Humfrey, and others, was based on the version by Davenant and Dryden, and further reconfigured as a dramatick opera in 1674 by Shadwell. *Psyche* was newly written in 1675, by Shadwell, with music by Locke and G.B. Draghi, as was *Circe* in 1677, by Charles Davenant, with music by John Banister. On these works see Price, *Purcell and the London Stage*, pp. 97–8, 203–4, 231–3, 296–7; and Peter Holman, *Four and Twenty Fiddlers: The Violin at the English Court, 1540–1690* (Oxford: Oxford University Press, 1993; rpt, 1995), pp. 334–55.
[13] *The English Opera; or the Vocal Musick in Psyche* (London: T. Ratcliff and N. Thompson, 1675).
[14] *Venus and Adonis*, John Blow's setting of an anonymous libretto, was first performed at court

in an attempt to establish tragic opera in England modeled more or less on the French *tragédie lyrique*.[15] *Dioclesian*, in 1690, thus represented a revival of the earlier tradition, with Betterton serving as he did in the 1670s as producer or impresario, and Purcell – too young to be involved in the works of the '70s – now enjoying something of a monopoly, composing the music for all of the dramatick operas from 1690 until his death in 1695.[16]

How does dramatick opera work? It would be difficult to explain the genre in terms of rigid musical conventions, since the musical landscape is determined by the play, and differences among the various examples significantly outweigh similarities. One overriding characteristic of dramatick opera is that the principal characters do not sing and the singing characters are auxiliary, brought in to entertain or divert, all of this requiring essentially two casts, one dramatic and one musical. The 1675 *Psyche* provides an exception in that Venus 'sings as often as she speaks, and the musical episodes do almost as much to advance the plot as the spoken dialogue.'[17] A further exception comes from *King Arthur* itself, where in Act II Philidel and Grimbald, described as 'Airy' and 'Earthy' spirits respectively,[18] alternate between speech and song. Grimbald here seeks to confuse Arthur and the Britons, offering to lead them to Oswald and the Saxons but intending to take them into a bog where they will 'fall, a furlong sinking' (p. 12); the honorable Philidel finally convinces Arthur that Grimbald is indeed a 'Malicious Fiend' (p. 12). Dryden makes clear to the listeners that this is not spoken dialogue rendered in music but rather that the characters are breaking into song: Grimbald leaves no doubt, declaring before his first solo notes that 'I had Voice in heav'n, ere Sulph'rous Steams Had damp'd it to a hoarseness; but I'll try' (p. 12); and the musical context further allows Purcell to create an echo chorus, sung by Grimbald's and Philidel's attending spirits, enhancing the confusion foisted upon Arthur at this moment. These exceptions help to underscore a general premise in dramatick opera that the spoken and musical realms remain separate, and that music should be heard by the listeners *as music*, not – as in a great deal of all-sung opera – as speech guised in musical notes.

While there is no firm template into which all dramatick operas fit, one that might explain the types and the sequencing of musical numbers required, and how they should interrelate with the text, a loose scheme outlining the 'Music (possibly) required in a dramatick opera' has been hazarded by Michael

in about 1682 and at Josias Priest's School for Young Gentlewomen in 1684; see Richard Luckett, 'A New Source for *Venus and Adonis*,' *Musical Times* 130 (1989), pp. 76–80. The first known performance of *Dido and Aeneas*, Purcell's setting of a libretto by Nahum Tate, took place in 1689, also at Priest's School, but recent scholarship has argued for earlier, court origins; see Bruce Wood and Andrew Pinnock, ' "Unscarred by Turning Times"?: The Dating of Purcell's *Dido and Aeneas*,' *Early Music* 20 (1992), pp. 372–90, and subsequent articles and communications by Martin Adams, Curtis Price, Andrew Walkling, and Wood and Pinnock in various issues of *Early Music*, 1993–5.

[15] Peter Holman cautions that 'as so often in English music, foreign models seem to have influenced the planning of these operas rather than their musical style'; see his *Henry Purcell* (Oxford: Oxford University Press, 1994), p. 199.

[16] Michael Burden, 'Aspects of Purcell's Operas,' in *Henry Purcell's Operas: The Complete Texts*, ed. Burden (Oxford: Oxford University Press, 2000), p. 5.

[17] Price, *Purcell and the London Stage*, p. 5.

[18] *King Arthur* (1691 wordbook), p. [viii]. Hereinafter textual references to the opera will be given in the main text with page numbers referring to the original wordbook.

Burden.[19] This list depicts a set of emerging practices – act tunes to close each of the five acts, masques at the end of acts two and five, and act songs in each act – derived in part from 'the basic layout of act or "framing" music found in spoken plays.'[20] Burden's scheme intentionally mirrors the actual layout of *Dioclesian*, and he is quick to point out that there is a great deal of variance from work to work. Probably the most consistent (and consciously operatic) feature of the dramatick operas is the use of masques (or things loosely like masques), usually placed at the ends of acts, the presence of a chorus and often dancers resembling the *divertissements* found in the acts of contemporaneous French operas. *The Fairy Queen*, Purcell's next dramatick opera after *King Arthur*, is somewhat exceptional in that each of its Acts II–V ends with a full-blown masque. In *King Arthur*, by contrast, each act contains masque-like elements, with the use of chorus in all five acts and the use of dance in Acts II–V. This all suggests that the creators of dramatick operas drew upon a related set of resources rather than seeking to forge rigid conventions. This is how Dryden himself seems to describe the then in-progress *King Arthur* to his publisher Jacob Tonson, in a letter from August 1684:

> [A] Play, Of the Nature of the *Tempest*; which is, a Tragedy mix'd with *Opera*; or a *Drama* Written in blank verse, adorn'd with Scenes, Machines, Songs and Dances: So that the Fable of it is all spoken and acted by the best of the Comedians; the other part of the entertainment to be perform'd by the . . . Singers and Dancers.[21]

Text and Allegory

Dryden's selection of Arthur as subject reflects the period of its original conception – the anticipated celebration of Charles II's twenty-five years on the throne – and he understood that Arthur provided him with the leeway to spin a good patriotic yarn: writing in 1693, the old poet noted that the subject 'of King Arthur, Conquering the *Saxons* . . . being farther distant in Time, [gave] the greater scope to my Invention.'[22] He provided only a few other clues as to his sources in the preface to the 1691 wordbook: 'When I wrote it, seven Years ago, I employ'd some reading about it, to inform my self out of *Beda*, *Bochartus*, and other Authors, concerning the Rites and Customs of the Heathen Saxons.'[23] Dryden probably did scour the usual historical and contemporary sources in creating *King Arthur*, but Andrew Pinnock's recent assessment, cued by Dryden himself, is difficult to

[19] Burden, 'Aspects of Purcell's Operas,' p. 17.
[20] *Ibid.*, p. 16, on issues of genre see also Luckett, 'Exotick but Rational Entertainments'; and Robert D. Hume, 'The Politics of Opera in Late Seventeenth-Century London,' *Cambridge Opera Journal* 10 (1998), pp. 15–22.
[21] Cited in Winn, *Dryden and his World*, p. 393. Ellen T. Harris argues that the parallels with *The Tempest* run deeper than Dryden indicates; see her '*King Arthur*'s Journey into the Eighteenth Century,' in *Purcell Studies*, ed. Curtis Price (Cambridge: Cambridge University Press, 1995), pp. 257–9.
[22] John Dryden, 'Discourse Concerning the Original and Progress of Satire,' cited in Davies, '*King Arthur*,' p. 255.
[23] *King Arthur* (1691 wordbook), p. [v].

dispute: 'He was free to make most of it up: free to draw on non-Arthurian sources for details of plot and for "more poetical" flesh to cover the plot's bare bones.'[24] But there was surely a common context that seventeenth-century authors brought to Arthurian material: Dryden would have understood what Abraham Cowley meant in *The Civil War* some forty years earlier:

> If any drop of mighty *Uther* still
> Or *Uther's* mightier son your Veins does fill,
> Show then that Spirit; 'till all men think by you
> The doubtful Tales of your great *Arthur* true.[25]

As Roberta Florence Brinkley explains, 'Cowley associated the struggle of the British and the Saxons with the conflict between the king and the Parliament, and appealed for a display of the spirit of true Britains. . . . This is a very natural parallel since the Stuarts had emphasized their British descent, and the Parliament was basing its claim to power upon the ancient rights of the Saxons.'[26] Dryden thus found a highly workable subject not only for celebrating the anniversary of the Restoration but for emphasizing Charles's more recent success in overthrowing the Rye House Plot, and he left no doubt that he had both topics in mind, noting in the preface that at the time *King Arthur* was first written Charles had just 'overcome all those Difficulties which for some Years had perplex'd His Peaceful Reign.'[27]

As for the story of the opera itself, Dryden makes clear the journey his Arthur will take right from the opening lines. Conon, Duke of Cornwall, opens the first scene, along with royal friend Aurelius and Albanact, the captain of Arthur's guards:

> *Con.* Then this is the deciding Day, to fix
> Great *Britain's* Scepter in great *Arthur's* Hand.
> *Aur.* Or put it in the bold Invaders gripe.
> *Arthur* and *Oswald*, and their different Fates,
> Are weighing now with the Scales of Heaven.
> *Con.* In Ten set Battles have we driven back
> These Heathen Saxons, and regain'd our Earth,
> As Earth recovers from an Ebbing Tide,
> Her half-drown'd Face, and lifts it o'er the Waves.   (p. 1)

Ten times Arthur and the Britons have put down the Saxons and their leader Oswald, only to face them once again on this 'deciding Day,' which Conon explains

> [*Con.*] Is Sacred to the Patron of our Isle;
> A Christian, and a Souldiers Annual Feast.
> *Alb.* Oh now I understand you, this is St. *George of Cappadocia's*
> Day.   (p. 2)

---

[24] Pinnock, '*King Arthur* Expos'd,' pp. 244–5.
[25] Cited in Roberta Florence Brinkley, *Arthurian Legend in the Seventeenth Century* (Baltimore: Johns Hopkins Press, 1932), p. 102.
[26] *Ibid.*, pp. 102–3.
[27] *King Arthur* (1691 wordbook), p. [i].

Thus Dryden sets the context for a righteous battle, for Arthur to suppress the Saxons, recapture Kent and unify Britain, and, as we soon learn, win the hand of Emmeline, Conon's blind daughter, who was once courted by Oswald. Pinnock points out that the reference to St George's Day allows Dryden to nail 'his colours firmly to the mast' in celebration of the Restoration, for Charles II (and later James II) were both crowned on 23 April, St George's Day, 'marked each year in towns up and down the country with bell-ringing and bonfires.'[28] A poignant exchange between Arthur and Emmeline continues the first act, lasting until he is called away by a trumpet, a sound that Emmeline pictures as having 'an angry fighting Face' (p. 5). Oswald is then introduced in a decidedly grislier scene in which he and the Saxon magician Osmond offer a sacrifice of 'Six Fools' (p. 6) and three horses 'Battle won' (p. 7) to the Norse gods Woden, Thor, and Freya, replete with ceremonial music.[29] An offstage battle and a chorus of victorious Britons close the act.

Merlin opens Act II, descending 'on a chariot drawn by Dragons' (p. 10) and his ensuing exchange with Philidel, who describes himself as the 'The last seduc'd, and least deform'd of Hell' (p. 10) makes clears Philidel's key role in leading the Britons to safety. The exchange between Grimbald and Philidel, mentioned above, follows, allowing Arthur and his men to remain on course. In the next scene, Emmeline and her attendant Matilda await news from Arthur, until they are diverted by – Matilda identifies – 'a Crew of Kentish Lads and Lasses' (p. 15) indicating to the audience (if not the two women) that these are disciples of Oswald. The diversion eventually leads to Oswald and his companion Guillamar's arrival and unceremonious abduction of Emmeline and Matilda. An alarm sounds, Arthur and the Britons are alerted to Oswald's actions, and a hasty meeting between Arthur and Oswald materializes, the central dramatic exchange of the opera:

> *Arth.* Then prithee give me back my Kingly Word,
> Pass'd for thy safe return; and let this Hour,
> In single Combat, Hand to Hand, decide
> The Fate of Empire, and of *Emmeline.*
> *Oswa.* Not, that I fear, do I decline this Combat;
> And not decline it neither, but defer:
> When *Emmeline* has been my Prize as long
> As she was thine, I dare you to the Duel.
> *Arth.* I nam'd your utmost term of Life: To Morrow.
> *Oswa.* You are not Fate.
> *Arth.* But Fate be in this Arm.
> You might have made a Merit of your Theft.
> *Oswa.* Ha! Theft! Your Guards can tell, I stole her not.
> *Arth.* Had I been present –

---

[28] Pinnock, '*King Arthur* Expos'd,' p. 245. Pinnock also suggests (p. 246) that Dryden adopted the name Oswald from William Davenant's *Gondibert*, wherein Oswald is 'a prince of the Lombard royal line, second only to Duke Gondibert in point of valour, dangerously ambitious and without his rival's statesmanlike qualities.'

[29] Pinnock identifies Dryden's source for the sacrifice scene, including the text of the sacrificial anthem, as Aylett Sammes's *Britannia Antiqua Illustrata* (London, 1676); see '*King Arthur* Expos'd,' pp. 247–9.

> *Oswa.* Had you been present, she had been mine more Nobly.
> *Arth.* There lies your way.
> *Oswa.* My way lies where I please.
> Except (for *Osmond*'s Magick cannot fail)
> A long To Morrow, ere your Arms prevail:
> Or if I fall, make Room ye blest above,
> For one who was undone, and dy'd for Love.   (p. 20)

Act III forms a kind of magical centerpiece for *King Arthur*. The spells of Osmond, who has created an enchanted grove, impede the Britons at the opening of the act, and even Merlin advises 'th'Attempt's too dangerous' (p. 22). Concerns about Emmeline are mitigated some by Merlin's revelation of a 'Vial' to 'restore her sight' (p. 22). Meanwhile, Grimbald captures and shackles Philidel, though Philidel eventually foils his pursuer, in time to be entrusted by Merlin with the 'Soveraign Drops' (p. 24). Emmeline's regained sight, witnessed by Arthur from behind the scene, leads to another moving exchange between the lovers, though short-lived, for Merlin indicates that they 'have hazarded too far . . . Osmond is even now alarm'd' (p. 29). Emmeline cannot join the retreat, however, Osmond's charms confining her to the grove. Arthur and Merlin depart reluctantly, Merlin comforting Emmeline: 'fear not . . . Th'Enchanter has no Pow'r on Innocence' (p. 29). Osmond enters once the Britons depart, at first unaware of Emmeline's restored vision. She of course finds him repulsive, though Osmond, having diverted Oswald and Guillamar with a 'Sleepy Potion' (p. 30), has intentions of thawing her love, quite literally in fact for he conjures up the most substantial masque of the opera: an exchange between Cupid and the Cold Genius, who is forced to rise through 'Beds of Everlasting Snow' (p. 31) to admit to love's warming powers. Emmeline is not moved by 'such Gay Shows' (p. 33), and Oswald warns 'if you will not fairly be enjoy'd, A little honest Force, is well employ'd' (p. 34). The act ends with Emmeline alone momentarily, praying, understanding she may soon be raped.

   The action carries over into Act IV, but Grimbald interrupts Osmond and Emmeline, announcing that Arthur 'is at hand' and that Merlin has been able to 'Counterwork thy Spells' (p. 35). Emmeline is apparently safe for the moment, though to rescue her

> Arthur must destroy the enchanted grove, where 'all is but illusion,' as Merlin warns him. With a struggle, he resists two musical temptations, remembering that the two naked sirens in the stream are 'Fair Illusions' and recognizing a trio of 'Nymphs and Sylvans' who sing an equally ravishing song as 'False Joys, false Welcomes.' . . . The third illusion, however, proves more difficult, even though there is no music involved. When Arthur hacks at a tree with his sword, a bleeding Emmeline appears, claiming that Osmond has imprisoned her in the tree and begging Arthur not to murder her. Caught between Merlin's injunction and his love for Emmeline, Arthur realizes that 'all may be illusion' and begs the 'thick'ning Fogs . . . that be-lye my sight' to break up. . . . When this Emmeline describes herself as 'A Love-Sick Virgin, panting with Desire,' he can no longer resist. . . . More susceptible than Emmeline to the blandishments of false visions, Arthur needs a more direct intervention by Philidel to save him. Just in time, Philidel strikes the false Emmeline with

Merlin's wand; the 'Infernal Paint . . . vanish[es] from her Face,' revealing her as the ugly Grimbald. Horrified by what he has almost done, Arthur energetically destroys the rest of the forest.[30]

Having overcome the temptations of Act IV, Arthur and the Britons prepare in Act V for the final battle with the Saxons. Armies assemble, but it is a duel between Arthur and Oswald that decides the day, the stage directions indicating that 'They Fight with sponges in their Hands, dipt in Blood; after some equal Passes and Closeing, they appear both Wounded' (p. 44). Magical intervention from Osmond and Merlin ultimately leaves Arthur with sword in hand and Oswald defeated:

> *Arth.* Confess thy self o'ercome, and ask thy Life.
> *Oswa.* 'Tis not worth asking, when 'tis in thy Power.
> *Arth.* Then take it as my Gift.
> *Oswa.* A wretched Gift,
> With loss of Empire, Liberty, and Love.   (p. 44)

The victorious Britons reassemble, and Arthur and Emmeline are reunited, 'so fitted for each others Hearts' (p. 45). Merlin gets the last word before the final, celebratory masque:

> Nor thou, brave Saxon Prince, disdain our Triumphs;
> Britains and Saxons shall be once one People;
> One Common Tongue, one Common Faith shall bind
> Our Jarring Bands, in a perpetual Peace.   (p. 45)

Thus a victorious monarch is celebrated, a country united, Dryden here building on the Arthurian scaffolding clearly to recognize the accomplishments of Charles II. But of course the opera premiered under William and Mary, making allegorical interpretation a more difficult task. Curtis Price sketches out a convincing plan for Dryden's original Arthur, intended for a mid-1680s audience: the Britons are the Royalists, the Saxons the Whigs. The context is the Exclusion Crisis, 'an intricate series of political manoeuvres intended to block the accession of the Roman Catholic Duke of York and to have the king's eldest son, the protestant Duke of Monmouth, declared legitimate.'[31] Arthur/Charles (with the aid of Merlin and Philidel, both of whom Price equates with the Marquis of Halifax, royal advisor, leader of the Parliament defeat of the Bill of Exclusion, and dedicatee of the 1691 wordbook) thus benevolently defeats Oswald/Monmouth (assisted by Osmond and Grimbald, standing in for the Earl of Shaftesbury, the chief exclusionist spokesman). Emmeline here becomes the 'national conscience,'[32] who – once her eyes are opened – redoubles her commitment to Arthur and recognizes the true ugliness of the Saxons. A convincing story for 1685, but in 1691, Price notes, audiences would presumably believe that 'Arthur was now clearly William III and Oswald the deposed James

---

[30] James Anderson Winn, *'When Beauty Fires the Blood': Love and the Arts in the Age of Dryden* (Ann Arbor: University of Michigan Press, 1992), pp. 299–300.
[31] Price, *Purcell and the London Stage*, pp. 291–2.
[32] *Ibid.*, p. 292.

II,' though 'an Arthur-as-James interpretation' is not farfetched.[33] James Anderson Winn expands on this idea: 'King Arthur lies open to a Jacobite reading'; in a Williamite reading 'the single combat between Arthur and Oswald at the end would represent the Battle of Boyne. But since Dryden considered William an "Invader," those who shared the poet's views might privately consider a reading reversing those roles, and see in the final combat a realization of their hopes that James would be restored.'[34] Thus in revising the opera for 1691 Dryden was forced to obscure a certain amount of the original Caroline theme, and it is intriguing to think that he found a middle ground between his own sympathies for James and his wishes not to offend, at least overtly, William. Winn continues: at the end of the opera 'Neither hero dies, and Dryden takes care to make both Britons and Saxons honorable men, treating the Saxon wizard Osmond as the villain . . . Dryden was doubtless correct in describing the lines he had been forced to excise from the original opera as "Beauties," but his skill in recasting the opera to make it open to either a Williamite or Jacobite reading has a beauty all its own.'[35]

The Music

King Arthur, like Dioclesian, was conceived as a dramatick opera, but it had the advantage over most other such works of having been expressly written by Dryden for this type of musical treatment rather than adapted from some previously all-spoken material. This means that individual songs, choruses, and masques take on a decidedly more integrated role than in many other dramatick operas. Roger Savage notes that 'the musical scenes in King Arthur are remarkably active. Almost every time the lively train of events in Arthurian Kent involves a piece of wizardry, a ceremony, a triumph or vision, music takes over without more ado and actively carries things forward.'[36]

Music first appears in the unfolding drama at the end of Act I, as priests join Oswald, Osmond, and Grimbald on stage and sing 'Woden, first to thee, A Milk white Steed, Battle won, We have Sacrific'd' (p. 7). The chain of solo and choral sections comprising this number approximates the general shape of a verse anthem, a sacred genre exceedingly familiar to Purcell from his work for the Chapel Royal and Westminster Abbey, and it makes sense that he would appropriate a familiar religious style to depict this ceremonial rite. This and other bits of choral writing throughout the opera probably elicited the remark from Thomas Gray upon hearing a revival of King Arthur that 'the songs are all-Church-Musick.'[37] The sacrifice scene stands in as the masque for Act I, and a

[33] Price, Purcell and the London Stage, pp. 293–4.
[34] Winn, Dryden and his World, pp. 448–9.
[35] Ibid., p. 449.
[36] Savage, 'Theatre Music,' p. 372.
[37] Letter from Gray to Horace Walpole, 3 January 1736, in W. S. Lewis et al., eds., Horace Walpole's Correspondence with Thomas Gray, Richard West, and Thomas Ashton, 2 vols. (New Haven: Yale University Press, 1948), vol. II, pp. 57–8. Cf. Price, Purcell and the London Stage, p. 299, and William Weber, The Rise of Musical Classics in Eighteenth-Century England (Oxford: Oxford University Press, 1992), p. 92.

turn of events as the priests exit – an offstage battle – allows a chorus of victorious Britons to enter to a trumpet and oboe fanfare and end the act on a happier note. Dryden's text for this chorus prefigures – assuming this was part of the 1680s version – his Cecilian ode, 'From Harmony, from Heavenly Harmony' (set first by Giovanni Battista Draghi in 1687 and more famously by Handel in 1739), at the text 'the double, double, double Beat of the Thundring Drum' (p. 9).

Purcell's music for the dialogue between Philidel and Grimbald and their attending fellow spirits, the first music in Act II, is some of the most remarkable of the opera. After Philidel initiates the angular melody to the words 'Hither this way, this way bend, Trust not that Malicious Fiend' (p. 12), his followers enter with the same tune but now in four-part harmony. Grimbald's spirits echo at the words 'this way bend' with an exact musical repeat, securing Arthur's confusion through musical means. But Purcell goes a step further, creating further echoes of the words 'this way' within each of the two spirit choruses, between the high and low voices, all of this resulting in a kind of multi-tiered antiphony. After Arthur realizes the deception, Purcell concludes the scene with further highly depictive writing, Philidel and several solo spirits singing 'Come follow me And me' (p. 12) in a rollicking, imitative style. The other music from Act II is the sequence of pieces sung by the diverting Kentish youth, beginning with the chorus 'How blest are Shepherds, how happy their Lasses, While Drums & Trumpets are sounding Alarms!' (p. 16). The stage directions indicate that after the first chorus (probably more appropriately after the instrumental prelude to the next number), in a bit of erotic interplay, 'the men offer their Flutes to the Women, which they refuse' (p. 16); a duet for two sopranos ensues, 'Shepherd, leave Decoying, Pipes are sweet, a Summers Day; But a little after Toying, Women have the Shot to Pay' (p. 16). The foresighted women are armed with marriage contracts, which the men quickly sign, leading to a lively chorus concluding the scene: 'whether Marriage bring Joy or Sorrow, Make sure of this Day, and hang to Morrow' (p. 17).

The best known music from the opera is that from Act III, the so-called Frost Scene, described in the wordbook as 'a Prospect of Winter in Frozen Countries' (p. 31), where Cupid in recitative style calls forth the Cold Genius: 'What ho, thou Genius of the Clime, what ho! Lyest thou asleep beneath those Hills of Snow? . . . Awake, awake, And Winter from thy Furry Mantle shake' (p. 31). He responds with 'What Power art thou, who from below, Hast made me Rise, unwillingly, and slow, From Beds of Everlasting Snow!' (p. 31), a remarkably inventive aria, with the Genius's ascent rendered by Purcell in a rising chromatic line, and with the singer asked to replicate shivering by singing his repeated notes with a tremolo.[38] After further exhorting from Cupid, the Genius finally adopts a 'warmer' style in his air 'Great Love, I know thee now . . . Every where Thou art obey'd' (p. 32). A 'Chorus of Cold People' (a designation found in several of the musical sources not the wordbook) enters for a dance and a shivering chorus, and Cupid and the Genius's duet, 'Sound a Parley, ye Fair,

---

[38] Lionel Sawkins, '*Trembleurs* and Cold People: How Should they Shiver?,' in *Performing the Music of Henry Purcell*, ed. Michael Burden (Oxford: Oxford University Press, 1996), pp. 243–64.

and surrender' (p. 33) – directed at Emmeline – closes the masque. This music became deservedly famous after Purcell's death; Roger North especially remembered the efforts of Charlotte Butler who portrayed Cupid (as well as Philidel) in the first performances:

> I remember in Purcell's excellent opera of *King Arthur*, when Mrs Butler, in the person of Cupid, was to call up Genius, she had the liberty to turne her face to the scean, and her back to the theater. She was in no concerne for her face, but sang a *recitativo* of calling towards the place where Genius was to rise, and performed it admirably, even beyond any thing I ever heard upon the English stage. And I could ascribe it to nothing so much as the liberty she had of concealing her face, which she could not endure should be so contorted as is necessary to sound well, before her gallants, or at least her envious sex. There was so much admirable musick in that opera, that it's no wonder it's lost; for the English have no care of what's good, and therefore deserve it not.[39]

The music of Act IV is less spectacular by comparison, though deftly composed, and far better integrated in the drama. The first two of the three temptations Arthur faces in rescuing Emmeline are musical ones. First, two naked sirens sing from an 'Aged Stream' encouraging Arthur to 'Come Naked in, for we are so; What Danger from a Naked Foe?' (p. 37). Price notes that 'the sirens answer their own question [or rather Purcell answers it for them] as they rise to ever more piercing dissonances'[40] especially at the words 'What Danger.' Purcell the musical dramatist shines here, the music intimating a dark side and allowing Arthur to say 'Farewell, with half my Soul I stagger off' (p. 37). Next, nymphs and sylvans try to divert Arthur in song and dance; he ultimately finds them less tempting, though not before they execute the longest musical number in the opera, an extended passacaglia (instead of the minuet Dryden had specified in the wordbook) for soloists, chorus, and dancers.[41]

The final masque of Act V is an unapologetic hodgepodge, or at least that is how it survives, with an inserted song lyric not by Dryden (indicated 'SONG by Mr. HOWE' in the wordbook, p. 49) and with part of the final song probably not by Purcell, perhaps a later substitution. Merlin calls all of this forth, his intention to display 'The Wealth, the Loves, the Glories of our Isle' (p. 45), but there is little overall integration between the pieces and one writer notes that the 'variegated verbal-musical approaches suggest that the nation's greatness depends on variety.'[42] The masque begins sturdily enough, with Aeolus appearing in the

---

[39] From North's manuscript, 'Some Memorandums, concerning Musick' (British Library, Add. MS 32532, fols. 1–26), excerpts of which are published in John Wilson, ed., *Roger North on Music* (London: Novello, 1959), pp. 217–18; the passage is cited and discussed in Roger Savage, 'Calling Up Genius: Purcell, Roger North, and Charlotte Butler,' in *Performing the Music of Henry Purcell*, ed. Michael Burden (Oxford: Oxford University Press, 1986), pp. 212–31. As Savage notes, North's final statement probably confuses *King Arthur* with *The Fairy Queen*, the principal manuscript of which was missing for some two hundred years.

[40] Price, *Purcell and the London Stage*, p. 308.

[41] The musical sources provide some confusion here, and it seems likely that the setting of the second stanza in this lengthy number may have been cut in performance. See Price, *Purcell and the London Stage*, p. 312; Pinnock, '*King Arthur* Expos'd,' pp. 255–6; Shay and Thompson, *Purcell Manuscripts*, pp. 244–5.

[42] Michael Alssid, 'The Impossible Form of Art: Dryden, Purcell, and *King Arthur*,' *Studies in the Literary Imagination* 10 (1977), p. 142; cited in Price, *Purcell and the London Stage*, p. 312.

clouds to sing a majestic air, 'Ye Blust'ring Brethren of the Skies . . . Retire and let *Britannia Rise*' (p. 45), and with Pan and Nereid following with the duet 'Round thy Coasts Fair Nymph of *Britain*' (p. 46), which quickly expands to a chorus. But things go astray a bit in the ensuing trio as Dryden connects '*Jasons* Fleece' with '*British* Wool' (p. 46). Next, the humorous 'Your Hay is Mow'd' (p. 47), sung by Comus and three rustics, surely yielded some laughs, but it seems too great a change musically and dramatically from what preceded it; more problematic, it serves as a ridiculous preamble to the sublime soprano solo 'Fairest Isle, all Isles Excelling . . . Venus *here* will chuse her Dwelling' (p. 48), one of Purcell's greatest songs. This leads to, 'You say, 'Tis Love' (p. 49), the song by Mr Howe,[43] and finally, after a brief interruption by Merlin, the patriotic finale 'St. *George* the Patron of our Isle,' with its problematic musical stemma. As the music ends Arthur praises Merlin 'Wisely you have, whate'er will please, reveal'd, What wou'd displease, as wisely have conceal'd' (p. 51). We might wish that Merlin had left just a bit more of it concealed.

But the problems of the final masque do not tarnish the opera as a whole: Dryden and Purcell's *King Arthur* remains one of the great musical-dramatic achievements of the seventeenth century. Built upon a loose Arthurian framework, with both author and composer capitalizing on the diverse resources of dramatick opera, the work effectively balances the spoken and musical realms, and allows the spectacles of the masques and other musical scenes to intensify (for the most part) the unfolding tale. Unfortunately, like all other dramatick operas, *King Arthur* enjoys no modern performance tradition. It survived long after its premiere, well into the nineteenth century, though suffering from heavy alterations,[44] apparently the general presumption being that audiences would not accept the separation of dramatic and musical casts. The Purcell tercentenary in 1995 provided a context for several substantially more faithful performances, particularly that of the Boston Early Music Festival; these helped to prove the idea that the work's original scheme is not a liability and made clear that *King Arthur*, though perhaps not in step with a longstanding dramatic or operatic tradition, nonetheless deserves at least an occasional, unimpeded path to the modern stage.

BIBLIOGRAPHY

Michael Alssid, 'The Impossible Form of Art: Dryden, Purcell, and *King Arthur*,' *Studies in the Literary Imagination* 10 (1977), pp. 125–44.
Joanne Altieri, 'Baroque Hieroglyphics: Dryden's *King Arthur*,' *Philological Quarterly* 61 (1982), pp. 431–51.
Jack M. Armistead, 'Dryden's *King Arthur* and the Literary Tradition: A Way of Seeing,' *Studies in Philology* 85 (1988), pp. 53–72.

[43] Probably John Grubham Howe; see Davies, '*King Arthur*,' p. 330.
[44] Harris, '*King Arthur*'s Journey'; Michael Burden, 'Purcell Debauch'd: The Dramatick Operas in Performance,' in *Performing the Music of Henry Purcell*, ed. Burden (Oxford: Oxford University Press, 1996), pp. 145–53.

Fredson Bowers, 'Dryden as Laureate: The Cancel Leaf in *King Arthur*,' *Times Literary Supplement* (10 April 1953), p. 244.

Roberta Florence Brinkley, *Arthurian Legend in the Seventeenth Century* (Baltimore: Johns Hopkins Press, 1932).

Michael Burden, 'Aspects of Purcell's Operas,' in *Henry Purcell's Operas: The Complete Texts*, ed. Michael Burden (Oxford: Oxford University Press, 2000), pp. 3–27.

——, 'Purcell Debauch'd: The Dramatick Operas in Performance,' in *Performing the Music of Henry Purcell*, ed. Burden (Oxford: Oxford University Press, 1996), pp. 145–62.

David Charlton, ' "King Arthur": Dramatick Opera,' *Music & Letters* 104 (1983), pp. 183–92.

H. Neville Davies, '*King Arthur; or, The British Worthy*,' in *Henry Purcell's Operas: The Complete Texts*, ed. Michael Burden (Oxford: Oxford University Press, 2000), pp. 255–335.

John Downes, *Roscius Anglicanus*, ed. Judith Milhous and Robert D. Hume (London: Theatre Research, 1987).

[John] Dryden, *King Arthur: or, The British Worthy. A Dramatick Opera* (London: Jacob Tonson, 1691).

Ellen T. Harris, '*King Arthur*'s Journey into the Eighteenth Century,' in *Purcell Studies*, ed. Curtis Price (Cambridge: Cambridge University Press, 1995), pp. 257–89.

Robert D. Hume, 'The Politics of Opera in Late Seventeenth-Century London,' *Cambridge Opera Journal* 10 (1998), pp. 15–43.

Margaret Laurie, ed., *The Works of Henry Purcell*, vol. 26, *King Arthur*, rev. edn (London: Novello, 1971).

Richard Luckett, 'Exotick but Rational Entertainments: The English Dramatick Operas,' in *English Drama: Forms and Development*, ed. Marie Axton and Raymond Williams (Cambridge: Cambridge University Press, 1977), pp. 123–41.

Andrew Pinnock, ' "From Rosy Bowers": Coming to Purcell the Bibliographical Way,' in *Henry Purcell's Operas: The Complete Texts*, ed. Michael Burden (Oxford: Oxford University Press, 2000), pp. 31–93

——, '*King Arthur* Expos'd: A Lesson in Anatomy,' in *Purcell Studies*, ed. Curtis Price (Cambridge: Cambridge University Press, 1995), pp. 243–56.

Curtis A. Price, *Henry Purcell and the London Stage* (Cambridge: Cambridge University Press, 1984).

Roger Savage, 'Calling Up Genius: Purcell, Roger North, and Charlotte Butler,' in *Performing the Music of Henry Purcell*, ed. Michael Burden (Oxford: Oxford University Press, 1986), pp. 212–31.

——, 'The Theatre Music,' in *The Purcell Companion*, ed. Michael Burden (London: Faber and Faber, 1994), pp. 313–83.

Lionel Sawkins, '*Trembleurs* and Cold People: How Should they Shiver?,' in *Performing the Music of Henry Purcell*, ed. Michael Burden (Oxford: Oxford University Press, 1996), pp. 243–64.

Robert Shay and Robert Thompson, *Purcell Manuscripts: The Principal Musical Sources* (Cambridge: Cambridge University Press, 2000).

James Anderson Winn, *John Dryden and his World* (New Haven and London: Yale University Press, 1987).

——, '*When Beauty Fires the Blood*': Love and the Arts in the Age of Dryden (Ann Arbor: University of Michigan Press, 1992).

Wagner: Tristan und Isolde *and* Parsifal

DEREK WATSON

Richard Wagner's creative grail quest may be viewed as his artistic progress from *Der fliegende Holländer* to *Parsifal*; that is from 1840 until the completion of his last opera forty-two years later. It spans ten musical dramas including the four parts of the *Ring* cycle. *Der fliegende Holländer* was conceived when he was twenty-six; *Parsifal* premiered when he was sixty-nine. Wagner was clear that these ten were the official canon of his works, dismissing three earlier operas as immature.

In *Der fliegende Holländer* (composed in Paris, 1841; premiere in Dresden, 1843) the eponymous character is a man in need of healing, of redemption from a curse. This he gains through the selfless love of a woman. As Thomas Mann pointed out, the Dutchman's language 'already contains such premonitions of the highly wrought religious language of *Parsifal* as the lines: "Ein heil'ger Balsam meinen Wunden/ Dem Schwur, dem hohen Wort entfliesst" [A holy balsam for my wounds/ Flows from your oath, your lofty words]'.[1] In the same essay Mann observes 'that the emotional world of *Tannhäuser* already antici-pates that of *Parsifal*, and that the latter work is simply the summation and supremely logical conclusion of a profoundly romantic-Christian *oeuvre*. Wagner's final work is also his most theatrical, and it is hard to imagine an artistic progression more logical than his. An art based on sensuous experience and recurrent, symbolic formulas . . .'[2]

Tannhäuser (completed and premiered in Dresden, 1845) indeed contains much that Wagner was to refine in *Tristan* and *Parsifal*. A striking image is the vision of a miraculous spring, the pure fount of grace pouring out refreshment to the human heart, which Wolfram von Eschenbach sings of during the Act II song contest. (The poet of *Parzivâl*[3] is a principal character in all three acts of *Tannhäuser*.[4]) The metaphor of a pure, bounteous spring is set up in contrast to the impure, erotic, destructive wells for which Tannhäuser thirsts. This duality of *agape* and *eros*, of an ordered Christian world (Thuringia) against that of pagan darkness and disorder (the sensual realm of Venus)

[1] Thomas Mann, 'The Sorrows and Grandeur of Richard Wagner', in *Pro and Contra Wagner*, translated by Allan Blunden (London: Faber, 1985), p. 111.

[2] *ibid.*, p. 94.

[3] Throughout this essay the spelling *Parzivâl* indicates Wolfram's epic and *Parsifal* the Wagner opera – a spelling the composer adopted only in 1877.

[4] Another link that Wagner would have observed was the folk lore that the grail was on the Hörselberg with Venus.

prefigures the bright, chivalric world of King Marke's Cornwall as opposed to the erotically abandoned night-realm of Tristan and Isolde who have drunk from the fatal cup of witchcraft and insatiable desire. In *Parsifal* the antipodes become the realms of Titurel and Klingsor. All these works involve characters who are afflicted with cravings they seemingly can never satisfy. Sexual longing, Wagner seems to be saying, must ultimately be overcome by some higher form of love. This begs the question as to whether the music actually 'says' this, for Wagner was supreme at expressing in dramatic music the joys of sexual love, doing so most fulfilledly in the *Ring* cycle.

Before moving on to the post-1850 music dramas, we must glance briefly at *Lohengrin* (music completed in Dresden, 1848; premiere in Weimar, 1850) which prefigures the *Ring* in its concerns with the desire for power, the corruption of innocence, and the tragic inability of love to flourish. In *Lohengrin* a knight of the grail appears among ordinary mankind to champion a virtuous woman wrongly accused by evildoers. The condition of his aid, and his espousal to the heroine, is that no one ever ask his name or origin. At the tragic denouement Wagner's text has the hero impart our first full knowledge of the arcane grail world:

> In fernem Land, unnahbar euren Schritten,
> liegt eine Burg, die Monstsalvat genannt;
> ein lichter Tempel stehet dort inmitten,
> so kostbar, als auf Erden nichts bekannt;
> drin ein Gefäss von Wundertät'gem Segen
> wird dort als höchstes Heiligtum bewacht:
> Es ward, dass sein der Menschen Reinste pflegen,
> herab von einer Engelschar gebracht;
> alljährlich naht vom Himmel eine Taube,
> um neu zu stärken seine Wunderkraft:
> Es heisst der Graal, und selig reinster Glaube
> erteilt durch ihn sich seiner Ritterschaft.
> . . .
> Vom Graal ward ich zu euch daher gesandt:
> mein Vater Parzival trägt seine Krone,
> sein Ritter ich – bin Lohengrin genannt.

[In a faraway land, reached by paths unknown to you, lies a castle known as Montsalvat; in its midst stands a bright temple, more splendid than any known on earth; therein is a vessel of wondrous power which is guarded as a sacred treasure: It was brought down by an angel host to be tended by the purest of mankind; each year a dove descends from heaven to fortify its wondrous strength anew: It is called the grail, and purest faith is imparted through it to its knighthood . . . From the grail I was sent here among you: my father Parzival wears its crown, his knight am I – and Lohengrin my name.]

From him we also learn that the grail sends emissaries into distant lands to serve the cause of innocence in peril. Such servants of the grail are armed with supernatural power to conquer evil.

Wagner's principal sources for this opera (many of which were of course to fertilise the text of *Parsifal*) include *Parzivâl* and *Titurel* by Wolfram von Eschenbach which he read in recent editions by Karl Simrock, Karl Lachmann and San-Marte,[5] and the anonymous late thirteenth century epic *Lohengrin* edited by Johann Joseph von Görres.[6] But he found his primary source of inspiration in a synopsis and commentary in the proceedings of the Royal German Society of Königsberg[7] – a volume Wagner first read in Paris in 1841 and which contained also the primary source for his *Tannhäuser* scenario. Another source for *Lohengrin* lay in his fruitful reading in Paris in 1840–2: the *Deutsche Sagen* of the brothers Grimm.[8] Ernest Newman noted that 'Wagner must have been familiar with most of the twelfth and thirteenth century variants of the Lohengrin legend, for his poem is a skilful amalgam of incidents and motives from various quarters'.[9] This ability to distil the mythic essence he required from a web of diverse material was one of Wagner's most valuable skills, born of innate dramatic sense and huge knowledge based on voracious reading. Newman cites his knowledge of the Walloon-French epic *Le Chevalier au Cygne* and its swan-transformation symbolism, and the figure of the Duchess of Cleves in the anonymous epic *Lohengrin* from whom Wagner evolved Ortrud, prime mover of evil intent. Creating her from mere hints in the sources is similar to his creation of Kundry in *Parsifal*: a highly complex invention who not only assumes a powerful, multi-faceted persona of her own (with references to several previous Wagner figures going back to the Ahasuerus-Dutchman) but gives the sprawling mythic tale necessary cohesion in three-act operatic form. The motif of the unasked question, and those of the swan and the dove, are thematic bonds between *Lohengrin* and *Parsifal*.[10]

Reference has been made to Wagner's omnivorous reading in his Paris period. It was a lifelong characteristic from his boyhood explorations among 'the chaotic mass of books' he found in the home of his paternal uncle, the writer, translator and philologist Adolf Wagner (in whose care much of his youth was spent) through to the many pages of Cosima Wagner's diaries where their reading was dutifully recorded. His Bayreuth library of more than two thousand volumes survives intact and, even more interestingly, so does the library he lovingly amassed in his period as Kapellmeister in Dresden. This first library was long thought (by Wagner and everyone else) to have been lost: the forfeit seized by a creditor when Wagner fled Dresden's failed revolution in 1849. Yet it survived against all odds and was duly catalogued and described by Curt von Westernhagen.[11] Adolf's library must have contained some material at least on the periphery of Arthurian literature and Wagner was undoubtedly acquainted with the outlines of the Parsifal and Tristan stories by the time of his Paris years. Aside from the reading he cites in his autobiographical writings and in letters, it is in the 400 volumes of his Dresden library that we first see exact evidence of the literary and historical works he kept instantly to hand.[12]

---

[5] Pseudonym of Albert Schultz.
[6] *Lohengrin, ein altdeutsches Gedicht, nach der Abschrift des Vatikanischen Manuscriptes von Ferdinand Gloekle*, ed. J. Görres (Heidelberg: Mohr und Zimmer, 1813).
[7] *Historische und literarische Abhandlungen der königlichen deutschen Gesellschaft zu Königsberg*, 1838.
[8] Two-volume edition, 1816–18.
[9] *Wagner Nights* (London: Putnam, 1949), pp. 130f.
[10] Indeed the musical motif of the swan in *Parsifal* is an exact reminiscence of that in *Lohengrin*.
[11] *Richard Wagners Dresdener Bibliothek 1842–1849* (Wiesbaden: Brockhaus, 1966).
[12] As a royal employee Wagner also made significant borrowings from the Royal Saxon Library,

We know that in his Paris and Dresden years (i.e. in the 1840s) Wagner read everything he needed to provide him with texts for his musical dramas for the rest of his life, Arthurian material included. These were the golden years of the nineteenth century rediscovery of mediaeval literature. How much Arthur could be found on his own shelves? He possessed San-Marte's edition of *Die Arthur-Sage und die Mährchen des rothen Buchs von Hergest*,[13] three editions of Gottfried von Strassburg's *Tristan und Isolde* with all its sources, variants and completions,[14] *Erec*[15] and *Iwein*[16] of Hartmann von Aue, the Grimm brothers' translation of *Irische Elfenmärchen*,[17] Johann Wilhelm Wolf's *Niederländische Sagen*,[18] Ulrich von Zatzikhoven's *Lanzelet*,[19] four editions of Wolfram von Eschenbach's works[20] and the other sources relating to *Lohengrin* cited earlier.

Five and a half years separate the completion of *Lohengrin* in 1848 and the commencement of the music of *Das Rheingold* in 1853. The period saw Wagner's precipitate exit from Dresden into Swiss exile, a large corpus of prose writing and the evolution of the text of *Der Ring des Nibelungen*. One step towards his concept of the Siegfried myth was an essay of early 1849 in which he grappled with legend and history: *Die Wibelungen: Weltgeschichte aus der Sage* [The Wibelungs: World History revealed in Saga]. This is worth a mention insofar as Wagner regards the Wibelungs or Ghibellines as successors to the legendary Nibelungs, and identifies their hoard, which Siegfried won, with the later quest for the holy grail. The grail is thus seen as a spiritualised form of the Nibelung hoard.

It is no accident that the final lines of *Siegfried*, where hero and heroine exclaim 'Leuchtende Liebe, lachender Tod!' [Luminous love, laughing death!], remind us of the imagery of *Tristan und Isolde*. Before being able to compose the third act of his third *Ring* drama, where the discovery of erotic love is joyfully celebrated, Wagner felt the need to explore another aspect of love: love as unfulfilled yearning, or as he put it, 'love as fearful torment'.[21] Thus he broke off

---

the importance of which for the *Ring* sources has been recounted by Elizabeth Magee in *Richard Wagner and the Nibelungs* (Oxford University Press, 1990).
[13] Quedlinburg and Leipzig: Gottfried Basse, 1842.
[14] The translation (into modern German) by Hermann Kurtz (Stuttgart: L.F. Rieger, 1844); two editions of the Middle High German original: that by Hans Ferdinand Massmann (Leipzig: G.J. Göschen, 1843) and the two volumes of Gottfried's works edited by Friedrich Heinrich von der Hagen, including the continuations and completions of *Tristan und Isolde* by Ulrich von Türheim and Heinrich von Freiberg (Breslau: Josef Max, 1823). Gottfried was Wagner's main source but he would have known versions of the tale by Gottfried's predecessors from Hagen's *Minnesinger* (Leipzig: J.A. Barth, 1838) which he also owned.
[15] ed. Moriz Haupt (Berlin: Weidmann, 1839).
[16] ed. George Friedrich Benecke and Karl Lachmann (Berlin: G. Reimer, 1843); also *Iwein mit dem Löwen*, ed. Wolf Grafen von Baudissin (Berlin: Alexander Duncker, 1845).
[17] Leipzig: Friedrich Fleischer, 1826.
[18] Leipzig: F.A. Brockhaus, 1843.
[19] ed. K.A. Hahn (Frankfurt am Main: H.L. Brönner, 1845).
[20] Karl Lachmann's edition (Berlin: G. Reimer, 1833); San-Marte's translation into modern German – *Parcifal, Rittergedicht* (Magdeburg: Creutz, 1836); San-Marte's *Lieder, Wilhelm von Orange und Titurel von Wolfram von Eschenbach und der jüngere Titurel von Albrecht in Uebersetzung und im Auszuge, nebst Abhandlungen über das Leben und Wirken Wolfram's von Eschenbach und die Sage vom heiligen Gral* (Magdeburg: Creutz, 1841); and Karl Simrock's edition – *Parzival und Titurel, Rittergedichte* in two vols. (Stuttgart and Tübingen: Cotta, 1842).
[21] Letter to August Röckel, 23 August 1856.

work on his *Nibelungen* tetralogy and wrote *Tristan und Isolde*. Of this 'searing love which devours' he told Cosima: '. . . it was very remarkable that in the middle of my work on the *Nibelungen* I felt the need to deal exhaustively with this one aspect, which could not be dealt with fully in my huge poem, and so I worked out *Tristan*. All of it subconscious, just always driven on.'[22]

In the preface to his 1844 New High German translation of Gottfried's *Tristan* (Wagner's principal source) Hermann Kurtz had noted what a tremendous tragic drama the epic would make. Wagner must have been struck by this but the catalyst for the project was a different writer entirely. In October 1854 he had immersed himself in the writings of the philosopher Arthur Schopenhauer. He told Liszt in December: 'I have found a sedative which has finally helped me to sleep at night; it is the sincere and heartfelt yearning for death: total unconsciousness, complete annihilation, the end of all dreams – the only ultimate redemption!' Later in the same letter: 'since I have never in my life enjoyed the true happiness of love I intend to erect a monument to this most beautiful of dreams, in which from beginning to end this love shall for once be truly and utterly satisfied. I have sketched a *Tristan und Isolde* in my mind . . .' In January 1855 he revised his old *Faust* Overture with a new motto for it from Part I of Goethe's drama that resounded with his current poetical and philosophical mood:

> Existence is become a mere, dead weight:
> would death could free me from the life I hate.[23]

Schopenhauer viewed worldly existence as a perpetual round of suffering from which the only release is the denial of the 'will', in annihilation or the Buddhist state of Nirvana.

Although he did not finally postpone work on *Siegfried* until 9 August 1857, dramatic and musical ideas for *Tristan* intruded insistently upon his creative consciousness for a year or two beforehand. Significantly, many of these ideas also connected with *Parsifal*, which from now on never wholly left his thoughts. Early in his consideration of *Tristan* he noted down his identification of the suffering Tristan with Wolfram's Anfortas. And late in 1855 he conceived the idea (never actually used) of having Parsifal, on his quest, visit the ailing Tristan in Act III: the man of renunciation visiting the man of insatiable longing. In 1856 he sketched a Buddhistic drama *Die Sieger*, dealing with concepts later explored in *Parsifal*: Mitleid (compassion) and Schadenfreude (pleasure in the suffering of others); he also penned the first musical sketches for *Tristan* in December 1856. Wagner noted later that an 1857 spring morning in Zurich brought bright thoughts of the Good Friday scene in *Parzival* and he made a sketch for an opera on the subject. The text of *Tristan und Isolde* was written in Zurich in August and September 1857; the music composed there, in Venice, and completed in Lucerne in August 1859. It was premiered in Munich in 1865. During the musical composition in Venice letters and a diary kept for Mathilde

[22] *Cosima Wagner's Diaries*, vol. I, ed. Martin Gregor-Dellin and Dietrich Mack, translated by Geoffrey Skelton (London: Collins, 1978), p. 699.
[23] Translation by Robert David Macdonald (Birmingham: Oberon Press, 1988).

Wesendonck are full of references to *Parsifal*. By 1860 Wagner had formed the notion of Kundry's character and importance. Many further parallels could be drawn between the worlds of *Tristan* and *Parsifal*. Both heroes are the orphans of grief-stricken mothers and of fathers who died in distant battle. The fact that the *Tristan* subject encroached upon Wagner's *Siegfried* is significant for precisely the same reason, for Siegfried's father too died in combat in a place unknown to his son, and his mother died in pain and grief. Siegfried, like Tristan in the sources, is also a dragon-slayer, a sword-bearer, whose ultimate fate is decided by the drinking of a potion and whose tragedy is bound up with the procuring of the woman he loves for a kinsman (Isolde for Tristan's uncle Marke; Brünnhilde for Siegfried's blood-brother Gunther).[24]

Gottfried's famous preface to his unfinished epic embraces several antitheses: bitterness/sweetness, sorrow/bliss, death/life, damnation/salvation, pain/joy. Wagner's drama develops this with a further series of such polarities:

Some Antithetical Symbols Related to *Tristan und Isolde*

Night	Day
Darkness	Light
Unconsciousness	Consciousness
Inner Reality	Outer Reality
The World of Sensation – Dionysian	The World of Form – Apollonian
Nearness	Distance
Joy	Sorrow
Love	Honour
Fidelity	Infidelity
Death (Eternity)	Life (Transitoriness)
Music	Drama
The 'black' keys A♭, C♯, F♯, B	The 'white' keys F, C, G, D
Schopenhauer's 'Wille' (Will)	Schopenhauer's 'Vorstellung' (Representation)

Just after the second verse of the young sailor's song at the opening of Act I, Isolde sings of her love for Tristan, acknowledging it as a force that is driving them into the arms of death. Note again the use of paradox:

Mir erkoren –	Chosen for me –
mir verloren –	lost to me –
hehr und heil,	glorious and strong,
kühn und feig:	bold and cowardly:
Todgeweihtes Haupt!	Death-devoted head!
Todgeweihtes Herz!	Death-devoted heart!

That death is the undoubted goal is clear from the striking musical phrase Isolde sings to the last two lines, and which recurs at significant moments in all three acts.

The idea of atonement is also intrinsic to *Tristan und Isolde*. The 'cup of oblivion'

[24] Links between the Siegfried myth and Arthurian subject matter are explored in Maike Oergel's *The Return of King Arthur and the Nibelungen: National Myth in Nineteenth-Century English and German Literature* (Berlin and New York: Walter de Gruyter, 1998), cf. pp. 208–99.

which they drink is also the cup of atonement, the cup of death.[25] The ambivalent meaning of the potion – love, atonement, death – is subtly played upon by Wagner. His musical symbolism, indeed the whole 'sound language' of *Tristan*, is commensurately richly allusive and ambiguous, through use of ceaselessly shifting chromatic harmonies and avoidance of cadences in the lovers' music. The appropriateness of extreme chromaticism to express yearning, frenzy, unfulfilled striving and sexual desire finds its perfect and essential foil in the feudal world of ordered loyalty represented by Kurwenal, Marke, Melot and the sailors. It is represented in sturdily diatonic style: mainly straightforward major and minor chord progressions. Here stability and rationality are opposed to the instability and near-delirium of Tristan and Isolde. When the two worlds impinge fatally upon one another at the conclusion of Act I, the dramatic dichotomy is brilliantly handled: the lovers embrace in an intoxication of bewildered joy, with surging, dangerously unstable chromatic currents of music, while bright C major fanfares intrude from the 'real' world with thrillingly theatrical *élan*.

The brightness of day is the discordant musical symbol that opens Act II. The core of that act, the long scene of the lovers, after an erotically hyper-charged start, takes up that musical image of day until gradually their colloquy reflects on their true and ideal sphere, the world of night and nothingness, unconsciousness, bliss of eternal union. As Bryan Magee points out this pervasive imagery of day and night 'functions on many levels at once. Day is what keeps the lovers apart, while night and darkness unite them – so much is obvious. But Wagner relates the distinction between day and night to Schopenhauer's division of total reality into the phenomenal and noumenal realms: the realm of day is the realm of the phenomenal, the realm of night is the realm of the noumenal. We may say that it is night which makes the lovers one, and unites them, but in fact it is in the realm of the noumenal alone that they are literally, that is to say metaphysically, one.'[26]

This opera is uniquely and quintessentially a product of Kantian-Schopenhauerian philosophy. In the musical language chosen to express its philosophical content *Tristan* has been viewed as a harbinger of the breakdown of tonality in twentieth century music. It certainly laid the foundations for later dramatic composers whose operas embrace music, poetry and philosophy: Richard Strauss, Schoenberg, Pfitzner, Britten, Tippett and Henze. Does this mean Wagner strayed too far from Gottfried, his source? There may still be some staid academic disapproval concerning his radical re-shaping of his mediaeval sources. This is to miss the point, especially the point about mythic material which every age feels the need to re-tell in its own language.

Wagner's skill as narrative poet is to fuse diverse elements of complex tales, reducing and regrouping his material. He simultaneously simplifies the epic sources, so that their essentials are capable of exposition in three-act form, and yet permits the expansion of certain aspects in ways that modern audiences would find psychologically necessary.

---

[25] On the significance of potions in general, in *Tristan* and other Wagner dramas, cf. Ulrich Müller and Oswald Panagl, 'The Potion as Symbol and Prop in Richard Wagner's Music Dramas', in the *Bayreuth Festival Programme Book* (1998), pp. 112–53.

[26] *Wagner and Philosophy* (London: Allen Lane, 2000), p. 218.

He is also diligently faithful in retaining key elements from his mediaeval source. The expansive passages in which Tristan and Isolde express the wish to dissolve into one entity take their cue directly from Gottfried: 'You and I, Tristan and Isolde, shall forever remain one and undivided! Let this kiss be a seal upon it that I am yours, that you are mine, steadfast till death, but one Tristan and Isolde!'[27]

One ancient ingredient of the story found in sources generally thought to be precursors of Gottfried, is not only present in Wagner's re-working of the tale but assumes significant symbolic and structural importance dramatically and musically. It is akin to the motif in the tenth century Irish tale *The Wooing of Emer* of the princess's recognition of the bandages of the man who saved her from sea-robbers. Often called the 'Blick', 'Liebesblick' or 'love-glance' motif, it is heard early in the Act I Prelude but its meaning becomes fully clear only later in the act when (in one of several great narratives Wagner adroitly uses to introduce 'the story so far') Isolde recalls the moment she stood poised with her sword ready to slay Tantris, the man she had once healed, when she had realised he was in fact Tristan, the killer of her betrothed. At that moment he looked up, not at the sword, not at her hand, but glanced directly into her eyes:

> Seines Elendes jammerte mich;
> das Schwert, ich liess es fallen!

> [His wretchedness awoke pity in me; I let fall the sword!]

Compassion (Mitleid) for the suffering helplessness of a wounded being, the overcoming of hatred by new awareness of fellow feeling, the abandonment of the solution of vengeance and violence, are all tellingly important factors. No matter that Isolde presently and emphatically rejects her moment of loving weakness. The music speaks truest of all: as she sings a meltingly beautiful descending chromatic phrase, a solo viola carries the poignantly tender 'love-glance' theme over an accompaniment of sustained *divisi* cellos. The idea recurs unmistakably when the lovers look at one another anew after drinking the potion, and at the moment of Tristan's death as he glimpses the long-yearned-for Isolde.

The most famous, richly-suggestive and distinctive musical symbol in the opera is the 'Tristan chord' – the first harmony heard in the Prelude and which alone has engendered a small library of commentary. The existence of these countless learned articles and analytical theses bespeaks its enigmatic quality. It defies one definition in terms of structure, harmonic function or extra-musical meaning. Its occurrences and significance in the opera can of course be observed. It is developed in a huge variety of ways. As a discord it is resolved by various means. When, either as a single chord or in a harmonic sequence, it accompanies text, it is used to highlight important words. The 'love-glance' idea referred to above is an extension of the opening paragraph of the Prelude of which the chord forms an integral part. The first note of the opera is an A. A is the first note of the 'love-glance' theme at bar 17 of the Prelude. All the music up

---

[27] Translation by A.T. Hatto (Harmondsworth: Penguin, 1960), p. 282.

to that point can be seen as a rising chromatic journey from the first A to another A in bar 17. This sequence is recalled in full at vital points in the drama. A linear development of the chord is Tristan's memorable vocal line in the central part of Act II, 'O sink' hernieder, Nacht der Liebe' [O sink upon us, Night of love]. The chord is heard for the last time in the final five bars of the opera, where two striking transformations occur. First the rising, yearning phrase that emerges from the chord (as at the start of the opera and innumerable times thereafter) is resolved onto B major harmony. The significance of this resolution is enhanced by the orchestration. The cor anglais, so identified as the sound of endless longing, sadness and despair, is suddenly silent in the transfigured closing chords.

The mystical, ultimate union of the lovers is therefore achieved by a simple musical device: resolution onto a tonic chord of a phrase denied this through three long acts. The resolution is of course far profounder and more complex than this glib sentence allows. In a work full of dichotomy, there is a final one. Although the goal has been death the final music seems to many listeners ecstatically life-affirming. And although the lovers' realm has been symbolised by night, Isolde's final words speak of ever more brilliant, radiant light.

Michael Tanner has noted that 'what is heroic about Wagner's characters is precisely their striving for more abundant life'.[28] His heroes and heroines are invariably wounded figures, scarred and torn by conflicting experiences. They need and they struggle for the resolution of healing and wholeness. The transformation may be posthumous in earthly terms. The pope's staff bursts into green leaf after Tannhäuser's demise to tell the world that the hero, like Faust, is redeemed. This symbol of healing and wholeness is akin to the Good Friday music in *Parsifal* Act III, showing nature restored with the advent of Parsifal and the end of years of blight, futility and wasteland. The ailing kingdom and its sick king are made whole by the return of the spear to the grail. This metaphor, like most in Wagner, works on several levels: the lance that harmed is also the agent of healing; the opposites of male and female are symbolically united.

The subject of *Parsifal* was perfect for Wagner's final music drama, dealing as it does with the conflict of flesh and the spirit and the concept of a society which, through misuse of love and power, can only be healed by the one who discovers, through fellow-feeling with the suffering, the highest form of love and thus new wisdom. Wagner was faithful to Wolfram's core conception: 'a brave man made slowly wise'. The promise the grail makes to the wounded Amfortas[29] is:

> Durch Mitleid wissend, der reine Tor,
> harre sein, den ich erkor.

> [Made wise through pity, the pure fool, wait for him, the one I choose.]

[28] 'The Total Work of Art', in *The Wagner Companion*, ed. Peter Burbidge and Richard Simon (London, Faber, 1979), p. 187.

[29] Wagner's re-spelling of Wolfram's Anfortas. The *m* is for ease of projection in singing, and perhaps for alliterative purposes as in Titurel's 'Mein Sohn, Amfortas, bist du am Amt?' [My son, Amfortas, are you at your place?]. On Wagner's nomenclature in *Parsifal* see articles by Thomas Lindner and Oswald Panagl in the *Bayreuth Festival Programme Book* (1995), pp. 106–19. Note also that in *Parsifal* Titurel is father to Amfortas, not grandfather as in Wolfram.

The innocent fool made wise through compassion[30] had accompanied Wagner's thoughts from at least 1845 when he first read Wolfram von Eschenbach's *Parzivâl* (c. 1205–1210).[31] We observed how thoughts of *Parsifal* persistently filtered through during the period of *Tristan's* creation, just as *Tristan* had intruded upon composition of *Siegfried*.[32] The first extant prose sketch of *Parsifal* was written in four days in 1865: *Die Meistersinger von Nürnberg* was then only half finished. At Bayreuth in 1877, after the premiere of the *Ring* the previous year, he wrote another prose draft, quickly followed by the full text, and commenced the music in September. *Parsifal* was composed both at Bayreuth and in Italy where Wagner repaired with his family for the sake of his health. The full score was completed in Palermo in January 1882 and the premiere followed at Bayreuth in July. Wagner wrote no more music and died in Venice in February 1883.

The image of a sacred vessel is one of the oldest in the human psyche and elements of the grail story such as cup and spear, healing and regeneration, are traceable in the legends of many ancient civilisations. In Wolfram the grail is a stone. In the unfinished poem *Perceval* or *Li contes del Graal* written (by 1180) by Chrétien de Troyes the grail is a dish. Only in later continuations of Chrétien (e.g. by Wauchier de Denain) are grail and spear given Christian symbolism. In Robert de Boron's *Joseph d'Arimathie* (by 1199) the grail is identified with the chalice used at the Last Supper, which was also the vessel in which Joseph of Arimathea caught Christ's blood from the Cross. The nature of Wagner's grail and the relic lost by Amfortas to Klingsor is made clear by Gurnemanz in Act I when he speaks of the founding of the grail sanctuary by Titurel:

> ihm neigten sich in heilig ernster Nacht
> dereinst des Heilands selige Boten:
> daraus er trank bei'm letzten Liebesmahle,
> das Weihgefäss, die heilig edle Schale,
> darein am Kreuz sein göttlich Blut auch floss,
> dazu den Lanzenspeer, der diess vergoss,
> der Zeugengüter höchstes Wundergut,
> das gaben sie in uns'res Königs Hut.

[one solemn sacred night the Saviour's holy messengers descended to him: they gave into our king's care the sacred vessel from which He drank at the Last Supper, the holy precious cup into which His divine Blood flowed from the Cross, and with it the lance which shed that Blood.]

The use of these Christian relics as stage props does not imply Wagner's reversion to Christianity (as Nietzsche's notorious denunciation of him purported) nor that this is a Christian work. Wagner's treatment of human frailty,

---

[30] In the German word *Mitleid* the sense is clearly 'suffering *with*'.

[31] Cf. the sources in note 20 above; the commentary by Görres to *Lohengrin*, cf. note 6 above, was also important. Later he studied San-Marte's three-volume commentary *Parzival-Studien* (1861–62).

[32] The cauldron of ideas constituting Wagner's artistic mind is nowhere better seen than in the summer of 1845. He conceived simultaneously the outline of *Lohengrin* and *Parsifal* and also that for *Die Meistersinger von Nürnberg*. He was in fact on a month's holiday or 'cure' with doctor's orders to take things easily.

sexual guilt and redemption is no more Christian in an orthodox sense than it was in *Tannhäuser* three decades or so before. Buddhism and the renunciatory philosophy of Schopenhauer are strongly evident too. As Barry Millington has summarised it: 'The second act of *Parsifal* recalls a pivotal event in Buddha's life, where, in a state of deep meditation, he expects the ultimate enlightenment that will make him a Buddha, or Enlightened One. There is a similar parallel in the immediately-preceding episode in the Buddha's reported life, when the tempter Mara tries to lead him astray by letting loose on him his seductive daughters and armed warriors. In the opera it is Klingsor who tries to tempt Parsifal with his seductive flower maidens.'[33]

The multi-faceted nature of Kundry is symbolised in her series of incarnations over the centuries, her soul's long journey 'from world to world' to expiate her sin of Schadenfreude – her mocking laughter at Christ's crucifixion. She embraces many other aspects: the mother, the temptress, the healer and the penitent. The curse she lays on Parsifal towards the close of Act II is her own curse of eternal wandering. In it we may read a metaphor for Wagner's philosophy of religion. 'Irre! Irre!' she cries. The verb *irren* means to go astray, to err. Mankind's great error as Wagner saw it was lovelessness. It is the condition he addresses in every one of his dramas. In a letter to Liszt of 13 April 1853 he continues a discussion between them on the nature of belief. Affirming *his* belief in the future of the human race and its capacity for love, he cites the only evil as *lovelessness* – and that he views as *Verirrung* (going-astray, an aberration) from which humanity may come to 'a *knowledge* of the uniquely beautiful necessity of love'.[34]

In *Religion und Kunst* (Religion and Art), an essay of 1880, Wagner speaks of art 'salvaging the kernel of religion, inasmuch as the mythical images which religion would wish to be believed as true are apprehended in art for their symbolic value, and through ideal representation of those symbols, art reveals the concealed deep truth within them'.[35] The seemingly inexhaustible store of symbolism embedded in *Parsifal*'s text and music has ensured it a most lively dramaturgical history.

As with Gottfried, Wagner's realisation of his requirements from Wolfram is through razor-sharp reduction of characters and situations. Gawan's defection from the brotherhood becomes but a passing reference in scene 1, but is sufficient to illustrate the weakness and guilt of Amfortas through his reaction. Gurnemanz is elevated to a structurally vital role as narrator of history, instigator of plot (divining Kundry's part in the scheme of personal redemption and recognising Parsifal both as fool and as the one made wise) and initiator of much important music. As the Act I forest transforms into Grail castle and the processional music begins, he explains to the puzzled boy at his side,

[33] *The Wagner Compendium*, ed. Barry Millington (London: Thames & Hudson, 1992), p. 307.
[34] *Selected Letters of Richard Wagner*, translated and edited by Stewart Spencer and Barry Millington (London: Dent, 1987), p. 284.
[35] Translated by Stewart Spencer in *Richard Wagner: Theory and Theatre* by Dieter Borchmeyer (Oxford: Clarendon Press, 1991), p. 386. Borchmeyer's chapter 'Summation and Consummation: *Parsifal*' is an excellent discussion of the metaphysical and religious aspects of the opera.

Du siehst, mein Sohn, zum Raum wird hier die Zeit.

[You see, my son, here time becomes space.]

These words could fittingly describe the opening six bars of the Prelude, which contain three main ideas that prove immensely fertile. The floating, enigmatic rhythms and the luminous glow of the orchestration instantly convey a sound-world found nowhere else in Wagner. Debussy described the scoring as 'lit from within'. The Luciferic realm of Klingsor, and all its effects on the world, is coloured with anguished chromaticism, ranging from passionate voluptuousness outstripping even that of *Tristan* to relentless dissonance that undermines orthodox tonality. Wagner holds things in balance with contrasting, firmly diatonic material like the Dresden Amen, and through masterly use of key contrast. His chosen tonalities are symbolic too in their polarities. As this opera, more than any of his dramas, deals with the reconciliation of opposites, it is significant that keys at opposite sides of the tonal spectrum are brought into conjunction.[36] For example D minor (associated with the idea of the hoped-for 'reine Tor', or pure fool) with B major (the fulfilment of that hope with Parsifal as grail king). Or A flat (the key of the 'sick' realms of the grail knights and of the flower maidens) in opposition to D major (the key of healing, redemption, and the resolution of Good Friday). If lines are drawn between these pairs of keys on the circle of fifths, a perfect cross is formed, perhaps indicating symbolic links both with the origin of the name *Parzivâl* ('straight through the vale' or 'through the middle') and the Buddhistic concept 'the middle way'. A further example of reconciliation in musical symbolism is the device (similar to the conclusion of *Tristan*) of allowing the first theme of the opera only at its *last* appearances to resolve upwards to join the final A flat major chords (returning to the tonality of the opening of the opera). The utopian socialist Wagner of the eighteen-forties finally realised his ideal society in the last scene of his last work. He showed that Utopia was only won, healed and restored, by wisdom born of suffering and awakened compassion.

Integrating and interpreting the manifold layers of meaning in Wagner's works is a beguiling, treacherous and irresistibly fascinating pursuit. Linguistic analogy and analysis of mythic symbols should however never be divorced from the musical metaphors. These are intrinsically and notoriously hard to

Parry's Guenever: *Trauma and Catharsis*

JEREMY DIBBLE

By the time Hubert Parry embarked on his one and only operatic project in 1884, he was an accomplished composer of instrumental music, songs, and choral works. His stylistic terms of reference were wide. Schumann, Brahms, Liszt, Scharwenka, and Tchaikovsky had all, in their different ways, informed his instrumental technique as is apparent in works as diverse as the *Concertstück* in G minor (1877), the Wind Nonet (1877), the *Fantasie Sonate in einem Satz* for Violin and Piano (1878), and, perhaps the most vivid example of his eclecticism, the Piano Concerto in F♯ (1880). His preoccupation with 'intellectualism' and with Brahmsian processes of development did not, however, prevent him from pursuing an equally active enthusiasm for the music of Wagner. As a close confidant and disciple of Edward Dannreuther (England's foremost champion of Wagner's music and founder of the London Wagner Society), Parry was soon intoxicated with *Die Meistersinger, Tristan und Isolde,* and *Der Ring des Nibelungen.*[1] 'I worked at the great Trilogy', he confided to his diary; 'I shortly began to understand Dannreuther's enthusiasm about it. . . . He [Wagner] seems entirely master of himself and his resources and capable of carrying out his great intentions without a flaw in the result.'[2] Labouring over Klindworth's editions of *Der Ring,* Parry prepared himself thoroughly for the experience of a lifetime. With Dannreuther's assistance he obtained free tickets for the second cycle of the tetralogy in August 1876, the effect of which was cataclysmic:

> I give up all attempts to describe my own feelings. I never was so perfectly satisfied in my life. Rheingold was first of all perfect to my mind. The Walküre came up to my anticipations which were of the very highest. Then Siegfried I found certainly hard to understand; and I did not enjoy it so much as the others at the time – but on looking back upon it I got to enjoy it more, and the impression afterwards became very strong. As for Götterdämmerung it utterly surpassed my anticipations. I was in a whirl of excitement; and quite drunk with delight.[3]

Parry's assimilation of Wagner soon began to manifest itself in his compositions. His concert overture, *Guillem de Cabestanh,* based on a character and tale

---

[1] See J. Dibble, 'Dannreuther and the Orme Square Phenomenon', in C. Bashford and L. Langley, eds., *Music and British Culture 1785–1914* (Oxford, 2000), pp. 275–298.
[2] Diary of Hubert Parry [June] 1876, Shulbrede Priory, Sussex (*ShP*).
[3] Diary, [August] 1876.

drawn from Francis Hueffer's eponymous book, was performed at the Crystal
Palace by a highly critical August Manns, conductor of the orchestra, and
exhibited an unabashed indebtedness to *Die Meistersinger* and passages of
Tristan. Such overt devotion drew criticism from his friends and colleagues. It
was uncongenial to Manns, but to others such as his friend and amateur singer,
Hugh Montgomery, it was a worrying tendency in his style. The harmonic
apparatus of Wagner's language produced 'a tendency to promiscuous inter-
course with all sorts of loose keys instead of that faithful cleaving to one only –
in an enlarged sense – to which one is accustomed in the respectable masters.'[4]
Others such as Joachim and Ethel Smyth, devotees of Brahms, took a dim view
and believed that it was impossible to espouse both schools. Smyth's view, Parry
recalled, was typically polemic:

> She is the most extreme anti-Wagnerite I have yet come across. Every touch of
> him she feels with equal aversion; she is contemptuous both of his poetry,
> charm and music. We played the Brahms variations on the Schumann theme in
> E flat and when we got to the last one she said 'I can't bear this; it's like
> Wagner'. There, that ninth, it's Lohengrin. I have got to detest the very sound
> of a ninth from him. After she said 'It is impossible for anyone to like Brahms
> and Wagner.' I demurred. She answered 'Well Amateurs of course are
> different, and no professed musician can possibly accept the two. No man
> can serve two masters. They are so utterly opposed in harmonic principles, it's
> not possible.'[5]

But, following Dannreuther's catholic example, Parry cared little for alliances or
for the factional discourse still raging in Germany. He did, however, maintain a
strong belief in the mutual exclusivity of instrumental and dramatic music; '. . .
what is applicable to the province of "dramatic" music', he wrote to Montgomery, 'is entirely alien to instrumental music'.[6] It was a belief that kept him
firmly wedded to Brahmsian principles in his orchestral and chamber works,
but for music of a dramatic nature he longed for the chance to demonstrate his
adherence to Wagner's theories. When a commission arrived, therefore, from
Gloucester for the 1880 Three Choirs Festival for a secular choral work, Parry at
last had the opportunity to test his powers.

The performance of *Prometheus Unbound* at Gloucester raised many eyebrows.
No-one had yet heard a native composer espouse Wagner with such conviction,
nor were they entirely in sympathy with the politico-philosophical connotations
of Shelley's epic poem. Parry's work, in truth, showed many weaknesses and
stylistic inconsistencies, and Hueffer, himself an eminent Wagnerite, was right
to criticise, in *The Times*, the inchoate nature of the cantata's declamatory
technique. Nevertheless, it was clear to the British public that German modernism had crossed the North Sea and that any attempt to stave off the progressi-
visms of Wagner and Liszt by the old guard of critics (namely Chorley, Bennett,
and Davison) was futile.

It would be another four years, however, before Parry would look to make a

---

[4] Letter from Hugh Montgomery to Parry, 20 April 1879, *ShP*.
[5] Diary, 6 September 1881.
[6] Letter from Parry to Montgomery, 15 September 1879, *ShP*.

determined foray into the world of opera. By that time he had made a second pilgrimage to Bayreuth to hear three performances of *Parsifal* with Dannreuther in 1882 and, deeply impressed with the development of Wagner's genius, his verdict was that the opera was '. . . a work of art . . . at the very highest point of mastery'.[7] At home he had received the endorsement of his peers through his appointment as Professor of Music History at the newly opened Royal College of Music and through honorary doctorates at Cambridge and Oxford. He was the composer of two large-scale symphonies, incidental music for Aristophanes' comedy *The Birds*, and a second choral commission for Gloucester, *The Glories of Our Blood and State*. Only opera stood before him as the principal challenge, one which he was only too willing to take on given the new vigour and momentum of English opera under the direction of Carl Rosa at Drury Lane.

Carl Rosa's initiative to perform opera in English was a risky enterprise. The Royal Italian Opera at Covent Garden and the Italian Opera at Her Majesty's Theatre and their cohorts of highly paid singers and conductors not only enjoyed the monopoly of operatic productions, but also, by their very presence and *raison d'être*, accentuated the national acceptance of grand opera as a foreign, or more quintessentially, Italian commodity. Through a series of unfortunate circumstances, English opera, whether under Balfe, Pyne and Harrison or Mapleson, had not prospered, yet under Rosa there at last seemed the real prospect of an alternative opera company in which the language of the production was always the vernacular. Rosa's first production, of *The Marriage of Figaro*, took place at the old Princess's Theatre in September 1875. He expected at first to make a loss, but, with time and a sufficiently popular programme of a limited number of operas each season, he could turn loss into profit, not least since the cost of his singers was only a fraction of that of the 'stars' of the Italian opera. Success followed with *The Flying Dutchman*, Adam's *Giralda*, Hérold's *Zampa*, and Nicolo's *Jaconde* in 1876, and Nicolai's *The Merry Wives of Windsor* in 1878. *Rienzi*, *Tannhäuser* and *Lohengrin* were given between 1879 and 1882, productions which stood their ground alongside Richter's new series of German operas (which themselves challenged the monopoly of Italian as the established language of the opera house), and Angelo Naumann's four cycles of *Der Ring* at Her Majesty's Theatre in 1882.

It had always been part of Rosa's agenda that, if English opera could gain a firm enough footing in London, new British opera on a grand scale would form part of his annual repertoire. Early on, in 1876, he had in fact included Cowen's *Pauline* though its relatively minor success persuaded him to return to more mainstream works in order to be sure of the company's safe financial position. It was not until 1883 that Rosa introduced British opera to the public, but this time the impact was almost unprecedented. Goring Thomas's *Esmeralda* and Mackenzie's *Colomba* were extraordinarily successful and on tour were taken up on the continent, and enjoyed revivals. *Esmeralda* in particular was staged in Cologne and Hamburg, and was considered by some, including Verdi, as the first important English opera. In 1884 Stanford's third opera, *The Canterbury Pilgrims*, also sold well though perhaps less enthusiastically than either *Esmeralda* or

[7] Diary, 26 July 1882.

Colomba,[8] and in 1885 Goring Thomas produced an opera, *Nadeshda*, more substantial in its musical content than *Esmeralda*, but less kindly received by audience and critics. A similar fate befell Mackenzie's second opera, *The Troubadours*, in 1886, though Corder's *Nordisa* was more successful in 1887.

It was undoubtedly this environment of indigenous operatic creativity that encouraged Parry to try his hand. He had attended all the new English operas in London, including the debacle of Stanford's *Savonarola* at Covent Garden in July 1884, and was highly motivated to produce a work in the Wagnerian mould which could expand the more limited horizons of *Prometheus Unbound*. A further imperative for his opera was also one of national colour and character. Stanford had, to some extent, already pointed the way in his (extremely) free adaptation of Chaucer and the inclusion of 'Sumer is i-comen in' as a national leitmotiv in *The Canterbury Pilgrims*, a work Parry admired with some reservations. But it was to tragedy, not comedy, that he turned for his subject matter. Widely read in English literature and history, Parry searched for congenial material. He was almost certainly attracted to Tennyson's 'national' plays, *Queen Mary* and *Becket*, but any possibility of using them evaporated after Stanford provided incidental music for the former in 1876 and planned an opera on the latter.[9] He had read many of Scott's historical novels and Kingsley's *Hereward the Wake*, but in the end his love of the Arthurian legends (and more specifically the love of Lancelot and Guenever), with which he had become acquainted at Oxford (through the four sections of Tennyson's *Idylls of the Kings*), completely overwhelmed him.[10] It was a theme ideally suited to his Wagnerian ideal and one that no other contemporary native composer had decided to undertake.[11]

Parry's librettist, Una Taylor, was suggested by Sir George Grove. Taylor was the daughter of Sir Henry Taylor, diplomat, poet, and essayist, and a friend of Edward Poynter, Edward Burne-Jones, and G.F. Watts. She was inexperienced and knew nothing of the theatre, disadvantages which should have persuaded Parry to look elsewhere; but their mutual enthusiasm for the venture seems to have blinded them to any shortcomings for the two agreed to collaborate immediately. Not long before her death in 1922, Taylor spoke of the collaboration:

> His [Parry's] conception of the story and mine differed. As you know, the Morte [d'Arthur] is a medley of various versions of the stories it tells, and it seemed to

[8] Stanford had already enjoyed some success with *The Veiled Prophet of Khorassan* (Hannover 1881) and *Savonarola* (Hamburg 1884).
[9] Stanford's plans to write an opera on *Becket* with a libretto by Gilbert A'Beckett did not materialise largely because Rosa took fright after the fiasco of *Savonarola* at Covent Garden on 9 July 1884. Stanford did, however, compose incidental music for the play in its production by Henry Irving at the Lyceum Theatre in 1893.
[10] In his diary, letters and the manuscript of the opera Parry uses a variety of spellings for Arthur's queen – 'Guenever', 'Guinivere', and 'Guinever'. The one most often used – in the manuscript of the opera – is the one I have adopted in the text, though in the quotation of diary extracts and letters I have quoted the spellings as they appear.
[11] Sullivan had in fact considered the subject of 'Guinevere' in the 1860s. His friend, Lionel Lewin, who died young, had written a libretto for him, which Sullivan exhumed in April 1884. The author and journalist Andrew Lang was enlisted to rework Lewin's manuscript libretto, but nothing further came of the work. It is possible, perhaps, that Sullivan may have heard of Parry's operatic project though no evidence exists to confirm this conjecture; see A. Jacobs, *Arthur Sullivan* (Oxford, 1984), p. 195.

me one could legitimately base our plot on a less commonplace one than the generally received tradition, and make Gareth's death, not Guenevere's faithlessness, the main motive in the tragedy. After Hubert Parry had read up the chapters in the Morte which I thought justified this rendering, I think he agreed willingly to work on those lines.[12]

At first Parry may have been in two minds about Taylor's scenario. It seems probable that at first he saw Lancelot and Guenever as equal protagonists, and in the early stages, before his meetings with Taylor, called his projected opera *Lancelot* in discussions with Dannreuther.[13] After the two met on several occasions in June, however, Taylor's view of the opera prevailed and Parry set to work on a series of copious sketches.

After Taylor left Parry's seaside home at Rustington on 18 June, Parry's diary informs us that he began to sketch Act I two days later: 'Good day's work at 1st Act of Opera', he recorded cheerfully; 'finished the sketch before I went to bed'.[14] Sketches for the rest of the opera were disrupted by the need for his return to London for the Royal College's summer term. There was still time, however, to learn more about the stage by attending the opera, and he was able to take advantage of Richter's production of *Tristan und Isolde* at Covent Garden, and, at the same time, be appalled by the travesty of Stanford's *Savonarola* at the same theatre. No doubt he hoped and felt he could do better. After the summer term was over, Parry returned to Rustington to find Una Taylor in residence. She stayed for a week during which it was agreed that their original conception of the scenario should be radically altered by beginning the opera further back in the story and by excising many of the retrospective allusions (dramatic devices which not only encumbered the plot but also held back the momentum). In a letter to Dannreuther, on whose constant advice and experience Parry relied throughout the composition of the opera, Parry explained the new plan:

I've got my librettist here, and we have been discussing the alterations in Guenever; and it strikes us that it will simplify matters altogether if we take up the story further back. We shan't have to go in for so many retrospective allusions. What we have got to is this. Act I – opens outside the walls of Chester. People moving about, and anticipating good sport at the burning of Guenever; and making up the pile of faggots. Enter Mordred and Gareth; Mordred is trying to persuade the latter to join in enforcing the sentence on Guenever, and tells him that Lancelot is expected to try to and rescue her. Guenever is brought in and protests her innocence bravely, and tells Mordred he has slandered her to the King. Mordred answers more or less mockingly and persuades the people that the sentence of burning is quite just. Guenever is tied to the stake and the fire lighted. Lancelot charges in with a small party of knights, knocks over a few knights and people and kicks the faggots out of the way – breaks the chain that binds Guenever to the stake and exits with her. Gareth, unarmed, is seen lying wounded close by as Lancelot goes out, and the curtain comes down. The old first act as you have seen it then follows. The main alteration being that Arthur is obviously at war with Lancelot, and

[12] C.L. Graves, *Hubert Parry* ii (London, 1926), p. 210.
[13] Diary, 28 May 1884.
[14] Diary, 20 June 1884.

Lancelot tries to make it up with him but fails. There is no need to explain why Arthur is going out to battle, and Mordred merely makes use of his opportunity to fall traitorously upon Arthur at the beginning of Act 3 and so on as before . . .[15]

Though the libretto of the opera was destroyed by Taylor (along with all correspondence with Parry) 'after there seemed no prospect of the opera being ever performed',[16] one is able to piece together the scenario from the manuscript which survives in short score in the Royal College of Music.[17] Act II begins with a female chorus which anticipates the tragedy of the love triangle of Arthur, Lancelot, and Guenever by relating the hapless tale of Sir Tristram. A horn sounds outside and Mordred returns with his knights bearing the dead body of Gareth. Lyones, Gareth's wife (described in Malory as 'the Lady of the Castle Perilous') enters to mourn the death of her husband. With Mordred's encouragement, she swears vengeance on Lancelot and Guenever. With the departure of Lyones, Arthur enters to the news of Gareth's death and he too is persuaded by Mordred's mischievous account of his nephew's demise. Mordred departs leaving Arthur to receive Lancelot and Guenever. Swayed by Mordred's account of Lancelot's treachery and of Guenever's infidelity, Arthur is in no mood to believe their entreaties. Making his farewell to Guenever, Lancelot departs knowing he is at war with Arthur, a conflict which Guenever begs Arthur to repudiate. He forgives her but is determined to wreak revenge on Lancelot. The last part of Act II leaves Guenever alone to confront a repentant Mordred. In seeking the queen's forgiveness he is spurned as a traitor, but reveals that his own army of knights have sworn not only to avenge Gareth's death by slaying Lancelot, but also to make Mordred Lord of all England by slaying Arthur. Guenever's pleading is drowned out by Mordred's army and the curtain falls.[18]

From Parry's letter to Dannreuther in August 1884 it is clear that he envisaged a dramatic opening to Act III with Mordred's attack on Arthur, whose army, after its war with Lancelot, is exhausted and depleted. Yet, since this part of the plot is missing in the manuscript, it would suggest that this part of the plot was discarded. Instead a lament for Lyones was written as the first scene which was followed by the entrance of Mordred. He announces that he and his army have prevailed and that he administered a fatal spear thrust to Arthur in the heat of battle. Yet Arthur's body was not to be found among the dead. Mordred's puzzlement is answered by Arthur's entry; the two fight, Mordred falls, and Arthur collapses from his wounds. Lyones approaches the dying king still with

<hr/>

[15] Letter from Parry to Edward Dannreuther, 1 August 1884, *GB-Ob* MS Eng. Letters.e.117.
[16] C.L. Graves, *Hubert Parry* ii (London 1926), p. 210.
[17] *GB-Lcm* MS 4194. There are also sketches of *Guenever* in *GB-Ob* MS Mus.c.122 (fols. 20–53) but fol. 54, originally identifed as one leaf of full score, is in fact from Parry's incidental music to Stuart Ogilvie's romantic tragedy *Hypatia* produced at the Haymarket Theatre in January 1893.
[18] In the autograph manuscript of this part of Act II was bound between the conclusion to Act I and the beginning of Act II. Whether this was the result of incorrect binding or of Parry's later revisions is unclear, though the lack of a simultaneous German text suggests that Parry may have rejected this section in favour of another conclusion which has either not survived or which he left unwritten.

vengeance on her lips. Arthur appeals to her to lay aside her wrath, but she is not to be assuaged. He begs her to take his ring to Guenever. Lyones promises, but sees her task as a new opportunity to seek revenge. The remaining part of the act recounts the hurling of Arthur's sword into the lake and the appearance of the barge which conveys the dying king to Avalon.

The courtyard of an abbey is the setting for Act IV. Guenever has found refuge in an abbey where she hopes to find peace and expiation of her sins. She bids farewell to her past life and proceeds to enter the abbey. At this point Lancelot enters and begs her to come with him to Brittany. She finally agrees but as they are about to depart the couple are accosted by a vengeful Lyones bearing Arthur's ring and by knights and women sworn to avenge Gareth's death. Lancelot and Guenever manage to shut the doors of the courtyard, but they give way and Lancelot is left to fend off the advancing hordes. In the meantime Lyones slips past him unawares and stabs Guenever on the steps of the abbey. The fighting stops, Guenever prays for forgiveness and dies; her body is then conveyed into the church on a shield by the nuns.

This, or at least something close to this, was the scenario Parry settled on for his opera. It was to be an uphill task. First Parry was inundated with other work. He had promised Dannreuther a new piano trio, there were articles for Grove's *Dictionary of Music and Musicians*, essays for Miss Leith's *Every Girl's Magazine* (which eventually found their way into *Studies of Great Composers*), public lectures for the Birmingham and Midland Institute, as well as the many duties at the RCM. Secondly, and of more immediate concern, was his failing health. Exhaustion, encumbered by encroaching angina, left Parry unable to work. In January 1885 he confided to his diary: 'After tea when I hoped to begin at the Opera again at last I was too tired and distracted and could not do anything that satisfied me.'[19] He was able to carry on until early June when an examination by the doctor gave him a serious shock: 'He examined away for a long while and looked so awfully grave at first that I began to think he was going to condemn me.'[20] Abstention from alcohol, smoking, and exercise were prescribed and several months of convalescence were ordered. On 17 June, with his companion Sedley Taylor (a musicologist at Trinity College, Cambridge), he embarked from Liverpool on the *Jupiter* for South America. From Lisbon he crossed to Cape Verde, sailed down the coast of Brazil to Rio de Janeiro, to Montevideo, and on to Tierra del Fuego. Up the coast of Chile the ship's destination was Valparaiso whose population consisted of a well-established British colony. From there he and Taylor travelled into the Andes on the backs of mules. Travelling by train to Santiago he heard *Aïda* creditably performed in the opera house before returning to Valparaiso to reboard the ship. On 18 September he arrived back at Rustington where the doctor declared his heart had moderately improved, though an inflamed cyst on his neck required operation, one which took place under gas on the sofa in his house at Upper Phillimore Place.

Parry felt distinctly uncertain about the prognosis of his health. He had been

[19] Diary, 17 January 1885.
[20] Diary, 3 June 1885.

advised to refrain from physical work of any kind, but had not been able to resist returning to sketches of the opera in early November and 'did a good bit of the first act afresh'.[21] Fortunately, a consultation with a noted heart specialist, Andrew Clark, had a rejuvenating effect:

> . . . [he] said my heart was strong, and that its peculiar behaviour arose from my excitable temperament. He said he did not think the voyage was likely to have done me much good, except as keeping me from worrying myself about arrears etc. . . . That work is good for me, and that I should not keep well without it. He actually recommended tea and allowed moderate smoke; but condemned beer absolutely. . . . I went away feeling a different man . . .[22]

The specialist's verdict enabled Parry to return to the vigour of his former work pattern. On 2 December he finished a new sketch of the First Act of *Guenever* and five days later he reached the end of a revised version of Act II 'by dint of working all day'.[23]

In January 1886 Parry met with Una Taylor once again with the dread realisation that he had chosen a librettist with whom he had little personal sympathy:

> Una Taylor is one of the most singular miniatures of cleverness and silliness I ever met. She sees everything upside down, and is mad with affectation to boot. She begins a conversation by asking Maude if she thinks murder is so seriously wrong after all. She says enthusiastically without being asked for an opinion that she does so "admire a theatrical voice in women". . . . The stage is more real to her than life. . . . When she first came, she cackled and giggled incessantly and by degrees under our silent habits she toned down.[24]

By the end of her stay, Parry was sick of her. 'We were thoroughly glad to be rid of her. The utter want of genuine hearty sincerity in her talk is more and more trying . . .'[25] By the beginning of February Parry finished sketching the opera and started to transfer his first thoughts into a piano arrangement which he showed to Dannreuther. The opera was also shown for the first time to Stanford who was 'very amiable [and] professed to be pleased with the first act of Guenever'.[26] On 21 March a completed Act II was shown to an approving Dannreuther but when he tried to make progress with Act III the language of the libretto proved to be a real obstacle: 'Tried to get on with Act 3 but stuck miserably fast. Una's language sticks in my throat and I cannot find anything satisfactory to go to it. I wrestled all day and did next to nothing and was a complete wreck after it.'[27] Little progress was made the following day and on 28 March Dannreuther professed himself 'disgusted with Una Taylor's words and thought it inevitable to rewrite a good deal of it'.[28] A 'tidy revision' of Act III was finished in early

[21] Diary, 8 November 1885.
[22] Diary, 13 November 1885.
[23] Diary, 7 December 1885.
[24] Diary, 16 January 1886.
[25] Diary, 18 January 1886.
[26] Diary, 10 March 1886.
[27] Diary, 26 March 1886.
[28] Diary, 28 March 1886.

April which just left the final act. Parry was sceptical: '. . . it doesn't seem at all satisfactory' he wrote with frustration in his diary.[29] By 25 April Act IV was undergoing revision and three weeks later he was 'putting the last touches to the pianoforte arrangement . . . and copying out the libretto'.[30] All this pressurised work was undertaken so that he could obtain Stanford's verdict of the opera. On 21 May Stanford wrote from Cambridge:

> I have just finished playing it through, and I think it's quite superbo, *really* superbo. Dramatically and every way I bet my hat on its success. The words are fine, and the book is quite admirable in my humble judgment. I would like you to alter one or two small things which I will show you (stage waits) and one or two *Parsifal* effects . . . No time to lose. I want to strike while the iron is hot.[31]

Stanford's urgency was motivated by his desire to show the opera to Carl Rosa. Parry considered this an advantage. He did not know Rosa well and was unfamiliar with the whole business of theatrical logistics. Stanford was an experienced opera composer and was more likely to be able to 'sell' *Guenever* to Rosa. The next few days and weeks were tense. During a visit to Cambridge on 15 June when Stanford conducted Parry's incidental music to Aristophanes' comedy *The Birds* for the Cambridge University Musical Society, the two men went through the opera together while Stanford suggested various emendations. Ten days later Parry wrote to Dannreuther (who had known Rosa as an old student colleague and friend during their days at Leipzig in the 1860s):

> Stanford tells me he is going to take the affair to Rosa on Monday. He said he hoped you might go with him, but I don't think that would be very pleasant for you. Sitting and looking on and doing chorus is not agreeable. But you might say a word to Rosa by note if you see cause and occasion enough to do so. That might encourage him to give it good consideration . . .[32]

But in the rush to get the copy to Stanford, Parry already harboured doubts about its readiness. 'I don't think you ought to go to Rosa's with Stanford', he urged in a second letter to Dannreuther; 'it will be an awful bore for you. But if you do, don't be surprised to find some things unaltered – as for instance the end of the First Act, where you spotted some very unsatisfactory things.'[33]

The result of the meeting on 28 June was more demoralising than Parry could have hoped. Rosa disliked much of the opera and considered much of the libretto unworkable. A letter to his wife summed up his disappointment and frustration:

> The news is as bad as it well can be. I saw Stanford last night and he told me all about it. Rosa doesn't like the libretto at all. The 2nd act he thinks hopeless – quite impossible! And even the music drags, as well it may with Una's successive processions of 'mailed' knights, who all must come in to slow march time. He liked the last act best, and the tail end of the 3rd act – when the

[29] Diary, 16 April 1886.
[30] Diary, 19 May 1886.
[31] Letter from Stanford to Parry, 21 May 1886, in Graves 1926 ii, p. 211.
[32] Letter from Parry to Dannreuther, 25 June 1886, *GB-Ob* MS Eng. Letters.e.117.
[33] Letter from Parry to Dannreuther, 27 June 1886, *GB-Ob* MS Eng. Letters.e.117.

barge comes in. But he will have nothing to do with performing it so as I said it will go into a drawer for good, and all that work is done with. I suppose it was good practice for me.[34]

To Una Taylor he tactfully withheld Rosa's criticisms of the libretto, and instead laid stress on the fact that, in spite of commendations from both Stanford and Dannreuther, Rosa had been unimpressed with the opera's scenario:

> I finished the pianoforte arrangement of the opera about 6 weeks or 2 months ago. I went through it with Dannreuther and he expressed himself much pleased with it. Then Stanford took it and also was pleased and offered to take it to Rosa. He and Dannreuther went together yesterday and I am sorry to say he as good as declined to have anything to do with it. He says in the first place anything to do with Arthur 'means ruin' in this country. 2ndly the third act drags and will have to be entirely rewritten librettoly and musically – the whole conception of it changed in fact! What he likes best is the tail end of the 3rd and the 4th act entire. I am so accustomed to disappointment that I shall probably soon shake it off after a bad night or two, when as last night bits of it will keep ringing in my head whether I will or no. But I am very sorry for you. I think it will disappoint you. There is no help for it. The best that could be done was done for it and there it ends.[35]

With Rosa's refusal there was no realistic opening for Parry's opera in London. Stanford, who had suffered several disappointments himself – Rosa had declined to perform his first opera, *The Veiled Prophet of Khorassan*, and the agony of *Savonarola* at Covent Garden had involved an unpleasant court case – was more resilient. He suggested the possibility of a German opera house, and Dannreuther backed him. For this a German translation was necessary, so Parry hired the services of Friedrich Althaus, Professor of German Literature at University College, London. Althaus quickly produced a translation and during his summer holiday to the continent Stanford, who was also trying to pedal his own *Canterbury Pilgrims*, discussed the matter with Emil Neckel of the Mannheim Theatre; through the intermediary of Carl Armbruster, *Guenever* was offered to Häckel at Munich, and at least one further, unnamed conductor was approached but declined, principally because Goldmark's *Merlin* was due to be premiered at the Vienna Hofoper in November.[36] The rejections from Germany hardened Parry's pessimism: 'He [Dannreuther] gave me back the MS of my opera which has been returned from Germany and is not to be tried. I knew that before it went. [The] excuses are polite; Goldmark's "Merlin" is too near the same subject – and Stanford's [work] is better backed with money guarantees.'[37] *Guenever* was then committed to a drawer and Parry never again referred to it either in his diaries or in correspondence, such was the bitterness of his disappointment.[38]

---

[34] Letter from Parry to Lady Maude Parry, 29 June 1886, *ShP*.
[35] Letter from Parry to Una Taylor, 29 June 1886, *GB-Ob* MS Eng. Letters.c.2.
[36] Graves 1926 ii, p. 212.
[37] Diary, 9 January 1887.
[38] The fate of *Guenever* was also sealed by Rosa's untimely death in 1889. This event largely killed off the production of new English operas. Only Sullivan's *Ivanhoe*, written for D'Oyley Carte's new English Opera House in Cambridge Circus in 1891, enjoyed real success, but even the auspicious beginning of Carte's grand enterprise quickly foundered which left no national focus for English opera to flourish.

Ex. 1.

[GUENEVER]

Ex. 2.

[MORDRED]

Ex. 3.

Moderato

[GARETH]

Ex. 4.

[LANCELOT]

Ex. 5.

Although blame can be levelled at Una Taylor for an uninspiring libretto – unbalanced in its focus of the main characters and encumbered by Pre-Raphaelite language – the fundamental problem with *Guenever* was that Parry was unable to apply his understanding of Wagner's theories of music drama with any consistency. Those essential elements of Wagnerian technique – a manner of vocal declamation informed by prose and irregular periodicity, the symphonic dimension of the orchestra, the psychological dimension of the libretto (which in itself informs the symphonic aspect of the music) and leitmotivs (which form the cement for the larger passages of declamation as well as the raw material for musical *and* dramatic development) – appeared to be Parry's aim, but his application of them was erratic and inchoate.

In his use of leitmotiv throughout the four acts of *Guenever* Parry exhibits a more wholehearted deployment of Wagner's method than do any of his British contemporaries; indeed not until Elgar's *Dream of Gerontius* do we see a native composer able to use leitmotivs with greater thoroughness and diversity. Parry's leitmotivs were also varied in character, register, and length. Guenever's material, the simplest and most malleable of all, consists of no more than a brief rising arpeggiation similar in shape to the famous Brahmsian cryptogram (Example 1) which is heard as she is led out to the pyre at the opening of Act I scene i. Mordred's brief figure (Example 2), furtive in nature, has similar musical potential, and with its dotted rhythm is often subsumed into march rhythms used to accompany his knights. Gareth's representative theme has from the outset a tragic, dirge-like quality (Example 3) in its rising figure across the octave which contrasts markedly with Lancelot whose idea is spacious, passionate and, of all the leitmotivs, the most extensive in terms of tessitura and duration (Example 4), while Arthur's motive, with its allusion to the 'Good Friday' music of *Parsifal*, is the most overtly Wagnerian in sound and manner (Example 5).

An examination of some individual scenes of *Guenever* reveals a composer who had the ability to handle the apparatus of Wagner's seamless canvas. Act I scene iv, which constitutes Guenever's main soliloquy, not only demonstrates a coherent A3A macro-structure and well-defined tonal scheme (F – D flat – F), but shows an understanding of that quintessential interdependence between voice and orchestra in which a new syntax of free prose-like phraseology is held together by a continually shifting background of leitmotivs, ever-changing in their musical constitution and dramatic context.[39] A similar flexibility can be observed in the lyrical soliloquies of Arthur, Lancelot and Guenever in Act II, while the love duet in Act IV for Lancelot and Guenever shows an imaginative and fluid melodic invention.

In spite of these successful instances of Wagnerian emulation in *Guenever*, much of the solo music of the opera is inhibited by poor vocal rhythm which is especially prevalent in the more animated dramatic sections such as for example the scene between Mordred and Guenever at the end of Act II, and the confrontation between Mordred and Arthur in Act III. Invariably the irregular phraseology of Parry's lyrical moods, where his natural lyrical predisposition was given room to expand and develop, was replaced by stereotypical, repetitive, sequential formulae, suggesting in themselves declining inspiration and inexperience. This is even more acutely felt in the weak chorus material where endless processions of knights in armour punctuate the plot (often as 'prefix' or 'suffix' to the solos of Mordred or Lancelot) with deadening effect. It was an irrevocable weakness which Parry clearly acknowledged after Rosa's rejection but felt that such major revision was not worth the trouble without an entirely new librettist and a new libretto.

The tragedy of *Guenever* is that it was clearly a project that excited the composer Stanford and Dannreuther both believed in the work, not because they were unaware of the opera's serious flaws, but because the quality of the best material revealed a passionate side of the composer's personality which the public had not heard since the performances of *Prometheus Unbound* in the early 1880s. There Parry had demonstrated his powers as a colourful orchestrator, particularly in the melancholy Prelude, the Furies Chorus (a compelling scherzo, spoilt only by poor vocal rhythm), Jupiter's scene, and the sumptuous scoring of 'The Spirit of the Hour'. These brave, contemporary sounds were, however, those very elements Parry chose to jettison in his later work. In later years his Darwinist obsession with form and intellectual content (or, to use the synonyms he coined in *The Art of Music* of 1893, 'design' and 'expression') led him to eschew colour and, as Vaughan Williams commented, 'an almost moral abhorrence of mere luscious sound'.[40] It is nevertheless open to question that, in the dramatic context of *Guenever*, Parry would have been moved to return to the vivid palette of *Prometheus*. It is a tantalising conjecture, made all the more so by the absence of an orchestral score.[41] There is also evidence that the romantic

---

[39] Act I scene iv of *Guenever* was scored by the author for the BBC in 1995 together with a concert ending.

[40] R. Vaughan Williams, 'A Musical Autobiography', in *National Music and Other Essays* (Oxford, 1986/2), p. 182.

[41] In his biography of Parry, Graves mentions that 'Stanford always adhered to the view that with a certain amount of revision and *rescoring* [my italics], the production of *Guenever* would

narrative of the opera, particularly the love element between Lancelot and
Guenever, provoked Parry into the creation of unusually passionate musical
ideas, which in his later choral works was deliberately tempered in favour of a
more reflective, philosophical demeanour. This is evident in the striking
orchestral interludes that anticipate the individual entries of Lancelot and
Guenever in Act II, and Arthur's entreaties to Lyones in Act III, and the love
duet of Lancelot and Guenever in Act IV. This duet is also preceded by a short
orchestral passage of great beauty which accompanies the lovers' poignant
joining of hands, and shows off Parry's distinctive handling of diatonic harmony
(Example 6). It was precisely to this hot-blooded character that Una Taylor
referred when she asserted that one could 'find qualities in Hubert Parry's opera
which are totally absent from his later compositions',[42] and which Stanford
believed might 'reveal a wealth of unexpected beauties in his music'.[43]

Rosa's rejection of *Guenever* plunged Parry into depression, but his salvation
came soon after, in 1887, with the premiere of *Blest Pair of Sirens*, commissioned
by Stanford and the Bach Choir for Queen Victoria's Golden Jubilee celebrations. In this work Parry found his true niche in the noble imagery of Milton's
poetry. More importantly his assimilation of Wagner – which is clearly evident
in the orchestral introduction's paraphrase of *Die Meistersinger* – found a happier
medium in a language equally influenced by Brahms and the cathedral music of
Parry's English forbears. Parry's Wagnerian aspirations were not, however,
entirely extinguished by the negative experience of his one attempt at opera. The
latent passion of Lancelot and Guenever found voice in the lyrical *Tristan*-
inspired duet between soprano and tenor ('Love to Love calleth') in the
Invocation to Music written for the bicentenary of Purcell's death in 1895 at
Leeds, and Parry's lasting impressions of *Die Walküre* and *Götterdämmerung* can
be heard in the orchestral movements of his much neglected incidental score to
The Agamemnon written for Cambridge in 1900 and the *Waldwebung* of his scena
for baritone and orchestra *The Soldier's Tent*, composed for Birmingham in the
same year. But it is surely in Parry's most substantial and original experiment –
'The Lamentation of Job' from his hour-long oratorio *Job* – that his desire to write
an extended dramatic monologue was fulfilled. In this lengthy scene the variety
of Parry's declamation, organic evolution, and leitmotivic transformation match
the rapidly shifting moods of Job's emotional predicament and, in emulating
Wotan's psychological searchings in *Die Walküre* and the 'Wahnmonolog' of
Hans Sachs in *Die Meistersinger*, allow room for that vital exploration of
character and self-examination which Una Taylor's inadequate libretto did not
provide in *Guenever*. Moreover, the complexity and breadth of Job's philosophical exposition were precisely those attributes that might well have given
the equally complex characters of Parry's opera life and depth. Indeed, Job's
baritone role and plaintive disposition has much in common with Arthur,

enhance the composer's reputation . . .' This would suggest that an orchestral score was
made. Yet no mention of scoring *Guenever* is made in Parry's diaries (a feature of his work he
always mentioned in connection with the composition of other works) which leads me to
believe that he only ever produced a piano score.
[42] Graves 1926 ii, p. 210.
[43] *Ibid.*, p. 212.

Ex. 6.

whose *Parsifal* reminiscences find a parallel in Job's central meditation ('Man that is born of woman'). Replete with its D flat *topos* of Valhalla and the last pages of *Götterdämmerung*, this is undoubtedly one of Parry's most inspired solo utterances and one in which his abortive experiences of opera found their creative catharsis.

King Arthur and the Wagner Cult in Spain: Isaac Albéniz's Opera Merlin

WALTER A. CLARK

On 20 June 1998, a stage work already a century old finally emerged from near-total obscurity into the light of day. It was a work that had experienced a difficult and lengthy gestation, only to be doubted, disparaged, and reviled by many critics and biographers, even those otherwise kindly disposed to its creator. On that day, José de Eusebio's concert version of Isaac Albéniz's *Merlin* premiered in Madrid at the Auditorio Nacional, astounding performers, audiences, and critics alike with its atmosphere, color, dramatic force, and almost complete independence from the Spanish style that the composer normally cultivated. Here was ample reason not only to reconsider the opera itself but also Albéniz's standing as a musical dramatist and, indeed, the nature and stature of musical theater in Spain around 1900.

In this chapter I wish briefly to examine the history and significance of *Merlin* (including its revival) and the incomplete *King Arthur* trilogy of which it was a part. The trilogy utilized a libretto by the English poet Francis Burdett Money-Coutts (1852–1923), while the obvious inspiration for the work was Wagner's *Ring*. It thus represents a fascinating confluence of national traditions and speaks clearly to a cosmopolitan dimension of Spanish music culture during that epoch commonly characterized as insular and parochial.[1]

Isaac Albéniz was born in northern Catalonia in 1860. He was of Basque and Catalan descent, but he is best remembered today for his piano pieces steeped in the folklore of Andalusia. A child prodigy of remarkable gifts, he evolved into a composer relatively late, only in his twenties, at which time he determined to use the treasure trove of Spanish folk music as the basis for many of his works. But not all of them, and this is an important point to make regarding Albéniz: he never confined himself to the folkloric idiom that became his stock in trade. He was quite capable of writing music in an international manner, often with an obvious debt to Chopin and Schumann. His sonatas and one piano concerto reveal scarcely a hint of Hispanism; the same is true of most of his songs. It is nonetheless the case that

---

[1] Much, though not all, of the material in this paper appears in the author's *Isaac Albéniz: Portrait of a Romantic* (Oxford: Oxford University Press, 1999). A slightly revised paperback edition (2002) and a more extensively revised Spanish translation (Madrid: Turner Publicaciones, 2002) of that biography are now available. For thorough bibliographic and discographic information, as well as a summary biography, see the author's *Isaac Albéniz: A Guide to Research* (New York: Garland, 1998).

his reputation rests firmly on such collections for solo piano as the first *Suite española*, *Recuerdos de viaje* (both from the 1880s), *Cantos de España* (from the early 1890s), and *Iberia* (completed in 1908, a year before his death).

Albéniz's nationalism was heavily influenced by his mentor Felip Pedrell (1841–1922), a composer and musicologist of considerable importance in nineteenth-century Spain. Albéniz embraced Pedrell's pan-Hispanic aesthetic and his openness to foreign trends, especially Wagner. This sort of progressive openness to the world outside of Spain – a cosmopolitan, liberal nationalism that celebrated both national unity and the regional cultural diversity within the nation itself – put Albéniz in the vanguard of artists and intellectuals in that country. It also ensured that, given the repressive and reactionary political atmosphere that prevailed in Spain during much of his life, he would feel increasingly estranged and alienated from his homeland. This disenfranchisement was exacerbated by the limited opportunities in Spain and the somewhat provincial cultural condition of the country. Thus, at the height of his powers as a performer, he ventured beyond Spain to develop his compositional craft in a more progressive environment.[2]

In 1889 Albéniz left the womb of his homeland for good and launched out on a career that would make a name for him throughout Europe. After successful appearances in Paris and Britain, he settled in London in the following year and remained there until late 1893. At first he devoted himself to concertizing, but gradually he became more absorbed in writing and directing operetta. In fact, it had long been his ambition to succeed on the stage, and his increasing involvement with musical theatre coincided with the gradual attenuation of his concertizing.

In the summer of 1892, Albéniz began work on an operetta in two acts entitled *The Magic Opal*, with a text by a popular English librettist of the day, Arthur Law. The work premiered on 19 January 1893, at the Lyric Theatre. It initially proved so successful that a touring company was formed only three weeks after the premiere to perform it throughout Britain. The London run, however, ended ignominiously on 27 February, due in part to the mediocre libretto. A revision renamed *The Magic Ring* fared little better in April 1893, at the Prince of Wales's Theatre. But Bernard Shaw conceded that even 'the revised version of the opera leaves Albéniz easily ahead of the best of his rivals'.[3]

Early in his London tenure Albéniz had signed an agreement making the businessman Henry Lowenfeld his agent.[4] In June 1893, Albéniz entered into a revised agreement with Lowenfeld that now included a third party. This man was Francis Burdett Money-Coutts, later the Fifth Lord Latymer, a London solicitor, poet, librettist, and wealthy heir to the fortune of the Coutts banking

---

[2] Albéniz's remarks on culture and politics in Spain were sometimes very acerbic. For example, in a diary entry of 2 April 1902, he declared that 'the Spanish people sing a lot but think little'. This diary is located in the Museu de la Música in Barcelona; all future references to diary entries pertain to this manuscript.

[3] This review appeared in *The World* on 19 April 1893. It is reproduced in Dan H. Laurence, ed., *Shaw's Music: The Complete Music Criticism in Three Volumes* (New York: Dodd, Mead & Co., 1981), ii, p. 859.

[4] Lowenfeld was of Polish (Galician) extraction. He made a fortune through his association with Kops' Ale, a non-alcoholic beer. In 1865, he founded the Universal Stock Exchange.

family. Through his involvement with the finances of both the Lyric and Prince of Wales's Theatres, Money-Coutts became an avid admirer of Albéniz and his music. Over time he became an intimate friend and generous benefactor as well. But the essential nature of their association was a collaboration in which Money-Coutts supplied Albéniz with a large income in exchange for Albéniz's setting his poetry to music and bringing him what he craved most: fame as a writer and vindication of his *declassé* literary ambitions.

Money-Coutts (who adopted the pen name 'Mountjoy') was educated at Eton and later took advanced degrees at Cambridge. He eventually became a prolific author, his preferred vocation, and did a considerable amount of editorial work for his London publisher John Lane. Albéniz's first assignment from him was to set the libretto for an opera whose action takes place during the Wars of the Roses, eventually entitled *Henry Clifford*. Albéniz began work on this new opera about the time he decided to leave London, for various reasons, in the fall of 1893. He returned to Spain for a few months before taking up permanent residence in Paris the following year.

Work on the new opera proceeded for over a year before its premiere in May 1895, at the Gran Teatre del Liceu in Barcelona. The story concerns young Henry Clifford, who is forced into exile but eventually returns in triumph and ascends to the throne upon the death of Richard III at Bosworth. The score reveals only here and there slight intimations of Hispanism, but neither does it rely on English carols or much local colour of any kind. In fact, this was Albéniz's most Italianate effort and reminds one of Verdi. The opera even premiered in Italian rather than the original English, as that was the custom at the Liceu (in which Ricordi had a controlling interest).

The critics received *Enrico Clifford* politely, at times with enthusiasm, but generally found the subject matter too far removed from Albéniz's native temperament. Albéniz evidently agreed with this assessment and prevailed upon Money-Coutts to fashion a libretto from a Spanish novel by Juan Valera (1824–1905). This formed the basis for his most successful opera, *Pepita Jiménez*, which premiered in Barcelona in 1896 and was subsequently produced in Prague (1897), Brussels (1905), Paris (1923), again in Barcelona (1926), and finally in Madrid (1964).[5]

The final product of Albéniz's operatic association with Money-Coutts was a project on a truly grand scale, one that held tremendous importance for Money-Coutts, if not as much for Albéniz. This was an operatic trilogy based on the fifteenth-century Arthurian romance *Le Morte Darthur* by Sir Thomas Malory. The constituent parts of the *King Arthur* trilogy were to be *Merlin*, *Launcelot*, and *Guenevere*. The urgency Money-Coutts felt about this project can already be sensed in a letter of 4 January 1895, in which he relates the following:

> I am feeling very much upset by the coming production of a drama at the Lyceum taken from the King Arthur legend. 10 years ago I projected writing 3 operas on that theme, and have amassed a large quantity of material. But now

---

[5] A creditable recording of most of the opera is now available on a Harmonia Mundi CD (HMC–901537). It features Josep Pons conducting the Orquestra de Cambra Teatre Lliure, using the original English libretto rather than any of the myriad translations.

this wretch, this author, has got my precise idea! He has taken Morgan Le Fay
as one of the principal characters (which Tennyson never did) and in fact,
seems to me to have sucked my brains, probably through the perfidy of some
kind friend to whom I may have talked of the scheme![6]

His devotion to *King Arthur* did not wane with the passage of time. In a letter
of 23 May 1903, Money-Coutts wrote to Albéniz's wife, Rosina, in response to
her concerns about the financial arrangements between him and her husband.
She felt that Albéniz was not producing a quantity of music commensurate with
the generous stipend he was affording them. To this he responded:

> The process, in the case of music, is of course slow; but it has been no slower
> than I anticipated, & when it is finished, my dear Madame, remember this:
> whatever "The Public" may think of our operas, we shall have done, to the
> utmost of our ability, a work that in England can never be disregarded; we
> shall have written *The National Trilogy* . . .[7]

We begin to appreciate the fact that Albéniz was not only involved in the
creation of Spanish national opera, but English as well. However, Albéniz's usual
facility of composition failed him as he waded into a musical swamp from which
he had increasing difficulty extricating himself. It took him several years to finish
the first opera, and the trilogy as a whole remained incomplete at his death.[8]

This Arthurian episode is treated in the secondary literature as an incredible
aberration in Albéniz's career, a totally misguided effort that was foisted on him
by the eccentric Maecenas in whose hands he had unwisely placed his financial
well-being. However, one could see the project as consistent with Albéniz's
devotion to Wagnerism, a love affair that went back perhaps as far as his days
as a student of Louis Brassin in Brussels in the 1870s. During his London years he
made a deep impression on Bernard Shaw with his performance of Brassin's
transcriptions of selections from *Das Rheingold* and *Die Walküre*.[9] Albéniz attended
performances of Wagner's operas whenever possible and even conducted
rehearsals of *Tristan und Isolde*. Detailed annotations made by him in his personal
copies of the full scores to the *Ring* reveal a profound knowledge of the music.[10]

The fact that Albéniz would compose an opera upon this subject should not
strike us as so strange, considering the fascination with things Arthurian that
gripped *fin-de-siècle* artists and musicians. In fact, Albéniz was preceded by his
Catalan countryman Amadeu Vives, who also wrote an Arthurian opera,
entitled *Artus* (1895). Of course, there was the influence on him of Pedrell,

---

[6] This letter is in the Biblioteca de Catalunya in Barcelona.
[7] This letter is in the Museu de la Música in Barcelona.
[8] Albéniz nearly completed *Merlin* in 1898 but then got bogged down in numerous revisions.
    In fact, he never finished the orchestration of Act I, and this was done posthumously (at
    Money-Coutts's behest) by León Jehin, director of the Monte Carlo orchestra.
[9] In the *Star* (6 December 1889), Shaw enthused that Albéniz's rendition of selections from *Die
    Walküre* at a recent concert of the Wagner Society produced a 'dead silence' in the audience
    that was 'the highest compliment he could have desired'. See Laurence, ed., *Shaw's Music*, i,
    p. 868.
[10] Reference to his conducting rehearsals of *Tristan* is made in *La música ilustrada hispano-
     americana* 2/20 (10 October 1899), p. 10. His *Ring* scores are now in the library of the Escuela
     Superior de Canto in Madrid.

who had composed his Wagnerian trilogy *Els Pirineus* only a few years earlier, in 1891.[11] In connection with the publication in 1892–93 of the music and libretto for his new opera, Pedrell published *Por nuestra música* ('For Our Music') as a guide to his compositional method and as a manifesto, presenting his adaptation of Wagner's philosophy to the Spanish nationalist impulse in music.

It is not generally known that the Wagner cult gained a foothold in the Iberian peninsula. Consequently, little research has been done on the production and reception of Wagner's operas in Spain, and the influence his music and writings had on local composers. The appeal Wagner had for citizens of Catalonia in particular is not hard to comprehend. Like the Germans, they too were striving for a sense of national and racial identity. Moreover, the fact that Parsifal declares himself from Montsalvat, and the association of that place with the Holy Grail, made Catalonia one of the locales outside of Germany most closely associated with Wagnerian myth. Appealing, too, was the combination of old and new in Wagner's work, his glorification of a haloed medieval past through a very forward-looking artistic language. This blending of the archaic and the modern was in harmony with the spirit of the *Renaixensa*, a nineteenth-century revival of Catalan literature, language, and culture.

Pedrell, along with the Catalan composer and conductor Enric Morera, became the high priest of Wagnerism in Spain. But the Spanish fascination with Wagner had actually begun in the 1860s in Madrid, when the Sociedad Artístico-Musical de Socorros Mutuos presented *Madrileños* with their first taste of Wagner (excerpts from *Tannhäuser*). The Sociedad de Conciertos, founded in 1866, performed the overtures to *Rienzi* and *Lohengrin*, and Wagner's works remained a staple of the Sociedad's repertoire into the twentieth century. The Teatro Real in Madrid responded to increasing interest in German opera by staging several of Wagner's works. The Madrid critic Antonio Peña y Goñi was a confirmed Wagnerite and did his part to promote an appreciation of Wagner's operas, although he was opposed by *amatori* of Italian opera such as the critic Luis Carmena y Millán. The year 1911 witnessed the rather belated birth of the Asociación Wagneriana de Madrid.

The Wagner cult took deepest root, however, not in Madrid but rather in Barcelona. During the first half of the nineteenth century, Italian opera had reigned supreme in Catalonia, as elsewhere in Spain. But selections from *Tannhäuser* were performed in Barcelona in 1862, and by 1870 there was a Wagnerian society in that city. The young music critic Marsillach i Lleonart was an enthusiastic Wagnerite who attended a performance of the *Ring* cycle in Bayreuth in 1876. Still, before Wagner's death in 1883, few in Barcelona were familiar with his music. The production of a complete opera by Wagner had to wait until 1882 with the performance of *Lohengrin* at the Liceu. As was the custom there, it was done in Italian translation. The most powerful impetus toward the popular appreciation of Wagner's music came in 1899 with the production at the Liceu of *Die Walküre*, which inspired a genuine passion. For many years thereafter Wagner's operas dominated the repertoire of that theatre.

Albéniz and Coutts, then, had good reason to believe that a *King Arthur*

---

[11] This work did not premiere until 1902, at the Liceu in Barcelona. Albéniz wrote an effusive review praising its virtues in *Las noticias* (2 January 1902).

trilogy could gain success not only abroad but also in Spain itself. When precisely the project commenced is not known. All three librettos were published in 1897 by John Lane in London. Albéniz finished the orchestral score for *Merlin* in 1902, but it was only published in a piano-vocal arrangement, by Édition Mutuelle in 1906. Unfortunately, Albéniz completed only the piano-vocal score of the first of *Launcelot*'s three acts. Marginalia in the libretto represent his furthest progress with the four acts of *Guenevere*.[12]

Merlin is scored for piccolo, three flutes, two oboes, English horn, three B-flat clarinets, bass clarinet, three bassoons, contrabassoon, four F horns, four trumpets, three trombones, bass trombone, tuba, timpani, tam-tam, snare drum, two harps, and strings. The orchestration is not only rich but highly imaginative. The Prelude to Act I establishes a mood of mystery reminiscent of the beginning of *Das Rheingold*. It features a timpani roll juxtaposed against sustained notes in the string basses, horns, and contrabassoon, with the gradual addition of bassoon, bass clarinet, clarinet, and cello. Later on, Albéniz pits tremolandi strings against a melody in the low woodwinds (English horn, clarinet, and oboe). In addition, he employs divisi strings to fill out the texture called for by the rich harmonies. His mixing of colors is also remarkable. At one point in this Prelude, a trombone choir plays triple pianissimo against a melody in the string basses. This is followed by a haunting theme in the English horn. Such mixtures of strings and brass are frequently found throughout the score and reveal a newly found confidence in orchestration, the product not only of his experience in the theatre but also of the assistance he received from his friend Paul Dukas.

Albéniz's commitment to Wagnerian principles in the trilogy is apparent in his use of leading motives and their presentation and development almost exclusively in the orchestra. It is also apparent in his avoidance of simultaneous singing and his treatment of the voices, that is, in the emphasis on clarity of declamation and renunciation of *fioritura*. The chromatic harmony, relative absence of separable numbers, Arthurian subject matter, and overall conception of an operatic polyptych also clearly derive from Wagner. Moreover, the English scholar Clifford Bevan has identified four significant leading motives in *Merlin* that were apparently inspired by or taken directly from Wagner's *Ring*. The motives appear singly and in combination, and they migrate to the only completed act of the second opera, *Launcelot*. This opera also presents new motives, similarly derived from the *Ring*.[13] But Albéniz finds a way to sneak out from behind the facade of the work to reveal his true identity as a Spaniard, and in the middle of Act III occur two enchanting Spanish-style dances.

The story adheres fairly closely to Malory's, with a few notable exceptions, and is well known to all. It will suffice here simply to cover a few highlights. The opera is in three acts. Act I takes place outside of St Paul's church, in London, where the famous sword Excalibur is embedded in a marble block. Inside the church, monks are chanting; it is Christmas Day. Albéniz and Coutts employ

[12] He began work on the orchestral score of Act II in 1903 but quit after thirty-one pages. The manuscripts are now in the Biblioteca de Catalunya and Museu de la Música.
[13] See Clifford Bevan, 'Albéniz, Money-Coutts and "La Parenthèse londonienne"' (Ph.D. dissertation, University of London, 1994), pp. 191-9, for a discussion of Albéniz's Wagner borrowings.

here a hymn attributed to St Ambrose (340–97 C.E.). Albéniz carefully simulates the metric freedom of plainchant by eschewing a time signature (Ex. 1).

Ex. 1. *Merlin*, Act I: 'Veni redemptor genitum', bars 1–6

Arthur extracts Excalibur from the stone and is proclaimed king. The act ends with an ensemble passage (six soloists, chorus, and orchestra) whose grandeur is without precedent in any of Albéniz's earlier stage works.

Act II transpires in a hall in Tintagil (*sic*) castle. Merlin conveys to Arthur the glad tidings that the rebellion of Morgan and Mordred has been put down and that they have been taken captive. Merlin is aware, however, that Arthur is in love with Guenevere and advises him against giving in to his passion, which advice Arthur sternly rejects. Nonetheless, as long as Merlin remains puissant, Arthur is safe; therefore, Morgan casts about for a way to incapacitate Merlin. At this juncture, Nivian, a Saracen dancing girl, enters and explains the nature of the spell Merlin has cast upon her and her dancing sisters. It seems they are compelled by his magic to dance for the Gnomes, who, thus enticed, leave their grottoes unguarded so that Merlin is able to steal their gold. Nivian implores Morgan to break this spell, whereupon she enters into a scheme of Morgan's devising. Of course, no such money lust was part of Malory's romance, but the banker in Money-Coutts could not leave this situation unaltered. He was also no doubt inspired by the *Ring* cycle, which centres around precisely such gold fever.

An enchanting prelude is heard at the beginning of Act III, while the curtain is still down (Ex. 2).

Ex. 2. *Merlin*, Act III: Prelude, bars 5–12

Merlin enters and warns Arthur yet again about the perils of his attraction to
Guenevere. For his pains, however, Merlin is merely dispatched to ask for
Guenevere's hand in marriage on Arthur's behalf. Before setting out, Merlin
decides to raid the Gnomes' store of gold. Nivian now appears with her troop of
dancers, captivating Merlin and the Gnomes with their undulations, performed
in time with music in a very stylized Spanish manner that has reminded most
commentators of the *polo* by Manuel García on which the *entr'acte* before Act IV
of *Carmen* is based (Ex. 3).

Ex. 3. *Merlin*, Act III: Dance of Nivian and the Saracens, bars 493–7

The Gnomes are seduced out of their cavern and disappear in pursuit of the
Saracens, leaving Nivian and Merlin alone. Night descends, and a choral
number is accompanied by a bewitching play of lights across the stage.
Nivian now dances alone for Merlin, so enchanting him that he agrees to her
request to hold his staff. This dance is also very stylized but seems most akin to
the *malagueña* (Ex. 4).

Ex. 4. *Merlin*, Act III: Nivian's Dance, bars 937–40

These dance numbers compensate for a lack of dramatic action in Act III. This
produces an effect that, while entertaining, retards the momentum towards the
conclusion and is anti-climactic. Soon Merlin descends into the cave to plunder
the gold, whereupon Nivian strikes a nearby boulder with the staff, causing it to
roll over and seal the cave. Nivian rejoices in her freedom and determines to
return to her homeland. Morgan exults in their victory, and the curtain descends.
    The story continues in the next two operas. In *Launcelot*, Guenevere, now the
queen, is falsely accused of poisoning one of Arthur's knights, and Launcelot
steps forward to be her champion. This development is accompanied by their
mutual romantic attraction. In *Guenevere*, Launcelot is caught with the queen in
her chamber (where he has been lured by a forged letter) and Arthur declares
war on him. Arthur soon realizes, however, that Mordred is his real enemy, and
they slay one another in mortal combat. Guenevere retires to a convent, and
Launcelot is left alone to reflect ruefully on the demise of chivalry.

One of the chief problems any composer would have working with this libretto is Money-Coutts's penchant for archaisms and stilted poetry. Even Money-Coutts himself acknowledged as much in a letter to Albéniz of 26 June 1905, saying that he was 'anxious to eliminate ancient & obsolete words'.[14] This was fortunate, for some of the expressions he uses definitely impede comprehension (though Money-Coutts thoughtfully included a glossary in the published libretto). What agonies must the composer of Cantos de España have endured when he attempted to wrap his music around the following:

> When flowerets of the marigold and daisy are enfolden,/ And wingless glow-moth stars of love englimmer all the glades,/ The paynim fairies footing forth in every forest olden/ Dance hand in hand the saraband with fair enchanted maids! (Merlin, Act III, 30)

Still, one must give Albéniz credit. He always managed to set Money-Coutts's poetry with a sure sense of the accents of the language, no matter how contrived it was. But it is also easy to see why Albéniz resorted to a recitative style of vocal writing. Making any sort of lyric material out of this poetry would have stymied him completely.

Above and beyond his penchant for stilted and archaic language, Money-Coutts's prudishness comes to the fore in the following instructions to Albéniz:

> It is very important to maintain the strict idea of the Opera that Nivian wins the rod from Merlin without any *sexual* cajoleries at all. Such a disagreeable episode, however inevitably suspected by the *French* mind, would go far to ruin the Opera in England, besides being contrary to the *plot* of the Opera, which is that Nivian merely acts under Morgan's directions, in order to gain her liberty, and that Merlin regards her as *a child*, and for that very reason is quite off his guard.[15] [Emphasis in original]

Money-Coutts was evidently not very familiar with Freud or he would have seen that, even without 'sexual cajoleries', Nivian's 'winning the rod' was already heavily freighted with erotic innuendo. Interestingly, we encounter the 'woman-as-child' motif that runs like a thread through their correspondence.[16] Yet, such a woman-child has the ability to rob a man, even a mighty sorcerer, of his powers and imprison him (a woman's potential for distracting a man from his duty is a theme in all three of their completed operas).

Merlin was never produced during Albéniz's lifetime, though it was performed in a concert version at the home of a M. Tassel in Brussels in 1905 (Albéniz himself accompanied the singers at the piano). The Prelude to Act I was performed that same year at the concert hall Grand Harmonie in Brussels. The opera finally premiered on 18 December 1950, in Spanish, at the Tívoli in

---

[14] This letter is in the Biblioteca de Catalunya.
[15] From an undated list of corrections, now in the Museu de la Música.
[16] Albéniz's letters to Money-Coutts have not survived, but the Englishman's response to a letter from his Spanish friend sheds light on this issue: 'Where did you learn your theory of women. That they are mere children; and we are fools to treat them otherwise?' This appears in a letter from Money-Coutts to Albéniz dated 6 February 1901, which is now in the Museu de la Música.

Barcelona, performed by the Club de Fútbol Junior (Junior Football Club), whose annual custom it was to produce an opera. Though the Barcelona critics received the work with general approbation, *Merlin* rapidly retired to the oblivion whence it had emerged.

There was, however, earlier praise for the work. Ernest Newman extolled the 'magical beauty' of the music and recommended the score 'to anyone who is on the look-out for something at once original, strong and beautiful', and who could appreciate with him the fact that 'the best opera on our sacrosanct British legend has been written by a Spaniard'.[17] To be sure, however, most commentators have condemned the trilogy as a total waste of effort, one out of keeping with Albéniz's artistic temperament.

Until recently, it was rather difficult to judge for oneself the quality and character of the work. With its recent revival and subsequent recording, this has been made much easier. José de Eusebio is a Spanish conductor who was intrigued several years ago by the 'myth of the missing *Merlin*'. He tracked down hitherto unknown publishers' proofs and other matierals to expunge errors in the published sources and assist in reconstructing the opera as Albéniz had originally intended it. He then went on to revive and record the work, conducting the Orquesta Sinfónica de Madrid and enlisting the aid of Plácido Domingo in the role of King Arthur.[18]

Eusebio confidently predicts that *Merlin* is destined to become part of the major international operatic repertoire. This may be hyperbole. *Aida* or *Carmen, Merlin* is not. But it is vastly superior to what most people thought it was, and it establishes without doubt one fact: Spanish operatic composers felt the allure of the Arthurian legend as keenly as their contemporaries elsewhere in Europe, and their contributions to this particular repertoire were far from inconsiderable.

---

[17] Ernest Newman, 'Albéniz and his "Merlin"', *New Witness* 10/254 (20 September 1917), pp. 495–6.

[18] I refer here to the liner notes written by Eusebio for the recording (Decca 289467096–2). These are followed by insightful remarks from Jacinto Torres, the leading Spanish authority on Albéniz, who assisted Eusebio in his research. In his enthusiasm, Eusebio occasionally overstates his case. Though he leads one to believe otherwise, he was not the first to take a serious look at this opera, as Bevan and the present author had done it years earlier (not to mention Torres). His knowledge of manuscript sources far outstrips his knowledge of the existing literature on the subject. Please consult Jacinto Torres, *Catalogo sistemático descriptivo de las obras musicales de Isaac Albéniz* (Madrid: Instituto de Bibliografía Musical, 2001), for a thorough treatment of the thematic incipits, manuscript sources, and publication history of the King Arthur trilogy.

Ernest Chausson's Le Roi Arthus

TONY HUNT

Arthur despairing, relinquished his arms. In the golden and purple glow of the sunset, invisible voices summoned the king whom fate had disappointed to the mysterious isles. All around, the solemn, consoling music drifted upwards, soothing the vanquished king's grief and celebrating his final glory. For our part, we were thinking of the man who had poured out his heart in these voices of glory and sadness. And we lamented the fact that he too, like the old king, had been snatched from us in the midst of his task.

[Arthus, désespéré, laissait tomber ses armes. Dans l'or et la pourpre du couchant, les voix invisibles appelaient vers les îles mystérieuses le roi déçu par la destinée. La mélodie grave et consolatrice s'élevait de toutes parts pour bercer la douleur du vaincu et célébrer son apothéose. Et nous, nous songions à celui qui avait mis tout son coeur dans ces chants de gloire et de tristesse. Nous le plaignions d'avoir été, lui aussi, comme le vieux roi, arraché à sa tâche.[1]]

In the words with which André Hallays greeted the first performance of Chausson's one and only opera, Le Roi Arthus,[2] given at the Théâtre Royal de la Monnaie in Brussels on the 30th of November 1903, we already find an acknowledgement of that affinity between the composer and the central figure of his lyric drama which was to become a locus communis of critical writings on the work. Begun in 1886 as Op. 23, Le Roi Arthus was to cause its composer much heartsearching and protracted struggles before his death in 1899 in a bicycle accident. A draft scenario had been sent to Paul Poujaud in 1886, but it was not until nine years later that Chausson made heroic efforts to complete the work, at San Domenico di Fiesole, putting the final touches to Act 3 on Christmas Day 1895. Thereafter, there were constant attempts to have the opera staged, beginning with proposals by the Belgian violinist Ysaÿe[3] for a production in

---

[1] A. Hallays, 'Le Roi Arthus', La Revue de Paris 6 (déc. 15 1903), pp. 846–58 at 846.

[2] 'Drame lyrique en 3 actes et 6 tableaux', it follows the Wagnerian pattern of continuous music and vocal writing, separated only by orchestral interludes, thus eschewing the more traditional sequence of recitative and aria. For a list of ten projected theatrical works by Chausson see Jean Gallois, Ernest Chausson: L'homme et son oeuvre (Paris, 1967; repr.1981), pp. 113f. La Vie est un songe, adapted from the most celebrated of Calderon's dramas, La vida es sueño, was planned as an opera of which the libretto was completed (1899), but not a note of music written.

[3] A friend of the composer, who dedicated the widely performed Poème Op. 25 to him, Ysaÿe not only gave the first performance of that work, but played it as a tribute to his dead friend, a week after his death, on 17 June 1899. Today the Poème is the best known of Chausson's works and was the subject of an unforgettable recording by the lamented Ginette Neveu in 1946 (with Issay Dobrowen and the Philharmonia Orchestra). Ysaÿe was also the dedicatee of the

Geneva and continuing with representations by the conductor Nikisch for a performance in Dresden, the Spanish composer Albéniz[4] for one in Prague, and Felix Mottl for its staging in Karlsruhe. Discouraged, Chausson had talked of leaving the field to 'Bruneau et Wagner' (!). In the event, his sudden death was to delay performance yet further, though his widow lived to attend the first night. Lacking confidence and afflicted with the severe self-criticism that also assailed Dukas, Duparc and Maurice Emmanuel, Chausson would scarcely have been prepared for the enthusiastic reception his work received in Brussels, an enthusiasm unfortunately not shared by Paris, where his publisher Choudens had high hopes. In his review of the first performance Hallays wrote,

> King Arthur compelled general admiration by virtue of the chivalric grandeur of its poetic conception, the charm and originality of the musical material, the richness of the orchestration, and the wonderful lyricism of Arthur's role.

> [Le Roi Arthus a forcé l'admiration générale par la grandeur chevaleresque de la conception poétique, la grâce et l'originalité des thèmes, la richesse de l'orchestration, le superbe lyrisme du rôle d'Arthus.[5]]

In another notice of the Brussels production Gustave Samazeuilh was warmly appreciative, whilst expressing some reservations about the orchestration of Act 1:

> Nor will we endeavour to catalogue all the themes, invariably expressive and characteristic, which support the orchestral polyphony of King Arthur. Nevertheless, we would be remiss if we did not praise the brilliance and warmth of the instrumentation, perhaps a little thick for the vocal writing of Act 1, as is often the case in other works of the same era as King Arthur. There is no doubt that if the composer were alive today, he would be the first to lighten the instrumental writing with a view to making the words more easily audible.

> [Nous ne nous évertuerons pas non plus à dresser le catalogue des thèmes, toujours expressifs et caractéristiques, sur lesquels s'échafaude la polyphonie orchestrale du Roi Arthus. Nous nous en voudrions néanmoins de ne pas louer l'éclat et la chaleur de l'instrumentation, peut-être un peu opaque au premier acte pour les voix, ainsi qu'il advient souvent dans d'autres ouvrages contemporains d'Arthus. Il est certain que l'auteur, s'il vivait aujourd'hui, serait des premiers à rechercher une atmosphère instrumentale allégée et plus propice à la perception des paroles chantées.[6]]

Particularly laudatory and perceptive were the remarks of Georges Eekhoud several months later, printed in the influential Mercure de France:

> The critics were unanimous in praising the firm, noble handling of the score in King Arthur. The orchestral scoring, dense and opulent without being over-

---

remarkable, if not totally successful, Concert in D major for piano, violin, and string quartet (1889–91).

4 Albeniz himself planned an operatic trilogy King Arthur, of which only the third part, Merlin, was composed. See Walter A. Clark's essay, pp. 51–60 above..

5 Art. cit., p. 847.

6 G. Samazeuilh, 'Ernest Chausson et Le Roi Arthus (Théâtre de la Monnaie, 30 novembre)', La Revue Musicale 3e année, no. 18 (15 décembre 1903), pp. 699–705 at 704. Gustave Samazeuilh, who died as recently as 1967, was, like his friend and teacher, Chausson, a law graduate and distinguished himself as a composer and critic, as well as preparing the French version of Tristan und Isolde. In 1947 he published a sketch, 'Ernest Chausson', in Musiciens de mon temps.

done, the harmonic richness, the elegant and refined writing which retains remarkable fluency and light; the exquisite tonal combinations, the attractive chromaticism, the endless modulations, the originality and expressive power of the musical themes, the pace and style of the spoken parts, the perfect judgement of emphasis, the symphonic accompaniment of the characters' gestures and actions, and above all the wonderfully descriptive preludes and interludes, not to mention the impressive choral ensemble at the end; all these features conspire to make the work one of the most beautiful works of which the young French school can be justly proud.

[La critique fut unanime à louer la ferme et noble tenue de la partition du *Roi Arthus*. Le travail orchestral, très fouillé et opulent sans surcharge, les riches harmonies, l'écriture élégante et recherchée quoique toujours aisée et lumineuse; les exquises combinaisons de timbres, le chromatisme si attachant, les modulations infinies, l'originalité et la valeur expressive des thèmes mélodiques, l'allure et le style des récits, la justesse de l'accent, le commentaire symphonique des gestes et des sentiments des personnages, et surtout les admirables préludes et interludes descriptifs, sans oublier le prestigieux ensemble choral du dénouement; tous ces éléments concourent à faire de cette oeuvre une des plus belles dont s'enorgueillera la jeune école française.[7]]

There is no doubt that Chausson was fortunate in the circumstances and choice of venue of the first performance of his opera. The Théâtre Royal de la Monnaie in Brussels had an enviable record of operatic first performances, including Reyer's *Sigurd* (7 Jan. 1884) and *Salammbô* (2 Feb. 1890), Chabrier's *Gwendoline* (10 April 1886), d'Indy's *Fervaal* (12 March 1897), and Blockx's *De bruid der zee* (1902). Albeniz's *Pepita Jiménez* was performed there. It was the first theatre to give the French versions of *Aida* (1871), *Tannhäuser* (1873) and *Meistersinger* (1885) and had performed Bellini, Donizetti and Verdi before Paris did. Chausson's early teacher, Massenet, whom he left to study exclusively with Franck, had his *Hérodiade* performed at the theatre, the première taking place on 19 December 1881. The production of *Le Roi Arthus*, meticulously supervised by d'Indy, was in fact the fulfilment of a promise given by one of the directors, Maurice Kufferath, shortly before the composer's death and evidently no efforts were spared to ensure the work's success. Georges Eekhoud wrote 'The work had a considerable success which has been confirmed in subsequent performances. It is currently enjoying its tenth performance and all the signs are that it will have a brilliant future.' ['Le succès de l'oeuvre a été considérable et s'est confirmé aux représentations suivantes. On est à la dixième et tout fait prévoir que la pièce fournira une carrière des plus brillantes.'[8]] According to Gustave Samazeuilh the first performance was marked by 'three curtain calls at the end of each act' ['un triple rappel à la fin de chaque acte'[9]]. The musical direction was

[7] 'Chronique de Bruxelles', *Mercure de France* 49 (1904), pp. 256–61. It should be pointed out, in fairness to Eekhoud, that the chapter on the opera in Jean-Pierre Barricelli and Leo Weinstein, *Ernest Chausson: The Composer's Life and Works* (Norman, 1955; repr. Westport, Connecticut, 1973), pp 187–202 contains the most deplorable plagiarism, being a tissue of unacknowledged literal translations of Eekhoud's review which the authors have the audacity to pass off as their own opinions. To add insult to injury, there is no mention of Eekhoud's review in their bibliography.
[8] *Art. cit.*, p. 256.
[9] *Art. cit.*, p. 700.

in the hands of Sylvain Dupuis, a Belgian composer (1856–1931), a friend of d'Indy and a Wagnerian enthusiast, who conducted at the Théâtre Royal de la Monnaie throughout the period 1900–11. The tenor taking the role of Lancelot was the highly gifted Frenchman Charles Dalmorès (1871–1939), who began his musical career as a horn player and made his operatic début at Rouen in 1899. After singing for a time in Brussels, he was in England taking part in the British première of *Hérodiade*, the *Hélène* of Saint-Saëns, and Charpentier's *Louise*. In the role of Lancelot he was acclaimed for his 'jeu dramatique et vibrant' which it was generally thought could not be improved on. Great critical praise was also accorded to Mme Paquot-d'Assy in the part of Genièvre[10] and Henri Albers as Arthus.[11] The production was given lavish material assistance and moral support by the directors of La Monnaie, Maurice Kufferath and Guillaume Guidé. Kufferath (1852–1919) was a director of the theatre from 1900 to 1914 and besides being a prolific writer on Wagner, also conducted Dukas's *Ariane et Barbe-Bleue* and Debussy's *Pelléas et Mélisande*. Kufferath made sure that the best artists were engaged in the production. The costumes, designed by Fernand Khnopff, were praised for their 'archaïsme assez discret' and the artist Dubosq and producer De Beer were both complimented on their substantial contribution to the effectiveness of the opera.[12] Alas! *Le Roi Arthus* did not achieve the brilliant future predicted for it.[13] There were several subsequent performances of Act 3 alone, including one at the Paris Opera in March 1916 and a radio broadcast on 25 April 1934.[14] The whole work was revived for a broadcast on 24 June 1949 and in 1981 Lionel Friend recorded the work complete for French Radio, the recording being broadcast by the BBC in the following year.

The literary interest of *Le Roi Arthus* stems in part from the fact that Chausson, an extremely cultivated and widely read man, wrote the libretto himself and displayed the same anxiety and meticulous care in its preparation and constant revision as he showed in the composition of the music. Hallays remarked that for this *poète-musicien* 'his culture and good taste made inventing and writing a libretto easy' ['son goût et sa culture lui rendaient aisée la tâche d'imaginer et d'écrire un livret'[15]]. Painters[16] and sculptors, musicians and writers flocked to

---

[10] In a letter of 1899 to Henry Lerolle, Chausson had suggested that Georgette Leblanc, whom he had visited on 30 March 1895 and who had sung the lead in his *Légende de Sainte Cécile*, would make an ideal interpreter of the role. This gifted woman, long-time companion of Maeterlinck and heroine of his dramas, possessed, like so many of Chausson's friends, both musical and literary talent.

[11] Samazeuilh, *art. cit.*, p. 704, praises his artistry, whilst regretting 'quelques défectuosités vocales'.

[12] The scenery was painted by Henry Lerolle. For Khnopff's involvement in opera productions see J.W. Howe, *The Symbolist Art of Fernand Khnopff* (Ann Arbor, 1982), p. 10: 'Khnopff's theatre designs deserve more study in themselves.'

[13] As has often been mentioned, the Brussels journal *Théâtra* conducted a poll of Belgian opera lovers in 1909 to discover which works would be most welcomed at the Théâtre de la Monnaie. The first four choices were *Tristan* (1273 votes), *Pelléas et Mélisande*, *Götterdämmerung* and *Le Roi Arthus* (1199 votes).

[14] A pre-war recording of two excerpts from Act 3 ('Pommiers verts, pommiers fleuris' and 'Ne m'interroge plus') was made by the baritone Arthur Endrèze in the role of Merlin (Pathé PCX 5006).

[15] *Art. cit.*, p. 853.

[16] For Chausson's own collection of paintings see Ralph Scott Glover, *Ernest Chausson: The Man*

his home in the Boulevard de Courcelles:[17] the list of his guests reads like a roll-call of the major cultural figures of late nineteenth-century France.[18] With many of these artists he shared his doubts and hopes, seeking their advice and explaining his difficulties, whilst offering constant encouragement to others who sought his assistance or requested his opinions. His correspondence with a number of musicians, including Debussy, Duparc and d'Indy, as well as with his lawyer friend Paul Poujaud and his wife's brother-in-law Henry Lerolle, provides a fascinating documentation of his struggles with the composition of *Le Roi Arthus*, which was a constant preoccupation from 1886 to 1895.

Chausson's interest in medieval literature is attested as early as 1882 by the writing of his symphonic poem *Viviane* Op. 5.[19] This enchanting piece, so unjustly neglected in the modern concert hall, was not a great success on its first performance (31 March 1883), but underwent successive revisions and was well received when the definitive version was given by Lamoureux on 29 January 1888. It was subsequently played in places as far apart as Glasgow, St Petersburg and Barcelona, so that in 1895 the composer was able to write to d'Indy:

> This *Viviane* just won't lie down. It's a hit in the provinces and abroad. And now it's playing again in Paris. All the same, I think it's high time I produced a companion piece. Be patient. Once *Arthur* is finished, we'll have a go.

> [Cette Viviane est vraiment infatigable. Elle fait la province et l'étranger. Et voilà encore qu'elle repique sur Paris! C'est égal, il me semble qu'il est grand temps de lui donner une compagne de route. Patience. Tout de suite après *Arthus* on s'y mettra.[20]]

For the performance of this work Chausson reports that he had had made a special pair of antique cymbals in F and C, which had unfortunately been lost, and then draws d'Indy's attention to the marking of the score:

> The exact title is: Viviane, symphonic poem. The setting is indicated at the head of the score.

---

and his Music (London, 1980), pp. 225–7, and compare Chabrier's collection of Impressionists, described in R. Meyers, *Emmanuel Chabrier and his Circle* (London, 1969), pp. 146–54.

[17] See Barricelli and Weinstein, *op. cit.*, pp. 34–6, and Glover, *op. cit.*, pp. 17–18, 34–5. It may be noted that Chausson wrote a novel, *Jacques* (1877), which he destroyed, and that Camille Mauclair dedicated to him his novel *Le Soleil des morts*. There would be value in a study of the literary relations of Chausson and his contemporaries along the lines of Arthur B. Wenk's *Claude Debussy and the Poets* (Berkeley etc., 1976). On Chausson's reading see Gallois, *op. cit.*, pp. 75–5.

[18] For surveys of his musical contemporaries see G. Samazeuilh, *Musiciens de mon temps: chroniques et souvenirs* (Paris, 1947); J. Tiersot, *Un demi-siècle de musique française 1870–1919*, 2nd edn (Paris, 1924); Romain Rolland, 'The Awakening: A Sketch of the Musical Movement in Paris since 1870', in *idem, Musicians Today*, transl. M. Blaiklock (London, 1915), pp. 246–324, also in R. Rolland and G. Jean-Aubry, *French Music of Today and Musicians of Today* [transl. E. Evans] (London, n.d.), pp. 246–324. The regular visitors to Chausson's home are listed by Glover, *op. cit.*, pp. 17f.

[19] The work was dedicated to Jeanne Escudier who shortly afterwards became Chausson's wife. A piano transcription of the piece was made by Samazeuilh (as well as by d'Indy) and published by Bornemann. The music is much superior to Guy Ropartz's *La Chasse du Prince Arthur* (1912).

[20] See 'Lettres inédites à Vincent d'Indy' in the special number (1 déc. 1925) of *La Revue Musicale* devoted to Chausson, pp. 128–36 at 132.

[Le titre exact, c'est: Viviane, poème symphonique. Le topo se trouve en tête de la partition.]

The 'programme' to which Chausson refers as prefixing the score was as follows:

Viviane and Merlin in the forest of Brocéliande
Love scene
King Arthur's men scour the forest for the Enchanter. He wishes to escape and join them
Viviane puts Merlin to sleep and surrounds him with hawthorn blossom.

[Viviane et Merlin dans la Forêt de Brocéliande
Scène d'Amour
Les envoyés du Roi Arthur parcourent la forêt à la recherche de l'Enchanteur.
Il veut fuir et les rejoindre.
Viviane endort Merlin et l'entoure d'aubépines en fleurs.]

A langorous introduction on muted strings, with its characteristic avoidance of a fixed tonality, establishes the sense of mystery which is so essential a feature of Chausson's style.[21] The forest setting is evoked throughout by a memorable motif on the horn. The theme of love is presented in bold, passionate themes on the violins and on the cellos, which are then contrasted with the individual voice of a solo violin. A most effective use is made of trumpet calls, including off-stage echo effects, to indicate the spatial movements of Arthur's men within the forest. Despite the occasional exploitation of certain Wagnerian devices, the piece is remarkable for its avoidance of clichés and for the young Chausson's masterly command of a dazzling range of atmospheric effects together with strong melodic lines.

Outside the Arthurian legends Chausson also showed a great attachment to the *Chanson de Roland*. In 1888 he wrote to his friend Poujaud from Biarritz:

For a long time now I've been wanting to take a trip to Roncevaux. So come. We'll go together. I've got the *Song of Roland* which we shall read in the inns.

[Depuis longtemps je veux faire une expédition à Roncevaux. Venez donc. Nous la ferons ensemble. J'ai la *Chanson de Roland*, que nous lirons dans les auberges.[22]]

Some time later (the letter is undated) Chausson writes again, from Ochaberrietra, that he has visited Saint-Jean-Pied-de-Port and Roncevaux:

. . . for four whole days I've done nothing but observe and not thought about anything. Except the *Song of Roland*, since I am in Roncevaux. I've seen the fountain near to which he died and the stream from which Turpin went to

---

[21] Writing to Poujaud in 1886, sending him the scenario of *Le Roi Arthus*, Chausson reflects on the appearance of Merlin in Act 2, 'I am very tempted by the appearance of Merlin. You're probably thinking that the old Viviane is going to rise up from the ashes and restore her image. It could be objected that this scene has not been very well prepared for, but the way it is introduced makes it, I think, perfectly acceptable' ['L'apparition de Merlin me tente beaucoup. Vous pensez bien que l'antique *Viviane* va renaître de ses cendres et se refaire une virginité. On pourra objecter que cette scène n'est pas préparée, pourtant à la manière dont elle arrive, je crois qu'elle peut être défendue']. See 'Lettres inédites à Paul Poujaud', in *ibid.*, pp. 143–74 at 155.
[22] *Ibid.*, p. 160.

fetch water. Do you have a fierce love of the *Song of Roland*? Yes, I'm sure you do. I find a Homeric beauty in the second canto, which is the real reason for my making the trip to Roncevaux.

[. . . pendant quatre jours, je ne me suis servi que de mes yeux, je ne pensais plus à rien. Sauf pourtant à la *Chanson de Roland*, en étant à Roncevaux. J'ai vu la fontaine près de laquelle il est mort et le ruisseau où Turpin alla chercher de l'eau. Aimez-vous férocement la *Chanson de Roland*? Oui, sans doute. Je trouve le second chant beau comme de l'*Homère*. C'est bien à cause de lui que j'ai fait le voyage de Roncevaux.[23]]

There is no indication, however, that Chausson ever contemplated a musical composition based on the *Roland*.[24]

A brief study of the genesis of *Le Roi Arthus* will clarify its central position in Chausson's *oeuvre* and demonstrate the pains which he took to refine his conception of the tragedy and to deal with the dangers posed by the inevitable analogies with *Tristan*. In 1886 whilst in Cannes Chausson sent Paul Poujaud a sketch of the scenario for the opera:

The subject matter fascinates me, despite the many parallels with *Tristan* which scare me . . . The greatest drawback with my drama is obviously the parallel of its subject matter with that of *Tristan*. That wouldn't be so bad, if I could somehow dewagnerise myself. Wagnerian in its subject and Wagnerian in its music, isn't that a bit too much all at once?

[Le sujet me plaît beaucoup, malgré les nombreuses analogies avec *Tristan* qui m'effrayent . . . Le plus gros défaut de mon drame est sans doute l'analogie du sujet avec celui de *Tristan*. Cela ne serait rien encore, si je pouvais arriver à me déwagnériser. Wagnérien par le sujet et wagnérien par la musique, n'est-ce pas trop à la fois?[25]]

Despite numerous difficulties, Chausson's attachment to the work could not be broken:

As for poor old *King Arthur*, Bouchor pulled it to pieces so much, I foresaw so many difficulties, that I momentarily despaired of it. Now I'm starting to think about it again. Despite all that's being said about it, I truly love it, as dear old Franck would say.

[Quant au pauvre *Roi Arthus*, Bouchor me l'a si rudement éreinté, j'y ai tant vu de difficultés de toutes sortes, que pour un moment j'en ai désespéré. Je me remets à y songer. Malgré tout ce qu'on en dit, *je l'aime*, comme dirait le bon Franck.[26]]

[23] *Ibid.*, p. 172.
[24] The Italian composer Luigi Dallapiccola set a number of passages in his *Rencesvals (Chanson de Roland)* for mezzo-soprano/baritone and piano (1946). He had earlier written *Rapsodia, studie per la morte del Conte Orlando* for chamber orchestra (1932–3).
[25] *Art. cit.*, pp. 150/155.
[26] *Art. cit.*, p. 156. The poet Maurice Bouchor (1855–1929), who had varied interests in music and the theatre (esp. the Petit Théâtre des Marionnettes), successfully collaborated with Chausson on a number of occasions. The beautiful setting of his *Poème de l'amour et de la mer* is one of Chausson's most inspired compositions. Chausson also wrote the music for Bouchor's translation of Shakespeare's *The Tempest*, for his drama *La Légende de Sainte Cécile*, the four *Chansons de Shakespeare* (Bouchor's translations) and the *Quatre Mélodies* (verses by Bouchor).

Already the composer, inclined to pessimism, foresees the uncertainties which might frustrate the development of a new lyric theatre and ruefully reflects that it would be his luck to submit his work to a company or theatre on the eve of their bankruptcy proceedings! – 'Et qu'importe après tout? Le principal n'est-il pas d'abord de faire ce que l'on sent de son mieux, sans s'occuper d'une réalisation plus ou moins problématique?' ['But then what does it matter? The most important thing, surely, is to do what one feels to be one's best, without getting involved in a realisation which may be more or less troublesome?']²⁷ In another letter of dejection in which he explains the depression which has delayed his writing ('C'est Arthus, toujours, qui en est la cause' (It's always Arthur which is at the root of it')), Chausson informs Poujaud,

> *Arthur* is slowly progressing and I don't really know what to think of it. In some places I can see clearly that it's bad. There are others where I'm not sure what to say. That's exactly why I'm writing to you while waiting for dinnertime . . . I'm beginning to gain a bit of confidence, not in what I've already done, but in what I shall make of this drama. I even reproach myself for liking my subject too much.

> [*Arthus* avance lentement et je ne sais trop qu'en penser. Il y a des endroits où je vois clairement que c'est mauvais. Il y en a d'autres où je ne sais plus que dire. C'est même pour cela que je vous écris en attendant l'heure du déjeuner . . . Je commence à avoir un peu de confiance, non dans ce que j'ai fait, mais dans ce que je ferai de ce drame. Je me reproche même de trop aimer mon sujet.²⁸]

Chausson received much valuable advice from Duparc in a document which we shall examine later and this had included suggestions about how to arrange Genièvre's death. In a letter of 3 September 1893 Debussy inquired 'Avez-vous fait décidément mourir cette pauvre Genièvre? La dernière chose que vous m'avez montrée me fait présager d'excessivement belle musique de vous!' ['Have you really ensured that poor Guinevere dies? The last thing that you showed me makes me expect some excessively beautiful music from you!']²⁹ Chausson was concerned with more than musical and dramaturgical considerations, however, for he was constantly revising the text of his libretto. To Debussy he confides, of *Le Roi Arthus*,

> It's still causing me many headaches. And repeated headaches. For when I think that I've finished a scene, I realise clearly after a few months' rest that there are masses of things in the words which won't work; I change them, and naturally, I have to change the music as well. Everything is always having to be revised; will it ever come to an end? Yet it has to be done . . .

> [Il me cause toujours beaucoup de malheurs. Et des malheurs renaissants. Car quand je crois que j'ai terminé une scène, je m'aperçois après quelques mois de repos qu'il y a des tas de choses dans les paroles qui ne vont pas; je les change, et naturellement, il me faut aussi changer la musique. C'est toujours à refaire, et cela finira-t-il jamais? Il le faudrait pourtant . . .³⁰]

---

²⁷ Letter to Poujaud, *art. cit.*, p. 156.
²⁸ *Ibid.*, p. 157.
²⁹ F. Lesure, *Claude Debussy, Lettres 1884–1918* (Paris, 1980), p. 52.
³⁰ 'Correspondance inédite de Claude Debussy et Ernest Chausson', *La Revue Musicale* (1 déc. 1925), pp. 116–26 at 119.

Debussy, in trying to alleviate his friend's burden, advises Chausson to avoid 'the obsession with the lower harmonies' ['la préoccupation des "dessous" '], a Wagnerian temptation, and to take as a model the music of Bach 'where everything miraculously comes together to bring out the musical idea, the important material unhindered by the lightness of the lower harmonies' ['où tout concourt prodigieusement à mettre l'idée en valeur, où la légèreté des dessous n'absorbe jamais le principal'[31]]. Chausson, as usual, is not reluctant to act on the suggestions of his friends:

> I've gone back, without too much trouble, to Act 3. I'm not dissatisfied by what I'm writing at the moment. I think things are becoming clearer and dewagner-ised. My wife, when I played the first act to her, said she hardly recognized me . . . You're absolutely and totally right in what you say of preoccupation with the 'lower harmonies'. Whilst you were writing to me, I was more or less thinking the same thing, the opening of my third act is proof enough. I think I owe this preoccupation above all to the aesthetics of the National Society.

> [Moi, j ai repris, et sans trop de peine, mon troisième acte. Je ne suis pas mécontent de ce que j'écris en ce moment. Il me semble que ça se clarifie et déwagnérise. Ma femme à qui j'ai joué la première scène m'a dit qu'elle ne me reconnaissait presque pas . . . Vous avez mille fois raison dans ce que vous me dites de la préoccupation des 'dessous'. Pendant que vous m'écriviez je pensais à peu près la même chose, le commencement de mon troisième acte en est une preuve. C'est je crois, surtout à l'esthétique de la Société Nationale que je dois cette préoccupation.[32]]

The most successful period of work on *Le Roi Arthus* appears to have been 1895 when Chausson was working at San Domenico di Fiesole, near Florence. He writes to Poujaud,

> With the passage of time this interminable *Arthur* had begun to turn sour and poison me, so to speak. After a number of violent disagreements, I eventually got on top of it and now am happily interring it in a heap of orchestral pages (the second act alone runs to 235 pages of rough copy)!

> [Cet interminable *Arthus* avec le temps avait sûri et m'avait comme empoi-sonné. Après quelques explications violentes, j'ai fini par avoir le dessus et maintenant je l'enterre fort gaîment sous un monceau de pages d'orchestre (le second acte seul a 235 pages de brouillon)![33]]

---

[31] Lesure, *Claude Debussy, Lettres*, p. 58. Debussy himself planned an opera on Tristan, using a libretto by Gabriel Mourey and based on Bédier's *Le Roman de Tristan*, which had already inspired the composer on its first appearance. The project remained in Debussy's mind from 1907 till 1916 when he abandoned it. See R. Orledge, *Debussy and the Theatre* (Cambridge, 1982), pp. 251–3. On Frank Martin's Tristan oratorio, also based on Bédier, see U. Müller, 'Mittelalterliche Dichtungen in der Musik des 20. Jahrhunderts III: Das Tristan und Isolde-Oratorium von Frank Martin (nach Joseph Bédier) . . .', in *Tradition und Entwicklung. Festschrift Eugen Thurnher zum 60. Geburtstag*, ed. W. M. Bauer *et al.*, Innsbrucker Beiträge zur Kulturwissenschaft, Germanistische Reihe Band 14 (Innsbruck, 1982), pp. 171–86. A brilliant production by Paul Hernon was presented at the Jeannetta Cochrane Theatre, London in January 1983. See pp. 6–7 above.

[32] Letter to Debussy, *art. cit.*, p. 123. This is an undated reply to Debussy's letter of 24 Oct. 1893.

[33] *Art. cit.*, p. 171. According to Gallois, *op. cit.*, p. 51, Act 2 was finished by the end of 1892. Chausson worked on the battle scene of Act 3 in the company of Debussy at Luzancy in 1893.

And to d'Indy,

> As a result of all the work I've been doing on the orchestration of *Arthur*, I
> notice with astonishment that it is making progress and I'm sometimes seized
> with the desire to finish it before I return to this great city of horse-drawn cabs
> and news-vendors . . . I hope to make a start on the orchestration of the third
> act on the first of January.

> [A force de travailler à l'orchestre d'*Arthus*, je m'aperçois avec étonnement
> qu'il avance et parfois l'envie me vient de le terminer avant de rentrer dans
> cette capitale des fiacres et des marchands de journaux . . . J'espère entamer
> l'orchestre du troisième acte le 1er janvier.[34]]

The opera was completed in the knowledge that Act 3 was the most successfully
reworked part of the drama and that there remained weaknesses in the first two
acts which the composer did not feel he had the stamina to deal with. It is,
indeed, the third act which has drawn the most favourable critical response
since the first performance[35] and which alone was the subject of the few attempts
in more recent times to perform part of the work.

Before undertaking an analysis of *Le Roi Arthus* it remains to consider briefly
the question of Wagnerian influence on Chausson. The neglect of many of the
latter's most beautiful compositions is not a little due to exaggerations like
Martin Cooper's sweeping statement that Chausson's opera is 'impeccably
Wagnerian from beginning to end'.[36] It is certainly not Wagnerian in spirit, as
we shall see.[37] Chausson's anxiety about the influence of Wagner stems from the
days (1883–6) when he was labouring on his lyric drama *Hélène* Op. 7 (two acts,
after Leconte de Lisle), of which only a female chorus has been published.[38]
Chausson had attended a performance of *Tristan* in 1880 which made a great
impression. Yet, a few years later he was to write complainingly of 'the baleful
spectre of Wagner which constantly haunts me . . . I've come to hate him' ['ce
spectre rouge de Wagner qui ne me lâche pas . . . J'en arrive à le détester'[39]].

---

[34] *Art. cit.*, p. 171.
[35] See, for example, the comments of L. Davies, *César Franck and his Circle* (London, 1970), p. 198:
'Act 1 is overburdened with a pallid and derivative love duet, as well as a bardic chorus that
harks back suspiciously to the days of Grand Opera . . . The moving farewell which Arthur
bids must rank among the best finales in modern French opera.'
[36] M. Cooper, *French Music from the Death of Berlioz to the Death of Fauré* (London, 1951), p. 66.
Cooper's judgement is strongly contested by Glover, *op. cit.*, p. 185. In the *Revue Musicale*
(1 déc. 1925) Maurice Bouchor argues that *Le Roi Arthus* marks little advance on Wagner and
that it 'must have seemed, even to its composer, the work of an epigone' ['devait apparaître,
aux yeux mêmes de son auteur, comme l'oeuvre d'un épigone'] (p. 181). The same prejudice
concerning alleged Wagnerian influence has deprived us of the chance of hearing any of Karl
Goldmark's operas with the exception of *Die Königin von Saba*. His opera *Merlin* was
performed at the Vienna Opera on 19 Nov. 1886 and was revised in 1904.
[37] A. Hallays justly wrote in the *Revue de Paris* (15 déc. 1903), p. 852, 'Ernest Chausson greatly
admired Richard Wagner. It would be difficult to discover any evidence in his musical
works: he is one of the few French composers of his time who remains almost entirely free of
Wagnerian imitation' ['Ernest Chausson admirait beaucoup Richard Wagner. On en
surprendrait difficilement la preuve dans ses oeuvres musicales: il est un des rares
compositeurs français de son temps à peu près indemnes de toute imitation wagnérienne'].
[38] See the brief assessment of this work in G. Samazeuilh, *Musiciens de mon temps, Chroniques et
souvenirs* (Paris, 1947), pp. 126–8.
[39] In a letter of 1884 to Poujaud, *art. cit.*, p. 144.

Later, after the completion of *Le Roi Arthus*, he wrote contemptuously that 'the need to find parallels [with Wagner] has become a sort of pastime. A sad and vain pastime' ['le besoin de trouver des ressemblances [avec Wagner] est devenu une sorte de passe-temps. Triste passe-temps, et très vain'[40]]. These words were written in a review of the first performance of the medieval and 'Wagnerian' *Fervaal* by his friend d'Indy and this notice shows him reflecting on the nature of 'influence' and defending the opera *Fervaal* against the charge of Wagnerism:

> The greatest artists have always undergone the influence of the masters who preceded them, but the idea they borrowed, filtered through their brain, came to bear the imprint of their own temperament. It is only in this limited sense that the composer of *Fervaal* may with any justification be described as a Wagnerian. What most confers individuality on any artist is his sensibility. The technical means by which he displays it are of much lesser importance.

> [Les plus grands artistes ont toujours subi l'influence des maîtres qui les ont précédés, mais l'idée empruntée, passant par leur cerveau, subissait l'empreinte de leur propre tempérament. C'est dans cette mesure seulement qu'il est légitime de dire que l'auteur de *Fervaal* est wagnérien. Ce qui individualise surtout un artiste, c'est sa sensibilité. Les procédés par lesquels il la manifeste importent beaucoup moins.[41]]

Henri Duparc was no less percipient in the fifty-one pages of commentary on the libretto of *Le Roi Arthus* which he wrote at the end of 1888 when he was struggling with his own opera *Roussalka* (later destroyed) and sent to the composer with the comment that, whether it should prove useful or not, he had himself learned much in assembling his remarks:[42]

> It is clear that if we are to rid ourselves of our obsession with this man [i.e. Wagner] and his works, an almost superhuman effort is needed. But we *have* to make the effort, if we are to avoid the mere writing of impersonal works, for it would be a great mistake to imagine that, given similarities in the drama, the music will not reflect the fact . . . Wagner brilliantly realized his ideas, and in the execution of comparable ideas none of us can hope to equal him: our only merit will thus lie in having created something beautiful whilst conceiving of it in quite different terms.

> [Il est certain que pour nous débarrasser de la préoccupation de cet homme [i.e. Wagner] et de ses oeuvres, il faut un effort surhumain; mais cet effort, il *faut le faire*, sous peine de n'écrire que des oeuvres impersonnelles, car ce serait une grande erreur de croire que, s'il y a des ressemblances dans le drame, la musique ne s'en ressentira pas . . . Wagner a merveilleusement réalisé ses conceptions, et, dans des conceptions analogues, aucun de nous ne peut espérer l'égaler: notre seul mérite sera donc d'avoir su faire de belles choses en les concevant autrement.[43]]

[40] See 'Fervaal', *Mercure de France*, sér. mod. 22 (avril 1897), p. 135.
[41] *Loc. cit.*
[42] This fascinating document is printed, with an introduction, in Charles Oulmont, *Musique de l'amour*, t. 2 *Henri Duparc ou de 'L'invitation au voyage' à la vie éternelle* (Paris, 1935), pp. 109–73.
[43] *Ibid.*, p. 217. He also remarks (p. 126) 'A great weakness, which it seems to me *absolutely*

Duparc gives an example from *Le Roi Arthus* of the way in which an artist may be misled by the tyrannical power of Wagner's achievement. He argues that in his presentation of Lancelot and Genièvre Chausson has slipped too easily into the trap of conceiving them to be like Tristan and Isolde. The latter retain their capacity to move us, despite the disloyalty and adultery, because they act under fatality, symbolised by the potion. In this way Wagner could avoid alienating the audience and could preserve some sense of the lovers' honourable qualities. Chausson's Lancelot and Genièvre lack any justificatory equivalent to the potion and do not have the advantage of familiarity to the audience:[44]

> Mais nous, spectateurs, nous ne connaissons pas les légendes de la Table Ronde, et nous sommes bêtes: nous voulons qu'on nous explique tout.[45] [But we, the audience, are not conversant with the legends of the Round Table, and we are stupid wanting everything to be explained to us]

At some point in the opera, not necessarily at the very beginning (which Duparc finds satisfactory as it was submitted to him), we must be brought into a sympathetic relationship with Lancelot ('Je trouve indispensable que . . . tu nous attaches à Lancelot' ['I consider it indispensable that you establish a relationship between us and Lancelot']). As it is, he appears as 'a nasty piece of work, who will merit the punishment – whatever it turns out to be – which will be his' ['un très vilain monsieur, qui n'aura pas volé le châtiment, – quel qu'il soit, – qu'il va recevoir']: we know too little about his virtues and have little reason to excuse his vices. We must be shown, therefore, that he is initially esteemed by Arthur's knights and that he is capable of revolting against his own conduct – 'the lover cannot have completely destroyed the hero in him' ['l'amant ne peut pas avoir tué complètement le héros en lui']. In addition, there must be a final trans-figuration of the hero through the triumph of conscience over passion, a 'réveil complet' of his true self.[46] This is what will best explain his refusal to fight against Arthur, and Duparc suggests that it would be fittingly inspired by a treacherous deal offered by Mordred which renders the hero indignant (Chausson does not adopt this procedure). *Le Roi Arthus* thereby becomes a *drame de conscience*, exploring the effects of shame, remorse and renunciation. What Duparc calls 'ces nuances' will not only generate true human tragedy, but, even more important, 'their inclusion will remove any idea of similarities to *Tristan*' ['leur mise en oeuvre éloignera toute idée de rapprochement avec *Tristan*']. And Genièvre? She earns Duparc's complete approval – 'elle est très femme'.

---

necessary to eliminate . . . is the obsession wth Wagner's music dramas and, particularly, *Tristan*' ['Un très grand défaut, qu'il me semble *absolument nécessaire* de faire disparaître . . . c'est l'obsession des drames de Wagner et surtout de *Tristan*'].

[44] A typical example of Duparc's forthright style in this connexion is his claim that we condemn adultery 'unless it can be amply demonstrated that the two suppliers of horns could not have acted otherwise' ['à moins qu'il ne nous soit bien prouvé que les deux confectionneurs de cornes n'ont pas pu faire autrement'].

[45] *Op. cit.*, pp. 129–30.

[46] L. Davies, *op. cit.*, p. 198, argues that Chausson does not really make the theme of betrayal convincing and that the remorse of Lancelot in Act 3 rings more truthfully than his earlier turpitude.

Chausson acted on most of Duparc's suggestions and consequently the implications of his drama are far removed from Wagner's. The apotheosis of the lovers in the *Liebestod* stems from the acknowledgement, as in Gottfried von Strassburg of the transcendental nature of passion, which exceeds the bounds of social order and sexual morality. In Chausson the love of Lancelot and Genièvre is sterile, destructive of individual integrity through conflict with conscience, and symptomatic of the human weakness which will lead to the breaking up of the fellowship of the Round Table. What we have is a drama of Christian repentance, incorporating the power of guilt, the value of renunciation and the expiatory role of death. Paul Dukas, shortly after the first performance of *Le Roi Arthus*, made the following shrewd observations on the nature of Chausson's drama:

> Chausson's chief concern in writing this lyric drama was clearly to produce not a work of symbolism or philosophy, but one directly born of the emotion produced by the contrast of situations and characters; in a word, a drama in the true sense of the word, and not a more or less theatrical musical poem like so many spawned by imitation of the Wagnerian music drama. In certain respects *King Arthur* serves such an end, largely through the way the external action acts on the spirit of the characters, in contrast to those works conceived on the lines of the master of Bayreuth's aesthetic notions where the action is most often presented as the influence of the world of appearances on creatures bearing the stamp of a preconceived, inner physiognomy, works in which the play of events is designed to render palpable their conscious or unconscious changes.

> [La préoccupation évidente de Chausson, en écrivant ce drame lyrique, a été de produire une oeuvre non pas symbolique ou philosophique, mais directement engendrée par l'émotion qui naît du contraste des situations et des caractères; en un mot, un drame au sens propre du mot, et non pas un poème musical plus ou moins scénique, comme en a fait éclore à foison l'imitation du drame wagnérien. A certains points de vue, le *Roi Arthus* répond à ce but, principalement par la façon dont l'action externe réagit sur le moral des personnages, au contraire des oeuvres conçues selon l'esthétique du maître de Bayreuth, dans lesquelles l'action nous est présentée le plus souvent comme le reflet du monde des apparences sur des êtres de physionomie intérieure préconçue et dont le jeu des événements est surtout destiné à rendre sensible les variations conscientes ou inconscientes.[47]]

Lancelot's tragedy, a sort of Christian morality, is played out against the contrasting presence of Arthus, who stands for heroic perseverance, noble stability and unflinching faith, all of which set in relief the vicissitudes of ignoble passion and emphasise the need for redemption. Perhaps Chausson remembered here the role of Charlemagne in his beloved *Chanson de Roland*. It is also difficult to deny that Arthus embodies some of Chausson's own characteristics – generosity, faith in constant effort,[48] equanimity, and acceptance of death.

---

[47] Quoted from his essay 'Le Roi Arthus et le Wagnérisme', in *La Revue Musicale* (1 déc. 1925), p. 215.

[48] See his letter of August 1888 to Poujaud, *art. cit.*, p. 161, and Debussy's letter to him of 26 Aug. 1893 Lesure, p. 47.

Some critics have even gone so far as to see in the fellowship of the Round Table
a poetic transposition of the companionship enjoyed by 'the followers of Franck'
['la bande à Franck']. Much of all this can be detected in the last moving
exchange of monarch and knight:

> Arthus   Mon honneur!
>   Crois-tu donc qu'il dépende
>   d'un autre que moi-même?
>
>   . . .
>
>   Ah! J'ai cru à la puissance
>   De l'effort, a l'énergie de la volonté.
>   Sans relâche, j'ai lutté.
>   Et maintenant, que reste-t-il
>   De toute ma vie?
>   Espérances déçues!
>   Inutiles, inutiles efforts.
>
> Lancelot   Qui peut connaître la force
>   Des pensées et la durée des choses?
>   A travers les âges, ton nom peut-être périra,
>   Mais, plus durable que son éclat sonore,
>   Ta pensée, Arthus, est immortelle.
>   L'amour, dont ton coeur s'enivra,
>   Jaillit de la flamme éternelle.
>   Tu vivras! Tu vivras!
>   Pour d'autres, la mort est l'éternel oubli.
>   Ils disparaissent pour jamais,
>   Hélas! hélas! comme moi . . .

The centrality of Arthus and the moral reawakening of Lancelot (Hallays found
his death 'le chef d'oeuvre' of the piece), who finally recognises the supreme
values represented by the man he has betrayed, form a unity which was over-
looked by some of the opera's earliest commentators. André Hallays complained,

> However, the libretto has one serious fault, an unexpected one to anyone who
> was familiar with Ernest Chausson's classical taste: it lacks unity. In fact, it
> contains two dramas: that of Lancelot and that of Arthur. When the curtain
> rises, we see Arthur in the palace at Carlisle. Then, suddenly, Lancelot and
> Guenevere emerge as the protagonists. Lancelot's remorse and Guenevere's
> passion appear to represent the heart of the tragedy, when in the middle of the
> action, in the fourth scene, Arthur is restored to prominence and dominates the
> drama thereafter. This mistake in the design and handling of the poem rather
> throws the spectator. Maybe it also explains certain hesitations in the music.
>
> [Ce livret a pourtant un défaut très grave, et très inattendu pour qui
> connaissait le goût classique d'Ernest Chausson: il manque d'unité. A vrai
> dire, il renferme deux drames: celui de Lancelot et celui d'Arthus. Au lever du
> rideau, nous entrevoyons Arthus dans le palais de Carduel. Puis, tout de suite,
> Lancelot et Guinèvre sont les protagonistes. Les remords de Lancelot et la
> passion de Guinèvre paraissent le fond même de la tragédie, lorsqu'au milieu
> de l'action, au quatrième tableau, Arthus revient au premier plan et dès lors
> domine tout drame. Cette erreur dans le dessin et dans la conduite du poème

déconcerte un peu le spectateur. Peut-être explique-t-elle aussi certaines incertitudes de l'oeuvre musicale.[49]]

A more accurate judgement came from Gustave Samazeuilh:

The external similarities which it [viz. *King Arthur*] inevitably displays, particularly in the first part, with that [viz. 'the poem'] of *Tristan and Isolde*, which belongs to the same legendary cycle, are well known. The important thing, on the other hand, is to bring out how different, interpretatively, the two works are. Whereas in Wagner the figure of King Mark is relegated to the gloom of his laments and the whole interest is concentrated on the triumphant passion of the two lovers, here, quite differently, it is the great figure of Arthur, the founder of the Round Table and the defender of Britain, who dominates, gives his name to the work and embraces the philosophy of the entire drama. Set beside this figure, crowned in glory, the fates of Guenevere, consumed by her mad passion, and Lancelot, constantly torn between his love and his reverence for his king, pale and are finally extinguished in an end without honour. In life they have sought only a selfish and illusory satisfaction; for them death will be everlasting oblivion, and no great, noble achievement will preserve their memory, as it does in the case of Arthur, for posterity. It is on this truly personal idea, of great nobility, thanks to which the concluding pages of the work reach sublime heights, that the three acts of *King Arthur* have been based ...

[On sait les analogies extérieures qu'il [= *Le Roi Arthus*] présente forcément, surtout dans sa première partie, avec celui [= 'le poème'] de *Tristan et Yseult*, emprunté au même cycle légendaire. Mais il importe, par contre, de faire ressortir à quel point la signification en est différente. Tandis que chez Wagner le personnage du Roi Marke est relégué dans l'ombre de ses lamentations et tout l'intérêt concentré sur la passion triomphante des deux amants, c'est au contraire ici la grande figure d'Arthus, fondateur de la Table Ronde et défenseur de la Bretagne, qui devient prépondérante, donne son nom à l'oeuvre et contient en elle toute la philosophie du drame. A côté de la sienne, auréolée de gloire, les destinées de *Guinèvre*, toute à sa folle passion, et de Lancelot, sans cesse hésitant entre son amour et sa vénération pour son roi, disparaissent et s'éteignent dans une fin sans honneur. Ils n'ont recherché dans la vie qu'une satisfaction égoïste et trompeuse; pour eux, la mort sera l'éternel oubli, et une oeuvre noble et grande ne fera pas vivre, comme celle d'*Arthus*, leur pensée à travers les âges. C'est sur cette idée vraiment personnelle et d'une grande élévation grâce à laquelle les dernières pages de l'oeuvre atteignent au sublime, qu'ont été établis les trois actes du *Roi Arthus* . . .[50]]

Chausson's libretto is itself a poetic drama. Even in its early stages Duparc had recognised its beauty of form and expression:

The language is excellent, exactly what it needs to be, noble and natural: so far as your verses are concerned, I frankly confess to you that I am completely bowled over by them, and high though I hold you in esteem, I never imagined that you were capable of writing anything so beautiful. You amaze me! The general pace of the drama is perfect: I should have said that right at the

---

[49] *Art. cit.*, p. 856.
[50] *Art. cit.*, pp. 701–2.

beginning, before voicing my endless quibbles about details and nuances . . .

[Le langage est excellent, tout à fait ce qu'il doit être, noble et naturel: quant à tes vers, je t'avoue franchement qu'ils m'ont espatrouillé, et que, malgré la très haute estime en laquelle je te tiens, je ne te croyais pas capable d'en faire d'aussi beaux. Tu *m'épates*! La marche générale du drame est parfaite: j'aurais dû commencer par te le dire, avant de te chicaner si longtemps pour des détails et des nuances . . .[51]]

In the analysis which follows we shall try to show how carefully Chausson attended to the language and form of his lyric drama, particularly under the guidance of Duparc, who announced the sending of his fifty-one page 'colis' in a letter dated 29 December 1888.

The opera opens with an animated prelude, the first theme of which is a boisterous, galloping figure of triplets in C minor (later echoed in *Soir de fête*), which suggests the putting to flight of the Saxons.[52] In a shift to the dominant, a vigorous dotted rhythm in the basses beneath high trills in the violins is reminiscent of Wagner's *Die Walküre* (see p. 2, bars 9 *et seq.*)[53] and provides a tempestuous transition to the stately, triumphal theme in E flat major (p. 4, bars 11–21), given out on trumpets, and associated throughout the rest of the work with Arthus and the Round Table. The tempo picks up again and a theme of martial character, exploiting triplets over a striding bass, brings us to another statement of the Round Table theme on full orchestra (p. 8, bars 1–3) and the prelude ends with an unmistakable reminiscence of the *Meistersinger* overture (p. 8, bars 4 *et seq.*). The turbulence of battle and the noble strains of victory are admirably conveyed through strongly characterised themes and orchestration which is rich without being thick.

The curtain rises and Arthus sings 'Gloire à vous tous' against harp and solo trumpet. The setting is magnificent: a large hall in the royal palace at Carduel (Kamelot in the scenario sent to Poujaud). The first performance imitated the indications already contained in the early scenario: 'Grande salle, avec colonnades en pleins-cintres. Première époque du style roman.' Beneath Romanesque clerestory and arcade, to the left, is the royal throne. Beside the King sits Genièvre and her ladies. The hall is full of knights, squires and pages, the most prominent of the knights being Lancelot and Mordred. On either side of the set stand bards in long white robes. Arthus seems to be concluding an oration to mark the victory celebrations (the invading Saxons have been resoundingly defeated by the Bretons). In the hour of victory Arthus acknowledges the Round Table and the help of God ('Et, surtout, gloire à Dieu') 'dans nos communs efforts'. He thinks of the absent Merlin and there is a resurgence of the stately, triumphal theme at the words 'Ou que tu sois, du moins ton âme vibre/ au cri de guerre des Bretons' (p. 14, bars 3–6). The attendant knights cheer and the opening theme of the prelude is

[51] Oulmont, *op. cit.*, p. 170.
[52] Page and bar numbers refer to the vocal score published by Choudens in 1900.
[53] I cannot agree with Glover, *op. cit.*, p. 173, who says 'It would be difficult to find anything less Wagnerian than the Prelude to Act I'.

introduced, followed by a quieter section celebrating peace. The colourful, confident opening is completely different from the one sketched in the early scenario sent to Poujaud. There Scene 1 depicted Lyonnel, 'écuyer de Lancelot (entre 16 et 23 ans)', watching anxiously by the Queen's bedchamber. The final version makes clear how seriously Chausson took Duparc's suggestions that we must early on be provided with a sympathetic portrait of Lancelot and an indication of the jealousy of some of the knights (in preparation for Mordred's treachery and rebellion). Since Chausson followed them so closely, it is worth quoting Duparc's directions:

> The way to do it seems to me quite simple: I would make him [viz. Lancelot] the hero of the day; it is thanks to him that the battle has been won, and Arthur will be eager to tell him so: 'why do you look sad, when we are celebrating our greatest victory, a victory in which you are the hero . . .' (a bit more development wouldn't do any harm [e.g. the bards singing of Lancelot's victory] . . .) That would explain, first, that Lancelot, instead of simply being one of the company of knights, stands on his own beside Arthur's throne, occupying a place of honour, and that Guenevere descends from the throne to offer him the cup – a not unimportant move from the theatrical point of view, – it would offer a clear explanation (an essential point) of the knights' jealous fury, which I should like to see developed a bit more; in order to prepare for Mordred's treachery in Act 3, he needs to have exercised some sort of influence on them already, to have been irritated by their proposals, and from this moment, in an aside, to be muttering vague thoughts of personal revenge.

> [Le moyen me paraît bien simple: je ferais de lui [= Lancelot] le héros de la journée: c'est grâce à lui que la bataille a été gagnée, et Arthus le lui dirait avec enthousiasme: 'pourquoi sembles-tu triste, quand nous célébrons notre plus grande victoire, une victoire *dont tu es le héros* . . .' (Un peu plus de développement encore ne nuirait pas [e.g. the bards singing of Lancelot's victory] . . .) Cela expliquerait 1° que Lancelot, au lieu d'être mêlé aux autres chevaliers, se tienne seul près du trône d'Arthus, à une place d'honneur, et que Genièvre descende de son trône pour lui offrir la coupe, – ce qui, au point de vue scénique, n'est pas sans importance, – 2° cela justifierait clairement (point essentiel) la rage jalouse des chevaliers, que je voudrais un peu plus développée; il faudrait, pour préparer la trahison de Mordred au 3e acte, que celui-ci eût déjà une sorte d'influence sur eux, que leurs propos l'irritassent, et que dès maintenant, à part, il grommelât quelque vague désir de vengeance personnelle.[54]]

Accordingly, Arthus instructs the bards to sing the praises of Lancelot, the true victor (E minor chorus, p. 25, bars 8 *et seq.*). Mordred mutters darkly 'C'en est trop. Toujours Lancelot' and a separate group of knights echo the words, complaining 'Pour le Roi, nous ne sommes plus rien', all of which leads to Mordred's 'Bientôt, je vous vengerai tous . . .' and the knights' 'Oui, oui, vengeons-nous.' After the Round Table theme rings out again on the trumpets (p. 34, bars 2–6), Arthus comes down from his throne and asks Lancelot 'Quel nuage assombrit ton front?',

---

[54] *Apud* Oulmont, *op. cit.*, pp. 136–7.

whilst Mordred delivers a sarcastic comment, which his monarch silences with the rebuke 'Ne soyez pas hautain ni railleur, je vous prie,/ envers l'insigne fleur de la chevalerie.' At this point Genièvre, her vocal part marked 'doux, avec grâce', leaves her throne and presents a cup to Lancelot ('Recevez de mes mains cette coupe vermeille'). However, Mordred hears her whispered intimation to Lancelot ('Cette nuit . . . le signal . . . viens') and jealously reflects on how the Queen rejected his love. Genièvre and her ladies now exit. Duparc proposed an ending which clearly did not find favour with Chausson, namely, that Arthus should retire and that we should see the Queen in the doorway of her room looking for Lancelot and giving Lyonnel instructions to keep watch:

> The conclusion of this scene would offer a striking contrast with what went before, and would greatly help to clarify the scene that follows . . .
>
> [Cette fin de scène ferait un contraste saisissant avec ce qui précède, et rendrait beaucoup plus clair le tableau suivant . . .[55]]

It is possible that Chausson found this direct evocation of the adultery so soon after Arthur's celebrations and his thanks to Lancelot distasteful. He complains in one of his letters to Debussy: 'J'ai assez vécu avec l'adultère et le remords. Je suis fort tenté d'exprimer d'autres sentiments, moins dramatiques.'[56] At any rate he dropped the opening scene of the early scenario, replacing it with the court celebrations.

Following Wagnerian practice, the second scene is preceded by an interlude, beginning with the turbulent C minor theme of the opening of the opera and using fragments of Genièvre's 'aria' as well as other motifs of the prelude. The final section marked 'lent' (p. 47), with its oboe and cello solos, especially the beginning in rising fifths and a descending chromatic scale, irresistibly calls to mind *Tristan* (which gives so much scope to solo instruments, often in the same way that Chausson treats them). There is also (p. 44, bars 2–8) a brief, passionate suggestion of impending action, which, as Glover has argued,[57] is a quotation from the Prelude to Act 2 of *Tristan*.

The second scene is set on a terrace of the castle, with a porch in the foreground, behind which are the Queen's apartments. It is night and the moon is up. Lyonnel, Lancelot's squire, is seated on the steps of the porch in the role anticipated for him by Duparc in the first scene. Chausson pruned Lyonnel's monologue, at Duparc's suggestion, only to be told that he had shortened it too much! Lyonnel's words depict Lancelot's fall from honour:

> Hélas! Faut-il que mon coeur
> Malgré moi te condamne?
> Amour fatal, amour sacrilège et maudit!
> Lancelot, toi, l'ami d'Arthus,
> Son frère d'armes et de gloire,
> Parjure, déshonoré, félon!

---

[55] *Apud* Oulmont, *op. cit.*, p. 139.
[56] *La Revue Musicale* (1 déc. 1925), p. 119.
[57] *Op. cit.*, p. 177.

Comment cela peut-il être?
Son amour l'a pris tout entier,
Il vit comme en un rêve,
Sans comprendre son crime.

Duparc's recommendations again were carefully heeded here, several lines of the final version stemming from him; 'I'm not very keen on the ending: I'd like to see Lyonnel more appalled by Lancelot's guilt than preoccupied with his own role of watchman' ['Je n'aime pas beaucoup la fin: je voudrais Lyonnel plus accablé de voir Lancelot coupable que préoccupé de son rôle de veilleur'[58]]. The music is poignant. There is a melody, marked 'modéré' (p. 50, bars 3–6) of almost Elgarian tenderness introducing the words 'J'espérais un jour recevoir de ta main les armes de chevalier' and this is used as a motif to express the affection that Lancelot inwardly bears for Arthus (see Act 2, sc. 2, p. 163, bars 1–2 and Act 3, sc. 1, p. 232, bars 5–7). The reference to Mordred's jealousy is followed by the Tristanesque rising fifths and descending chromatic scale (p. 55, bars 1–6). Against a high C# on strings and flute we hear the cries of the nightwatchmen and then all is light as harp and clarinet in Ravelian combination (p. 55, bars 7 *et seq.*) introduce the lovers. The famous A flat major duet, whilst failing to reach the heights of its counterpart in *Tristan*, cannot conceal the latter's influence.[59] There is a certain lack of rhythmical subtlety in the way that the voices move together in Chausson's duet, but there is much to admire (Duparc found the whole scene 'admirable'). The duet begins:

Délicieux oubli des choses
De la terre, rêve enchanté,
Rêve d'amour et de clarté
Parfumé de suaves roses,
Profond et doux enivrement
Où nos deux âmes confondues,
Muettes d'extase, éperdues,
S'étreignent amoureusement . . .

There is no trace of 'Courtly Love', Genièvre declaring to Lancelot, 'Je suis à toi,/ je suis ta servante et ta femme' (later, in Act 2, sc. 1, 'Je suis ton butin, ta proie'). There is an obvious irony in the words 'Les amants sont d'éternels vainqueurs./ L'amour est le seul maître . . .', sentiments which are completely negated by the conclusion of the opera. In a more peaceful section ('Paisiblement entre les bras s'endort mon coeur'), against a background of harp arpeggios (p. 69, bars 1 *et seq.*) the lovers sink into each other's arms, oblivious of their surroundings, and Lyonnel approaches to warn them of daybreak, an event beautifully evoked in graded orchestral colouring (p. 80, bars 9 *et seq.*, p. 85, bars 5 *et seq.*, p. 87, bars 8 *et seq.*). Suddenly Mordred enters, sees the lovers and shouts for assistance. Lancelot strikes him, arranges to meet Genièvre in the nearby forest, but is already stricken with remorse:

---

[58] Oulmont, *op. cit.*, p. 140.
[59] See Glover, *op. cit.*, pp. 175–6.

Chevalier déloyal, j'ai tiré mon épée
Pour soutenir mon mensonge.

Returning to her apartments, the Queen finds Mordred alive. Soldiers arrive.

In the scenario sent to Poujaud there were four scenes in Act 1, the love scene being followed by a scene in which Mordred, thinking it to be Lyonnel who has visited the Queen, fights with him. In a fourth scene, Arthus arrived, received explanations from the two men, whilst Lancelot, observed, but unrecognised, made good his escape. Duparc found the third scene too long and suggested incorporating elements of it in the second scene. In addition, he observed, 'I'd get rid of this timorous development of Guenevere which recalls to no purpose the lark duet' ['Je supprimerais cette évolution craintive de Genièvre, qui fait penser bien inutilement au duo de l'alouette'[60]]. Chausson adopted Duparc's suggestions. The rest of the material forming scene 4 of the early scenario was dropped, as was revised material of this section submitted to Duparc.

Act 2 begins with a short prelude in which a calm, reflective theme in B major, played on the whole orchestral range in octaves, evokes a still, sunlit, rural landscape. Once again, Chausson makes use of solo instruments, here a solo cello in its high register (p. 89, bars 4 et seq.). The scene is the edge of a pine forest, a large expanse of fields forming the background. The sun is shining through the trees and to the right a moss-covered rock provides an area for sitting. The song of a distant ploughman is heard. Lancelot is agitated, anxious to discover whether he has been recognised and whether Mordred is truly dead. He is already overcome by remorse, for he has betrayed 'Arthus! Arthus!/ Le plus grand, le plus saint des rois!/ Lui, le chevalier du Christ,/ Le vainqueur des Saxons!' Despite having fallen so low, defiling his honour, word and name, he nevertheless recognises 'A jamais, je resterai fié,/ Je le sens bien, à celle qui m'enfièvre./ Tout, loyauté, serment, honneur est oublié/ Dès que mes bras étreignent ma Genièvre.' The music is sombre and, with Genièvre's arrival, characterised by nervous agitation (see dotted rhythms and offbeat notes at p. 106, bars 8 et seq. and, later, p. 117, bars 1 et seq.). Genièvre informs Lancelot that Mordred is not dead and has accused him of treachery, Arthus alone defending, albeit hesitantly, his trusted knight. Lancelot is now caught in a terrible dilemma in the face of Genièvre's mounting insistence that he save her by returning to Arthus and brazenly denying everything ('Un moyen te reste, l'audace!'). Throughout this scene much greater use is made than before of chromaticism and rising sequences to indicate great surges of emotion (often culminating in the Tristan chord). The more Lancelot hesitates, the more unsympathetic Genièvre becomes:

Lancelot   Mentirai-je à mon noble maître?

Genièvre   Un mensonge de plus, qu'importe?
               N'es-tu pas déloyal
               Et traître en m'aimant?
               . . .

---

[60] Oulmont, op. cit., p. 140.

Lancelot Mais froidement tromper
     Sa noble confiance
     Quand, malgré l'évidence,
     Il me veut innocent.
     Genièvre, est-ce possible?
     N'exige pas de moi
     Ce sacrilège horrible.
     . . .

Genièvre C'est odieux, je le sais,
     C'est infâme, mais il le faut:
     Mon honneur le réclame: le tien aussi.

Lancelot prefers to die, but this cannot save Genièvre. Increasingly desperate, she calls him 'ingrat', 'lâche', in the most insensitive terms: 'Un inepte scrupule/ t'interdit aujourd'hui/ de sauver mon honneur.' Chromaticism and agitated rhythms abound (p. 112, bars 5 *et seq.*, p. 124, bars 9 *et seq.*). Exhausted, Genièvre finally dismisses Lancelot: 'Notre amour fut un mauvais rêve,/ Je ne veux plus te voir./ Je te chasse. Va-t-en.' The crucial step has been taken. Lancelot, immobilised by grief, reflects that he is now no longer loyal even in love (note the typical dotted, chromatic figure in the bass, p. 128, bars 11 *et seq.*) and, seeing Genièvre 'pâle comme une morte', he summons up all his strength in a moment of sudden decision, 'Il faut la sauver avant tout. Puis . . .' A trumpet motif (p. 130, bars 2 *et seq.*) reminds him of Arthus and the bass clarinet, so distinctive a feature of the melancholy music of Acts 2 and 3, introduces the cry of the exhausted Genièvre (p. 130, bars 14 *et seq.*). Lancelot will lie to Arthus 'sans baisser la tête' in what will be 'l'épreuve suprême' and then, having saved the Queen, he will seek 'dans les combats . . . une mort noble et prompte'.

 Duparc understood 'la situation atroce' in which Lancelot is placed and advised Chausson to remove some of the more tender and sentimental reflexions on his love for Genièvre, also suggesting the intercalation of his ruminations with verses of the ploughman's song, so as to prepare the exclamation 'Arthus! Arthus!' (p. 100, bars 11–16):

This, as I explained to you, is the feeling that I should exploit, a feeling of inner revolt which will always bow to passion, right up to the moment of death, when it will conquer passion. Interpreted in this way, it seems to me, the character of Lancelot will be profoundly true, moving, and quite different from Tristan.

[Voilà, comme je te le disais, le sentiment que j'exploiterais, – sentiment de révolte intérieure, qui fléchira toujours devant la passion, jusqu'au moment de la mort, ou il vaincra la passion. Ainsi compris, il me semble que le caractère de Lancelot serait profondément vrai, émouvant, et tout à fait différent de Tristan.[61]]

Now there is a great resurgence of passion, as Genièvre begs forgiveness for her 'injuste parole' and 'mots odieux', emphasising their common fate, and

[61] Oulmont, *op. cit.*, p. 146.

proposing flight to a refuge where they can 'aimer librement au grand jour'.
Lancelot is won over: 'Il me semble que c'est un rêve que je fais . . . ne vivre
que pour notre amour . . .' Genièvre responds:

> Nos corps sont à jamais
> Enchaînés l'un à l'autre,
> Comme nos deux coeurs sont unis!
> Nul amour n'est semblable au nôtre.
> O délices d'aimer!
> O transports infinis!

From this scene Duparc cleared two elements. The first was Genièvre's account
of Mordred's love for her, which Duparc directed should be in Act 1. Then
Duparc wanted Lyonnel out of the way:

> But one thing which I find purposeless and off-putting, is Lyonnel's interven-
> tion: you have the feeling that this adolescent's reappearance keeps being
> engineered: I see no need for it at all; if I were you, I'd make him into an
> episodic, secondary character, otherwise you'll inevitably end up with a sort of
> Kurwenal, who has no real reason for existing . . . here . . . he is completely out
> of place. And then, why does he offer up his life? Much good it would do
> Lancelot to run through this fair young man!

> [Mais une chose que je trouve tout à fait inutile et refrigérante, c'est
> l'intervention de Lyonnel: on y sent la préoccupation de faire de temps en
> temps reparaître cet adolescent: je n'en vois nullement la nécessité: à ta place,
> j'en ferais un personnage tout à fait épisodique et secondaire, sans quoi tu
> tomberais forcément dans une espèce de Kurwenal qui n'a pas sa raison d'être
> . . . ici . . . il est tout à fait cheveu dans soupe. Et puis, pourquoi offre-t-il sa vie?
> Lancelot serait bien avancé s'il perforait cet éphèbe![62]]

Duparc's outspoken and earthy style is continued in his criticism of a number of
passages in which he finds the lovers' reflexions too sentimental:

> Will you forgive me if I say quite bluntly that I hate the cavatina: 'O beaux
> jours écoulés'? and that melancholy madrigal which follows: 'Ou porter mes
> pas irresolus' . . . 'What is Lancelot without Guenevere . . .' (What is Tristan
> without Isolde?) – 'But you, Guenevere, be happy' . . . no: I have to say this
> scent of operetta makes me queasy and want to throw up: I feel sure that the
> sacrifice of these two or three mawkish moments will not drive you to despair.

> [Me pardonneras-tu si je te dis sans périphrase que je déteste la cavatine: 'O
> beaux jours écoulés'? et l'espèce de madrigal mélancolique qui la suit: 'Où
> porter mes pas irrésolus' . . . 'qu'est-ce Lancelot sans Genièvre . . .' (qu'est-ce
> que Tristan sans Iseult?) – 'Mais toi, Genièvre, sois heureuse'. . . non: j'avoue
> que ce parfum d'opéra comique me donne de tièdes régurgitations: je
> m'imagine même que le sacrifice de ces deux ou trois mièvreries ne te
> rendra pas fou de douleur.[63]]

---

[62] Oulmont, op. cit., pp. 147–8.
[63] Ibid., pp. 148–9.

Chausson was not slow to act on these suggestions and the result is almost invariably a more impressive simplicity.

An interlude now brings an animated, passionate climax, dying down to a more sombre section (with bass clarinet again) which anticipates Arthus's anxiety and concludes with a sort of funeral march (p. 159, bars 6 *et seq.*).

In Act 2 Chausson finally interverted the two main tableaux as he had sketched them in the scenario sent to Poujaud, so that the second scene comprises material which formed the first scene in that scenario. In an atmosphere of gloomy foreboding we are introduced to an inner, cloister-like courtyard at Carduel. Arthus enters and joins a number of knights already talking together in hushed voices. On learning that Lancelot has not appeared, he dismisses the knights and ruminates on his growing anxiety against a musical background of sombre, rising chromatic scales and the ominous beat of the tympani:

> Toujours, toujours, cette pensée . . .
> La paix fuit mon âme angoissée,
> Je ne puis retrouver ma foi.
> Comment mettre fin à ce doute horrible?
> Genièvre! Lancelot!
> Non! Non! C'est impossible.

A motif associated with the friendship of Arthus and Lancelot here makes its second appearance in the opera (p. 163, bars 1–2). The martial theme representing the Round Table also makes an appearance (p. 165, bar 4) as Arthus piteously foresees the end of the institution which he founded:

> J'ai fondé la Table Ronde.
> Et je croyais mon oeuvre immortelle et féconde!
> Hélas! J'y découvre un germe de mort.
> Les chevaliers entre eux luttent de jalousie,
> Ils ne supportent plus sans un pénible effort
> La règle austère qui les lie.
> Ils écoutent Mordred
> Qui les pousse en secret à la révolte.

Arthus's distrust of Mordred makes him wonder whether there is a plot against Lancelot. As he sees less and less clearly, he yearns for the advice of Merlin. Suddenly the trees separate and in a greenish light Merlin is seen half reclining on a bed of apple tree branches.[64] He is old, with a long, flowing white beard, and attracts Arthus's attention by calling to him. There, in the garden of the cloister, Merlin sings the celebrated 'Pommiers verts, pommiers prophétiques' in which he announces that 'les jours marqués sont accomplis'. Faced with these enigmas, Arthus responds 'Ta parole est sombre comme le rire de la mer' and receives the stark message:

---

[64] This scene is referred to in a letter from Debussy of 24 August 1893. Chausson describes changes he has made in it in a letter to Henry Lerolle, see *La Revue Musicale* (1 déc. 1925), p. 177 (letter dated 1892).

N'espère rien de l'avenir,
Notre oeuvre commune est brisée:
Dégénérée et méprisée,
La Table Ronde va périr.

Arthus now realises that 'notre oeuvre impérissable' is doomed, but he still desperately searches for an explanation ('Suis-je le jouet d'un rêve?'). Merlin replies, 'Aveugles que nous sommes,/ nous avons trop compté/ sur la vertu des hommes':

Si l'emplacement consacré
Est envahi par les orties,
C'est qu'un crime encore ignoré,
L'orgueil, les basses jalousies
Ont fait mentir les prophéties.

He declines to reveal more, but in a poetic diction which evokes Celtic verse, he predicts Arthur's eventual rebirth:

Mais, quand viendra
Le jour du glorieux réveil,
O fils de Pendragon,
O guerrier sans pareil,
Alors, les chênes, dans leur joie,
De rouges fleurs se couvriront,
Vêtus d'argent, d'or et de soie,
Les guerriers morts s'élanceront,
Et le clair soleil qui flamboie
De son disque éclatant
Couronnera ton front.

This is followed by an energetic statement of the Round Table theme on the full orchestra (p. 184, bars 4 *et seq.*). There is nothing left to Arthus but to accept his coming death and at the same time to continue his anguished questioning about Genièvre and Lancelot. No reply is vouchsafed him and Merlin abruptly vanishes, leaving Arthus shouting for the Queen. A crowd of knights forms and soon divides into supporters of the rebellious Mordred and the champions of Lancelot. The curtain falls swiftly on this ugly scene of dissension.

The prelude to Act 3 begins with a sombre theme in D minor first given out on bass clarinet over a tremolo background and then passed to cellos and brass. Battle is evoked in an animated passage of dotted and triplet rhythms. The final act opens on the summit of a hill overlooking a battlefield. There are rocks and pine trees in the foreground; in the background, the sea. Genièvre appears anxiously observing the battlefield, convinced that Lancelot, having had the courage not to flee, will be victorious in battle. Mordred has proclaimed himself king and many of the knights of the Round Table have gone over to him. Doubts assail Genièvre – does Lancelot still love her? Just as, at the beginning of Act 1, Arthus asked Lancelot 'Quel nuage assombrit ton front?', Genièvre now, filled with foreboding, reflects on Lancelot's joylessness:

'Un farouche désespoir assombrit son visage.' The conflict of Act 3 is already expressed in her words,

> Ah! S'il était vrai!
> Si le remords qui dompte son âme
> Avait tué son amour?

Suddenly, Lancelot, unarmed, is seen approaching and confesses to Genièvre that he has fled, unable to bear arms against his monarch:

> Je l'ai vu, lui, Arthus!
> Alors, une soudaine et terrible clarté
> Envahit mon âme, une indicible honte me saisit.
> J'ai jeté mes armes, j'ai fui, j'ai fui, j'ai fui!

Genièvre revives the passionate vituperation of Act 2, calling Lancelot 'ingrat' and referring to the 'inutile lâcheté/ d'un coeur pusillanime'. Lancelot's sole duty is to defend to the death their 'indomptable amour', but he refuses to 'combattre en rebelle' and determines to go, if possible with Genièvre, to seek out his king and stop the fighting:

> Et j'obéis à la voix qui parle dans mon coeur.
> Genièvre, accepteras-tu de partager mon sort?
> . . .
> Unis dans l'amour,
> Unis dans le péché,
> Le serons-nous aussi
> Dans l'expiation?

There follows Genièvre's death scene. She is 'Trahie! Abandonée! Méprisée!' ['Betrayed, abandoned, scorned.'] She has lost to the 'lâcheté d'un coeur tout éperdu d'amour' ['the cowardice of a heart consumed by love']. The noise of battle dies down. Genièvre realises that Lancelot must be dead: 'Il a pu l'accomplir,/ le suprême abandon!' [He achieved the supreme sacrifice] Determined to die, she strangles herself with her own tresses:

> Ornaments d'une vaine beauté,
> Cheveux sombres et bleus
> Comme la nuit, vous,
> Qui n'avez pas su retenir Lancelot
> Dans vos filets soyeux,
> Prêtez-moi votre secours ami!
> Vous fûtes mon orgueil
> Dans des jours heureux;
> Maintenant, aidez-moi,
> Aidez-moi à mourir.

The first conception of this scene, in the scenario sent to Poujaud, was completely different. Genièvre, after Lancelot's death, is packed off to a convent! This feature evidently survived in the version submitted to Duparc, who does not seem to have expressed any reservations about it. In the early scenario

Lancelot, mortally wounded, returned from the field of battle and died in Genièvre's presence. Duparc commented on the Queen's suicide as follows:

> Without actually wrapping her hair round her neck so tightly as to break her vertebral column – which would demand exceptional athleticism – she is forced to struggle furiously; and the better she does, the weaker she gets; consequently her suicide takes an age, and yet it seems to me absolutely essential that it should be over very quickly.

> [A moins de se serrer le cou assez fortement avec ses cheveux pour se casser la colonne vertébrale – ce qui demanderait de rares qualités athlétiques – elle est obligée de s'acharner: et plus elle réussit, plus elle perd ses forces; par conséquent son suicide est forcément long, et il me parait indispensable qu'il soit très rapide.[65]]

Duparc suggests than Genièvre might employ a scarf with which she had indicated their assignations to Lancelot, or, better, Lancelot's own arms which he might lay down after his refusal to fight.[66]

Duparc also had more general criticisms of Act 3 in the version submitted to him:

> From the very first reading the dramatic portion of Act 3 struck me as inferior to the rest of the drama . . . I should be very surprised if you do not agree with me that it is important, after gripping the spectator with a number of dramatic situations, to establish in him an emotional relationship – whether of affection or contempt – with each of your main characters . . . the situations, even the most tragic, are no longer enough; it is the spectator's very heart which must, as it were, make an appearance.

> [Dès la première lecture, la partie dramatique du 3e acte m'a paru inférieure au reste du drame . . . je serai bien étonné si tu ne penses pas comme moi qu'il est nécessaire, après avoir empoigné le spectateur par des situations très dramatiques, de l'attacher par des sentiments d'affection ou de mépris à chacun de tes principaux personnages . . . les situations, même les plus tragiques, ne suffisent plus; c'est le coeur même du spectateur qui doit, pour ainsi dire, entrer en scène.[67]]

Above all, claims Duparc, Arthus, with nothing more to lose, must direct a word of forgiveness to Genièvre. Lancelot's death must be not merely materially more poignant than that of any of the other characters, but must be qualitatively so, as a result of a final 'réveil de son vieil honneur'. Lancelot must be dominated, not by his love, but by anger at Mordred's treachery to Arthus. In fact, in the final version Chausson cut entirely the appearance and explanations of the traitor, whose role is reduced to a brief appearance in the two tableaux of Act 1. Chausson worked hard to simplify Act 3 after Duparc had made of it what he himself called 'un *monstre* en forme de scénario'. Duparc thought that Lancelot's return to honourable indignation might best be motivated by an attempt on the

---

[65] Oulmont, *op. cit.*, p. 111.
[66] The published score contains the directions 'She rises, and seems to be looking for a weapon . . .' ['Elle se lève, semble chercher une arme . . .'].
[67] Oulmont, *op. cit.*, pp. 150–1.

part of Mordred to win him over to the side of the rebels and he even designed a plan in which Mordred struck Lancelot with his sword.[68] Chausson rightly sensed that the action was becoming too complicated.

The prelude to the second scene combines the sombre rumination of the bass clarinet over timpani beats with offstage trumpets evoking the battle and with the Round Table theme. The scene is set at the end of the day, on a plain near the seashore. Lancelot lies dying. He could not stop the fighting and threw himself between the combatants. Arthus is griefstricken:

> Je n'ai plus rien d'humain que ma douleur.
> Tout, tout s'écroule à la fois, tout s'effondre.
> L'oeuvre de ma vie est brisée!
> Au cri de mon coeur blessé,
> Nul coeur ne peut plus répondre.

Lancelot urges Arthus to avenge his honour and kill him. There now takes place the exchange, which we quoted earlier, between the King and his vassal in which Lancelot fully recognises the merits of his monarch and predicts that his 'pensée . . . immortelle' will last for ever. With Arthus's words

> Mon courage est vaincu;
> Je n'ai plus d'espérance.
> Dans un sommeil sans lendemain,
> Endormez, s'il se peut,
> Endormez ma souffrance.

there are introduced two wordless choirs offstage, which are then joined by five soprano soloists in long, undulating, chromatic patterns, until finally the choirs take up the words,

> Viens!
> Celui qui nous envoie
> T'assigne un sublime sort.

The stage directions read,

In the background, in the pink and gold glow of the setting sun, a small boat full of ladies is seen approaching across the waters. One of the ladies, standing in the stern of the boat, spreads her broad wings like sails.

[Au fond du théâtre, au milieu des lueurs roses et dorées qui entourent le soleil couchant, on voit apparaître et s'avancer sur la mer une nacelle remplie de femmes. L'une d'entre elles, debout à l'arrière de la nef, étend de grandes ailes en guise de voiles.]

Gradually, Arthus takes his leave of life ('Les temps sont accomplis des grandes aventures') whilst the choirs sing of an island 'caressée par des flots d'or et

---

[68] Duparc's proposals included the words 'Ah! Mordred, this man who was once without stain on him, whom love of a woman succeeded in making me forget, your baseness has reawoken him in me . . .' ['Ah! Mordred, cet homme jadis sans tache, que l'amour d'une femme a pu me faire oublier, ton infamie l'a enfin réveillé en moi . . .'] (Oulmont, p. 155).

d'azur'. The Round Table theme is heard again (p. 327, bars 1–2; p. 332, bars 12–13; p. 337, bars 2 *et seq.*) and Arthus enters the barge and is borne into the sunset, apparently asleep on a couch within the boat.[69] In a calm and peaceful finale (C major) the choir sings:

> Comme un sublime manoeuvre,
> Sur terre, tu reviendras
> Pour reprendre ta grande oeuvre
> Et livrer de fiers combats!
> Arthus! Arthus!
> Sur ton front royal
> Qu'a dédaigné la victoire,
> Plane la suprême gloire
> D'avoir cru dans l'idéal!

In this final scene Chausson seems to have distilled musically that 'tristesse majestueuse' which Racine saw as the true pleasure of tragedy.

It is a paradox that an opera which enjoyed so markedly successful a first production should have been so entirely neglected since. Vincent d'Indy, who supervised preparations for the production with loving care, expressed himself delighted and surprised when he first heard parts of the score converted into real sound: 'The first act which I thought was the least good is a revelation; it is wholly theatrical and seems short despite being 42 minutes in length' ['Ce premier acte que je croyais le moins bon est simplement un éblouissement; il est tout à fait scénique, et paraît court malgré ses 42 minutes de durée'[70]]. The rewards of Chausson's painstaking attempts to simplify the action of the drama and of the minute attention which he paid to the practicalities of staging are still, in the absence of modern performances, perforce unappreciated. It is also a paradox that this work, which of all Arthurian operas[71] most clearly has Arthur himself as its central subject, should treat exclusively of the dissolution of the fellowship which he founded. Yet the gloominess of much of the music of Acts 2 and 3 is relieved by the harmony and tranquillity of the finale in which pessimism gives way to a serene resignation. After the 'passion' of Arthur, as

---

[69] In the scenario sent to Poujaud (*art. cit.*, p. 154) Chausson described the ending in the following terms: 'An irresistible power bears him [viz. Arthur] off to the enchanted boat. The calls become more urgent and softer. The chorus promises him oblivion and eternal rest. The boat remains in the background, even seeming to recede. Arthur advances into the sea. The water is already up to his chest, then suddenly the boat disappears. A shout is heard: Arthur vanishes beneath the waves.' ['Une force irrésistible l'entraîne [= Arthus] vers la barque enchantée. Les appels deviennent plus pressants et plus doux. Le choeur lui promet l'oubli et l'éternel repos. La barque reste toujours dans le fond du théâtre, elle semble même s'éloigner. Arthus s'avance et pénètre dans la mer. Déjà, l'eau lui monte jusqu'à la poitrine, puis, tout à coup, la barque disparaît. On entend un cri; Arthus disparaît sous les vagues']. For Chausson's hesitations concerning the first scene of Act 3 see his letter of 1894 to Henry Lerolle, *La Revue Musicale* (1 déc. 1925), p. 177.

[70] Quoted in Oulmont, *Musique de l'Amour* t. 1, p. 187.

[71] Space does not permit anything like a listing, but in addition to those already cited in the notes above, mention might be made of Tom Cooke's *King Arthur and the Knights of the Round Table* (1835), Frederick Corder's *La Morte d'Arthur* (1877–8), Rutland Boughton's Arthurian 'choral dramas' (1908–45), Luboš Fišer's *Lancelot* (1959–60), and Richard Blackford's *Sir Gawain and the Green Knight* (1978).

Oulmont rightly described the central portion of the opera, comes the apotheosis which enshrines the values exemplified by Arthur in a transcendental ideal which will endure, though the Round Table pass away. It is easy to understand how Chausson's best energies were engaged by this subject, for despite his constant striving for perfection, he often experienced the discouragement of isolation and neglect. Yet two years after he completed his opera and only the same number of years before his death Chausson wrote one of the jewels of French chamber music, the A major Piano Quartet (Op. 30) in which the composer, in the words of d'Indy, 'free at last from his doubt and his distress, thinks only of a flight to new and loftier regions of art'.[72] As the Arthurian ideal lives on, so Chausson endures through compositions which have been increasingly appreciated with the passage of time.

[72] Quoted in Glover, *op. cit.*, p. 93.

Rutland Boughton's Arthurian Cycle

MICHAEL HURD

Begun in January 1908, the five music dramas that make up Rutland Boughton's Arthurian cycle were completed in November 1945 – a massive undertaking that occupied, on and off, virtually the whole of his creative life. What began, however, as the story of King Arthur, retold in music as an inspirational symbol for the people of Great Britain, gradually became a record of Boughton's own spiritual and political development. It is therefore necessary first to chart something of his life and extraordinary achievements.

He was born on 23 January 1878 in Aylesbury, where his father was partner in a small grocery business. Although he showed clear signs of an exceptional talent for music, opportunities for advanced musical education (or, indeed, advanced education of any kind) were not available to a young man of his social background. The best his parents could do to foster his talents was to apprentice him, in 1892, to a London Concert Agency. But he was not the type to allow his self-taught efforts, already nothing if not ambitious, to go unremarked. By 1898 he had attracted the attention of several influential London musicians to such effect that a fund was raised to enable him to study at the Royal College of Music under Sir Charles Stanford. But the sum was not sufficient for a full course, and in 1901 he was obliged to abandon his studies and seek a living as best he could. Though he endured many privations, he turned his hand to a variety of musical hack-jobs while gradually making his way as a published composer. In December 1903 a moment of ill-judged chivalry led him into marriage – with Florence Hobley, the daughter of an Aylesbury neighbour. He was soon to regret it. Fortunately, in 1905, his career entered a more settled phase. He was invited to join the teaching staff of the Birmingham and Midland Institute of Music, then under the progressive leadership of the composer Granville Bantock.

It was a turning point in every respect. Not only was the work congenial (he taught singing), but the city's artistic life was vibrant and challenging. He was soon acknowledged not only as an inspiring teacher, choral trainer and conductor, but also as a significant member of a generation of composers judged to be worthy to follow in the footsteps of Parry, Stanford, and Elgar. He made new and stimulating friends – chief among them Edward Carpenter, poet and apostle of sexual liberation, and playwright George Bernard Shaw, with whom he was to enjoy a lifelong correspondence, half teasing, half genuinely admiring, and always affectionate. Even more important was the relationship he began to develop with a young art student, Christina Walshe.

Christina was everything that Florence was not. She was intelligent, idealistic, enthusiastic and, above all, a talented artist in her own right: someone who could understand the dreams that were beginning to take shape in his mind and was prepared to support them in any way she could. Artistic companionship soon blossomed into love, though it would not be until 1911, when Florence finally agreed to a Deed of Separation, that their relationship could be formally acknowledged.

By that time, however, Boughton was ready to turn his dream into reality. As a student he had planned a fourteen-day cycle of dramas on the life of Christ in which the story would be enacted on a small stage set in the middle of a large orchestra, while soloists and chorus commented on the action and revealed its significance to modern life.

It was a curious hybrid: Wagnerian in scale and in the role the orchestra would play; harking back to medieval mystery plays, so far as the dramatic presentation was concerned; and incorporating the choral principles of what he considered to be a peculiarly British mode of self-expression – the oratorio. He dubbed it 'Choral Drama'. But as time went on and the example of such writers as Tolstoy, Ruskin, Shaw, and William Morris began to influence his thinking, the need to emphasize its significance as an expression of what he referred to as the 'oversoul' of the Nation led to a change of direction. It was not Christ who would best tap into the mystical heart of Great Britain, but Arthur – the once and future King.

It seems probable that Boughton intended to write his own libretto. He had already done as much in 1901 for *Eolf*, an early operatic effort (in which Arthur plays a minor role) which progressed only as far as the vocal score stage before being abandoned. Moreover, he had made frequent contributions to such magazines as *The Musical Times*, and *The Music Student*, had acted as reviewer and music critic for at least two London dailies, and in 1907 had published a small volume, *Bach*, that would run to three editions before being expanded, in 1930, into a larger, and highly controversial, study. But events were to take an unexpected turn. Granville Bantock handed him the manuscript of a 'Festival Drama' by one, Reginald Ramsden Buckley. It was called *Arthur of Britain*.[1]

Buckley (1883–1919) had conceived his cycle of four dramas as a text for music and was eager to find a composer to take up the challenge. He sent it to Elgar, who sent it back; and then to Bantock, who evidently thought the undertaking too colossal even for his tastes. Boughton, however, was delighted. What Buckley had inadvertently provided was a text that would allow him to explore precisely those choral aspects he thought essential to his vision of a truly 'national' music drama.

In addition to the poetic dialogue through which the drama would unfold in the usual way, Buckley had provided preludes, interludes, and brief commentaries that variously set the scene, define the prevailing emotions, or act as stage directions. It is not clear whether he intended these to be sung by a chorus, or whether the words were to be transmuted into descriptive orchestral passages.

[1] In 1914 Buckley arranged for Williams & Norgate to publish the text of the entire cycle, *Arthur of Britain*, thereby confusing later audiences who, much to Boughton's dismay, expected the text to match what they were hearing.

Indeed, he does not seem to have considered how his ideas were to be made effective in theatrical terms, musical or otherwise. Nor, at this stage, did Boughton. He simply embraced the possibilities and, demanding very few modifications, began to set the 'libretto' as Buckley had shaped it. By 1908 a purely orchestral version of the Prelude to Act II of *Uther and Igraine*, as the opening drama was then called, was successfully performed at Leeds and Bournemouth, thus confirming that composer and poet were now fully committed to the realization of an exceptionally ambitious project.

An even stronger gesture of intent came in 1910 with the publication of the *Uther and Igraine* libretto, prefaced by explanatory essays – by Boughton on 'Choral Drama' and Buckley on 'The Growth of Dreams'. The book, *Music Drama of the Future*,[2] was as provocative a manifesto as its title suggests. Recognizing that their ideas would find no place in the conventional opera house, they proposed nothing less than a Wagnerian solution – in Boughton's brave words:

> Wagner's festival dramas necessitated the building of Bayreuth theatre. Our dramas necessitate the building of a place which Buckley has fitly forenamed the Temple Theatre. That theatre we are intent on making the centre of a commune. There have been many communes and they have failed – for lack of a religious centre. Our theatre supplies that. It shall grow out of the municipal life of some civically conscious place if we can get such a place to co-operate with us. Failing that, a new city shall grow around the theatre.

At first, true to Arts-and-Crafts principles, they set their sights on Letchworth Garden City. A 'Summer School' was to be held, after which the students, amateur and professional, would give a public performance of the work they had been studying. Despite massive publicity, the 1912 'school' failed to attract sufficient support. But Boughton was not to be deterred. In 1913 a nationwide appeal, backed by, among others, Bantock, Beecham, Galsworthy, Shaw, and Gordon Craig, was launched for the building of a 'National Festival Theatre for Music and Drama'. Elgar promised to lay the foundation stone – but not at Letchworth. Glastonbury was now the preferred site. A Summer School at Bournemouth, at which the second act of *Uther and Igraine* was successfully performed in the open air, convinced most of the Glastonbury supporters that some sort of 'festival' could be mounted. And despite a certain amount of opposition (largely on account of Boughton's equivocal marital situation), plans were announced for the following year.

Despite the fact that war had been declared on 4 August, the first Glastonbury Festival began at 8pm on 5 August 1914. It was not quite as originally planned: a grand piano took the place of Thomas Beecham's promised orchestra and the tiny Assembly Rooms became the theatre. The Festival culminated in a performance, on 16 August, of *The Immortal Hour* – a setting of Fiona Macleod's Celtic drama which had fired Boughton's imagination in 1912 and distracted him from Arthurian matters. The Festival was judged a complete success, and

---

[2] *Music Drama of the Future* was published by William Reeves. Few copies seem to have survived.

with modest financial backing from the Clark family (Quaker owners of a highly successful and philanthropically motivated shoe factory in the neighbouring village of Street) Boughton began the series of festivals that, with a brief interruption during his military service in 1917, were to run with increasing success and sophistication until 1927.

When the end came, it was not because of any failure in what had been achieved musically and socially, but because Boughton had allowed his political views to unsettle his supporters – already taxed by a break with Christina and the advent of a new 'wife', Kathleen. In 1926, in response to the injustices of the General Strike, he declared his communist sympathies by presenting *Bethlehem*, his 1915 setting of the Coventry Nativity Play, in modern dress: Christ born in a miner's cottage, and Herod as a top-hatted capitalist. The scandal, happily whipped up by the national press, was more than his supporters could cope with, and in July 1927 the Glastonbury Festivals went into liquidation.

But by this time Boughton, at least, could afford to be unconcerned. *The Immortal Hour* had attracted attention far beyond Glastonbury, and in October 1922 had commenced an unprecedented run of 216 consecutive performances at London's Regent Theatre, followed by a revival in November 1923 of 160 performances, and further revivals in 1924 and 1932. *Bethlehem* had also found success on the London stage. Moreover, Glastonbury itself had achieved miracles. By the time they came to an end Boughton had mounted no fewer than 350 staged performances and over 100 chamber concerts, had toured his works extensively throughout the West Country and founded a companion Folk Festival School in Bristol. Glastonbury had become a training ground for young singers anxious to learn the operatic trade, and had won the admiration and support of music lovers from all over the country. Although his own works formed the backbone of the proceedings, he also staged operas by Gluck, Purcell, John Blow, and Matthew Locke, and provided a platform for new operas by Edgar Bainton and Clarence Raybould.

Only the first two parts of the Arthurian cycle were completed in time for production at Glastonbury, and they appeared in reverse order: *The Round Table*, on 14 August 1916, and *The Birth of Arthur* (as *Uther and Igraine* was now known) on 16 August 1920. They were repeated, as a pair, at the 1920 and 1925 festivals. Buckley witnessed complete performances of only *The Round Table*, for in March 1919 he became ill and died. He was only thirty-six.

No longer urged on by an enthusiastic collaborator, Boughton's interest in the cycle seems to have diminished. Although he had accepted the first drama more or less as Buckley had written it, he had voiced considerable misgivings over the second, insisting on completely reshaping its structure, and partially rewriting the text himself. Buckley protested, but found it impossible to argue against what even he must have recognized as a superior instinct for the theatre. Although Boughton seems to have begun sketches for a third part of the cycle, which eventually emerged in 1934 as *The Lily Maid* and, significantly, had nothing to do with Buckley's original concept, he found himself drawn to subjects which fired his imagination to the same degree as *The Immortal Hour* and *Bethlehem* had done in previous years. *Alkestis*, a setting of Gilbert Murray's translation of Euripides, was staged at the 1922 Summer Festival, and *The Queen of Cornwall* (an adaptation of Thomas Hardy's 1923 'Mummers' play) in 1924.[3] Both furnished him with ample opportunity for the kind of choral commentary that was essential to his type of 'music drama'. More importantly, their subject matter – faithfulness and betrayal – had an intense personal significance for him, for he was now openly in love with the woman who would become his third and lasting partner.

With the collapse of the Festival, Boughton retired to a small-holding on the Gloucester-Herefordshire borders. In 1934 and 1935 he attempted to revive his festival schemes, at Stroud and Bath respectively, but neither took root.[4] At Stroud, however, the third part of the Arthurian cycle, *The Lily Maid*, received its first performance. The libretto was entirely Boughton's, and its composition motivated by the same feelings of helpless guilt that had drawn him to *Alkestis* and *The Queen of Cornwall*, but it is interesting to note that he was still advertising Buckley's remaining dramas, *The Holy Grail* and *The Death of Arthur*, as things to come that were 'not yet completed'.

In the event, they were dropped altogether. When in 1943 he began work on the last two dramas, *Galahad* and *Avalon*, they were utterly different from anything Buckley might have agreed to: entirely Boughton, idiosyncratic and largely autobiographical – as far removed from what had been begun in 1908 as time and experience could make them. The final page of the orchestral score was completed on 10 November 1945, but although Boughton had many more years to live (he died on 25 January 1960) no performances have yet taken place. Of the earlier parts, only *The Lily Maid* was to enjoy performances over and above its first production: in London, in 1937, and in Chichester in 1985.[5] If only for economic reasons, the chances of the entire cycle being performed are remote indeed. And, as we shall see, it is not only economics that make the prospect unlikely.

But before passing to a consideration of the cycle, it is important to understand the nature of Boughton's political beliefs. Although he was a member of the Communist Party of Great Britain from 1926 to 1929, and again from 1945 to 1956, it would be inaccurate to think of him as a rigid disciple of Marx and Lenin, Engels or Trotsky, or anyone else. His brand of 'communism' belonged firmly to the kind of idealism that moved such thinkers as John Ruskin, William Morris, Edward Carpenter, and George Bernard Shaw, who, appalled at the inhuman aspects of industrialization, commercialism, and colonialism, worked peacefully for a more humane vision of society – a vision founded upon the basic truths of Christianity. Indeed, Boughton's involvement seems to have been a search for a 'religion' that would replace what he perceived to have been

---

[3] Unlike Glastonbury, both festivals employed an orchestra. Both mounted *The Immortal Hour*, and while Stroud saw the first performance of *The Lily Maid*, Bath introduced a new work *The Ever Young*.

[4] Although *The Immortal Hour*, *Bethlehem*, *Alkestis*, and *the Queen of Cornwall* appeared in print (Stainer & Bell, Curwen, Goodwin & Tabb, Joseph Williams, respectively) the Arthurian cycle has remained unpublished. All Boughton's manuscripts are to be found in the British Library (Add. 50960–51012).

[5] Performances of *The Lily Maid* took place in London's Winter Garden Theatre (conductor Steuart Wilson) in 1937, and at Chichester in 1985 (conductor Michael Hurd) as part of the British Music Society's project, *British Opera in Retrospect*.

betrayed by the practice of the established church. Significantly, it was when Communism proved itself to be not merely fallible, but unforgivably culpable by crushing the Hungarian revolt of 1956, that Boughton resigned his Party membership once and for all. He remained convinced, however, that some form of communism was 'the natural goal of Christian civilization' and that peace and goodwill would only be secured in a world where people were able to live 'in conditions of approximate material equality'. It was this belief that motivated what he was ultimately to make of the Arthurian cycle.

The basic outline of *The Birth of Arthur* is straightforward and departs from the traditional story in only two respects: Igraine is shown to be eager for Uther's embrace, and Merlin brings Uther to her by cunning rather than magic. Arthur, the Hero-King, is thus born of a passionate, consenting union and we are spared the elements of deceit and rape that make the original tale rather less than palatable. Buckley's version takes the following shape:

ACT I   Uther, King of Britain, has seen Igraine at a banquet and fallen passionately in love with her. He now holds Gorlois, her husband, prisoner and is about to lay siege to Tintagel, where Igraine is in hiding. Merlin, dreaming of a Hero-King who will save Britain, spiritually and politically, decides to use Uther's obsession for his own ends.

ACT II   Igraine, attended by Sir Brastias, remembers Uther's passionate glances and contrasts them with her husband's coldness. She longs for a child. When Uther is brought secretly to the castle by Merlin, she welcomes him with a love that is as fierce as his own – even agreeing to Merlin's demand that the child of their union shall be given into his safekeeping.

Boughton found this scenario completely to his liking (and not entirely irrelevant to his dealings with Florence and Christina). He made very few changes to the basic structure, but cut, or reduced, some of the choral commentaries. With *The Round Table* his alterations went much deeper, affecting not only the structure and the plot but also the character of Arthur himself.

As Buckley planned it, *The Round Table*, begins with the boy Arthur releasing the Sword from the Stone and, vouched for by Merlin, being accepted as king both by the knights and the people. Guenevere is introduced, rather precipitately, as someone Arthur has already met and admired. She tells of a Round Table, that will be her dowry and which has the power to 'bind the kingdom' and bring peace and prosperity. The knights acclaim her as Arthur's bride and Britain's Queen.

In the second act, Arthur's reign has prospered. Though there is as yet no doubt about Guenevere's love for the King, it is clear that she is sympathetic to Lancelot, the knight on whom Arthur greatly depends. It is also clear that Lancelot is in love with her and greatly troubled by the betrayal of his friend and king.

In the third and last act, Arthur visits the Lake of Wonder and is given the Sword Excalibur by the Lady of the Lake. Thus armed, Arthur will be able to overcome all his enemies. Merlin has done all he can do. Led by the enchantments of Nimue he prepares for death, even though he foresees that it will not be Arthur who will find the Holy Grail.

To Boughton, Buckley's scheme was inadequate. Not only did the protagonists lack character and motivation, but the dramatic shape was awkward. It moved, if anywhere, only to an anticlimax. He therefore demanded radical changes. Merlin, he decided, should set the action in motion by visibly planting the Sword in the Stone, and Arthur would win it, not by magic but by releasing the secret catch which holds it in place. Arthur's lowly state was to be made explicit, so that his winning of the Sword becomes more unexpected and the knights' initial dismay more understandable. What was Buckley's third act now becomes the second – Arthur learning of his origins through Merlin and the Lady of the Lake, who also advise him to win Lancelot's allegiance by marrying Guenevere and gain control over the Round Table. Merlin, his task done, can now die. Buckley's second act becomes Boughton's third act and a natural climax to the drama. Guenevere is shown to be as much in love with Lancelot as he with her. She persuades him to support Arthur's bid to bring peace to the land through the Quest for the Holy Grail.

Just how much more theatrically effective Boughton's version is, may be judged from the following comparative table:

BUCKLEY	BOUGHTON
Act I: Outside the Cathedral Arthur wins the Sword, but is rejected by the knights until Merlin reveals his origins. Guenevere tells of the Round Table, a dowry that will bring peace to the land.	*Act I, scene i: Outside the Cathedral* Merlin places the Sword in the Stone and prophesies the coming of a Hero-King. *Act I, scene ii: Sir Ector's kitchens* Arthur works with the cooks, Sir Dagonet his only friend. *Act I, scene iii: Outside the Cathedral* Arthur wins the Sword, but is rejected by the knights until Sir Ector explains the mystery of his birth and Merlin's role in shaping his destiny.
Act II: Camelot At a great feast we learn of Lancelot's hopeless love for Guenevere, who is faithful to Arthur.	*Act II: The Lake of Wonder* Through Merlin and the Lady of the Lake, Arthur learns of his origins and mission. He is told to win Lancelot's allegiance by marrying Guenevere and claiming the Round Table. Merlin, his task complete, prepares for death.
Act III: The Lake of Wonder Merlin and the Lady of the Lake give Arthur the Sword Excalibur. His task complete, Merlin prepares for death.	*Act III: Camelot* At a great feast we learn of Guenevere's love for Lancelot, who agrees to support the Quest of the Grail which will bind the knights in brotherhood and ensure peace.

Buckley's version of the cycle is completed in two further dramas: *The Holy Grail* and *The Death of Arthur*. Boughton, however, inserts a complete digression: the tragedy of Elaine, the Lily Maid of Astolat, who falls in love with Lancelot. Though Boughton argued that Lancelot's unthinking philandering revealed his 'fascist' tendencies, the story has little to do with the main thrust of the saga. It is, however, a beautiful tale, beautifully told, and consequently drew from Boughton music of the highest order – far superior, indeed, to anything in the rest of the cycle.

Buckley's third drama introduces Morgan le Fay, Arthur's evil half-sister, who stirs up the ambitions and discontent of Mordred, his bastard son, by sowing doubts in his mind about Guenevere's faithfulness. The decline and disorder in Arthur's kingdom is, for a time, averted by the arrival of Sir Galahad, who proposes the Quest for the Grail. Though Arthur himself remains aloof, the knights take up the challenge.

In the final part of the cycle Buckley shows a kingdom wracked by discontent, Mordred openly plotting the King's downfall. Lancelot and Guenevere recognize the hopelessness of their love and go their separate ways. Led by Mordred's promise of a time of freedom when there will be 'No God, no King, no Grail', many of the knights rebel and Arthur is overthrown. Sir Bedivere returns Excalibur to the Lake of Wonder, and the Lady of the Lake bears the dying King away.

Though Buckley's scheme follows the traditional pattern closely, he fails to make his characters convincing as human beings with human emotions. They do not grow as a result of their experiences, but remain cyphers in a pre-ordained plot. Boughton found it impossible to proceed with the cycle as Buckley had planned it, and it was to be twenty-six years before he felt able to complete the project – this time on his own terms.

The two final episodes in Boughton's cycle, *Galahad* and *Avalon*, interpret the Arthurian tales in a way that is clearly autobiographical. In them he traces his personal 'quest' for an ethical basis to life that accords with the true message of Christ, as opposed to the interpretation put upon it by church dogma. The character of Galahad is therefore, to all intents and purposes, Boughton himself – filled with doubt and wonder, eager to find answers to the contradictions that life throws up, and anxious to reconcile its ugly realities with the eternal truths of art. It is an interpretation worth examining in greater detail:

Galahad

Scene i: Lancelot's castle

Galahad, unaware that he is Lancelot's son, is filled with wonder at the beauty and truth of Christ's teachings but cannot understand the Quest of the Grail. To him it is mere superstition. He questions three travellers: a knight, a monk, and a pedlar. Their attitudes to religion only add to his confusion: the knight scoffs at it, the monk believes only in its outward trappings, and the pedlar ignores it altogether. None seem able to understand what Christ actually taught.

Scene ii: A chapel in Lyoness

Galahad comes to a strange chapel. Before its altar there lies a wounded knight, grieving, it seems, over some lost, unhappy love. Galahad comforts him and receives the Silver Shield of Innocence and the Golden Sword of Truth.

Scene iii: Outside the Cathedral

The people wait to see King Arthur and his knights come from the Cathedral in splendid procession. Galahad joins them, but cannot understand why the poor are not allowed to enter a building that should be open to all men. As the royal procession emerges, the choir sing the Beatitudes according to St Luke's version of the Gospel. The clerics answer them with St Matthew's version. Galahad is struck by the subtle differences:

Blessed are ye poor, for yours is the Kingdom of Heaven.

Blessed are the poor in spirit, for theirs is the Kingdom of Heaven.

He questions the priests, but they regard him as impertinent and subversive of good order. The nobles and clergy depart, singing a hymn in praise of military might. Galahad is left alone with Will, the leader of the dispossessed. He offers to take him to friends who may be able to answer his questions.

Scene iv: A wood

Galahad meets Will's mysterious friends: Penimel and Melicora. They explain how life evolves – Nature both protecting and destroying her creatures indiscriminately. Only when human beings learn to help each other will they be able to rise above the hapless condition of the animals. Will hints that a new order is coming into existence, and promises to send for Galahad when the time is ripe. Left alone, Galahad ponders all that he has learned and decides that the solution to the world's ills must lie in the laws that govern music and turn the sound of many voices into one harmonious song. Full of joy, he decides to tell King Arthur of his discovery.

Avalon

Act I: Camelot

As Galahad waits for an audience with the King, he learns that Lancelot is his father. The knights assemble. Arthur tells them that although the Quest of the Grail has failed, they must give account of their adventures. Sir Gawaine hints that Lancelot's journeys have not been entirely without interest. A quarrel breaks out and is only brought to an end when Galahad asks to be allowed to sit in the Seat Perilous – the seat in which only the pure may safely sit. He comes to no harm, and immediately disproves the legend by making Sir Dagonet take his place. The priests are furious at the loss of a useful myth, but Lancelot, the sceptic, is pleased. Galahad tells Arthur that the poor must be set free and, encouraged by Queen Guenevere, explains the symbolic lessons to be learned from the laws of music. He is interrupted, however, by a messenger who speaks of a barge that has been found. It bears the body of a dead lady, guarded only by an old serving man. The knights depart, leaving Galahad alone with Lancelot. They talk of the unrest that stirs in the land and the dangers the country now faces. With Lancelot's blessing, Galahad leaves to join the people's uprising.

The knights now return with the body of the dead lady. It is Elaine, the Lily Maid, and Lancelot must do penance for his cruelty. Left alone, Arthur and Guenevere consider their lives. He thanks her for her loyalty and comforts her with the thought that their personal sacrifices have been made for the good of the country. When Lancelot returns, Arthur leaves him alone with the Queen. She tells him they must part: she wronged him when she married the King, just as he wronged the Lily Maid and, before that, Galahad's mother. Lancelot protests his innocence. But the damage has been done: Arthur, Guenevere, Lancelot have all failed – failed themselves, failed each other, failed the country. All that is left to Guenevere is to do penance in some remote nunnery. Lancelot curses the church and vows never to fight for it again.

Act II, scene i: Merlin's Cave beneath Tintagel

Led by Mordaunt and Mordred, an army of peasants has gathered. Mordaunt genuinely believes in their cause, but Mordred is motivated only by ambition. Galahad arrives, but the peasants will not listen to him. They bind him and leave him to the mercy of the rising tide, but he is saved by Will.

Scene ii: A battlefield

The rebellion has been crushed and Mordaunt lies dead. Mordred, however, still leads what remains of the peasant army. He is joined by Sir Gawaine, who offers to make a pact so that together they may seize power.

Scene iii: The Lake of Wonder

Attended by Sir Bedivere, King Arthur lies dying – his kingdom bitterly divided into rich and poor. Weapons have failed him as surely as corrupted Faith. He bids Sir Bedivere return Excalibur to the Lake from which it came, and tells him that it has no magic power – only the power that comes from superstitious belief. The Lady of the Lake appears and grants the King three visions: the Past, the Present, and the Future – the Star that rose over Bethlehem, the White Star that rose with Arthur himself, and the Red Star that will one day rise to unite all men in liberty and equality. Joyful at this promise of better things, King Arthur dies in peace.

Though events were soon to make it impossible to take seriously the denouement of Boughton's cycle, and cast doubt upon the possibility of ever performing it as a whole, credit must be given for the ingenuity with which he manipulated the legend. Despite the fatal flaws in its arguments, it remains a fascinating document of his personal odyssey. Particularly touching is his faith in the sanity of music, which must have seemed all the more poignant when the events of 1956 forced him to reassess his political certainties. Perhaps at that moment he recalled the advice George Bernard Shaw had given him in 1925: 'Do not introduce Glastonbury to Moscow, which will only let you down out of sheer clumsiness. Bach, Haydn, Mozart, Beethoven, Wagner, Strauss, etc., won't.'

Ultimately, an enterprise of this magnitude is only as good as the music it inspires. Written over so long a period, it is hardly surprising to find that, despite many moments of great power and beauty, Boughton's response proved to be uneven in quality and inconsistent in approach. This, in itself, would not necessarily rule out the possibility of a complete performance should sufficient financial backing ever be forthcoming. But there are other considerations to be taken into account, and they are far more inhibiting.

Boughton, as we have seen, became dissatisfied with Buckley's abilities as a librettist, and it is probably for this reason that he failed to complete the orchestration of *The Birth of Arthur*, even though the work exists as a vocal score and was successfully performed with piano accompaniment in 1920 and 1925. This alone makes an acceptable revival virtually impossible, though certain orchestral extracts (which Boughton sanctioned) might be salvaged. The score is frankly Wagnerian in concept and method. A series of bold representative themes that are woven into a glittering orchestral tapestry pinpoint the characters and salient ideas. But though the extended choral sections are impressive in purely musical terms, they inevitably hold up the action and pose an almost insuperable challenge to any producer. Boughton partially solved the problem by the use of 'living scenery'. Thus, to effect the opening of the second act the men of the chorus were dressed in stone-coloured tunics and required to stand to attention in architectural groups. The women, on the other hand, were clad in floating garments of blue and green which, when they danced, seemed like the billows of the sea:

> Dark and stark and strong
> Tintagel Castle stands!
>
> The splash and the surge of the sea on the rocks of Tintagel.
> The boom of the breakers.
> The echoes in chasm and cave . . .
>
> O hear ye the song of the surges
> That beat in the caves of Tintagel.
> The shrill of the pebbles.
> The hiss of backgathering waves.

With the full resources of the modern theatre, it is a solution that might well prove effective. In the cramped conditions of Glastonbury it can only have been the merest sketch of a possibility – comic, inevitably, to all but the most reverent.

Aware that the method behind *The Birth of Arthur* had turned it into an uneasy cross between music drama and oratorio which, by its very nature, could scarcely make for effective 'theatre', Boughton abandoned his theory of 'choral drama' when it came to *The Round Table* and moved into the world of orthodox opera. Gone are the choral commentaries: the chorus now takes part in the action as cooks, knights, lake-maidens – whatever the situation demands. The network of representative themes is still employed, but with a lighter hand. There are now set-piece arias which employ the simple, folk-like manner that Boughton adopted once the limitations of Glastonbury had made it obvious that a thoroughgoing Wagnerian approach was out of the question. There are solid choruses in four-part harmony for the cooks and the knights, and the lake-maidens chant their mystic lays in whole-tones that Debussy would have recognized. But if the mix was eclectic, it was also dramatically effective, and it is no surprise to find that, next to *The Immortal Hour* and *Bethlehem*, *The Round Table* was the work that Glastonbury audiences most enjoyed. In the unlikely event of a place ever being found in the modern opera house for romantic-historical works, *The Round Table* might well be a contender.

Much more so *The Lily Maid*, assuming that a sufficiently intimate theatre could be found – for *The Lily Maid* stands apart from the rest of the cycle and is best thought of as a chamber opera. The story is intimate and, though it casts light upon the character of Sir Lancelot, has little to do with the rest of the cycle. The action is framed by a series of choruses – some in the style of simple ballads, others more obviously 'choral'. The orchestra is scaled down and requires only single woodwind and a minimum of brass, with tympani, harp and strings. Musically, however, it is outstanding: opulently romantic in its orchestration, harmonically rich, and uninhibited in its reliance on simple, heartfelt melodies. It is the one part of the cycle that could be presented to a modern audience without apology, for it is the one part that touched Boughton's heart and drew from him some of his finest music.

The same cannot be said for the remaining parts of the cycle. In them Boughton returned to a large orchestra and a chorus that takes an active part in the drama. Though there are many beautiful passages, the general level of inspiration does not match the heroic nature of the action. What in *The Birth of Arthur* carried a great deal of Wagnerian conviction, and in *The Round Table* had the courage of grand operatc entertainment, is now watered down in an uneasy mixture of Mussorgsky-ish realism and folky lyricism. The second scene of *Galahad* further compounds the problems by being an almost verbatim tran-scription of a dramatic cantata that Boughton had composed in 1904 to William Morris's poem *The Chapel in Lyoness*. Effective enough in its own terms, the difference in style is all too obvious. And when, at the end of the cycle, Arthur is granted his vision of communism triumphant:

> A new red star I see in the East –
> Over a warrior's brow it is pressed –
> He calls the whole world to communion feast,
> And the star grows great as the sun.
> Flashes of sickles in chariots I see,
> Hammers engined in a whirling glee –
> Base-born are high-born when they are born free
> And the Red Star shines e'en to Avalon.

Boughton can only muster a perfunctory, four-square hymn tune by way of response – as banal as the text, in fact. Regardless of the trick that time has played on Boughton's political certainties, it seems unlikely that such musical virtues as *Galahad* and *Avalon* may possess (and there are many) would be sufficient to bear the weight of the cycle's other inadequacies.

Chiefly at fault are the libretti. Though Boughton's may have a stronger grip than Buckley's on character, motivation and dramatic effect, they are still woefully deficient in terms of the language he thought fit to employ. It fails, as so many attempts to lend conviction to dialogue set in mythic times are apt to fail, by adopting a type of 'Wardour Street' English that Hollywood mined from the novels of Sir Walter Scott and Harrison Ainsworth. Only when he was dealing with emotions he could relate to on a personal level (as in *The Lily Maid*) was he able to achieve what he presumably set out to find: the simplicity of folk poetry. Elaine's plaintive song:

> I have found the shadowy deer
> That you were hunting when you came here.
> Unto all ladies I make my cry,
> But you must offer my mass-penny.

is a case in point. But more often we are offered such gems as Mordred's plotting:

> I wit you know the King's dis-ease,
> No longer manly to hold the throne.
> So we are met, Sir Galahad,
> To 'stablish a braver rule of our own.

To which Galahad responds in terms that recklessly combine archaism with bathos:

> Witted I not things were so bad;
> But we do need Christian government.

Hard enough to disentangle on the page, scarcely understandable when sung!

Lest it be thought that Rutland Boughton was an incompetent composer whose ambitions far exceeded his reach, his failure to weld the five parts of the Arthurian cycle into a coherent whole must be set against what he achieved in those music dramas in which his emotions were deeply involved: *The Immortal Hour, Bethlehem, Alkestis, The Queen of Cornwall,* and *The Lily Maid.* The first two are currently available on disk in authoritative performances, while extracts from the other three have been broadcast effectively in recent years. CD recordings of two of his symphonies, several concertos and quartets are also readily available to demonstrate beyond any reasonable doubt that he was a skilled craftsman who possessed a highly original, if slightly quirky, musical personality.[6] Though the Arthurian cycle has fallen victim to time and political delusion, it cannot be entirely written off. It remains an extraordinary demonstration of artistic courage and determination – a ruin perhaps, but undeniably impressive.

---

[6] CD recordings of Boughton's music are available on the Hyperion label: *The Immortal Hour* (CDA 65101/2), *Bethlehem* (CDA 6666690), Symphony No. 3, and Oboe Concerto No. 1 (CDA 66343), Flute Concerto and Concerto for String Orchestra (CDA 67185), Oboe Quartet No. 1, String Quartets 1 and 2 (CDA 66936). Further recordings, sponsored by the Rutland Boughton Music Trust, will follow in due course.

Postscript

Although *The Queen of Cornwall* does not form part of Boughton's Arthurian cycle, its story – Tristram torn between his love for the two Iseults – belongs to the same canon. Boughton created his own libretto, adapting it from Thomas Hardy's 1923 play *The Famous History of the Queen of Cornwall* by making judicious cuts and adding several of Hardy's own poems at points which called for lyrical expansion. Hardy read and approved the adaptation and attended the second performance (on 22 August 1924), later speaking of the music as 'a glorification of the play' – which, indeed, it is.

Everything about it suited Boughton. The story echoed his own emotional crisis: he was in thrall to a new love – Kathleen replacing Christina – and felt every pang of Tristram's guilt. Moreover, Hardy had given his play a 'Greek' chorus consisting of the 'Shades of Dead Cornish Men and Women' who comment on the action as it unfolds and lend a sense of distance and eternity to all that happens. Boughton seized the opportunity to create some of his finest choral effects, including wordless passages that brilliantly suggest the wind and waves that beat against Tintagel, echoing the lovers' tempestuous passions. Christina, in turn, dressed the chorus in stone-coloured costumes, so that they appeared to melt into the very fabric of the castle walls.

Harmonically, it is Boughton's most astringent score – though it never loses his innate lyricism. Add to this the fact that Hardy's words, for all his recourse to archaisms and obscurities, are the words of a great poet. Together with *The Immortal Hour* it is Boughton's masterpiece and, as such, a signal contribution to the music of King Arthur.

Michael Hurd is, so far, the only person to have made a detailed study of Boughton's life and music. His biography, *Immortal Hour*, was published by Routledge & Kegan Paul in 1962, but revised and expanded in 1993, when it was published by the Oxford University Press under the title *Rutland Boughton and the Glastonbury Festivals*. He also contributed a chapter, similar to, but not identical with, the present one, to *The Arthurian Revival (Essays on Form, Tradition, and Transformation)*, edited by Debra N. Mancoff (Garland Publishing Inc., 1992).

Although opinions may be modified over the years, the facts remain the same. It is therefore inevitable that the basic contents of the present chapter will be found in the earlier publications. A few cherished phrases may also have migrated from one account to another, but each version is offered as an account in its own right and apologies are offered for any unintentional verbal repetition.

An Exotic Tristan in Boston: The First Performance of Messiaen's Turangalîla-Symphonie

NIGEL SIMEONE

Introduction: Messiaen's Tristan Trilogy

I've composed three 'Tristans', very different in dimension and instrumental media: the earliest is *Harawi*, an hour-long song cycle with piano; the second is the *Turangalîla-Symphonie*, for Ondes Martenot, piano solo and very large orchestra, lasting about an hour and a quarter; and finally the *Cinq Rechants* for a choir of twelve unaccompanied voices which should last from twenty to twenty-five minutes.[1]

The first performance of Messiaen's *Turangalîla-Symphonie* was one of the most important landmarks in the composer's career. It was his first overseas commission, and did much to establish his international reputation. One of several major works written at the behest of Serge Koussevitzky for his Music Foundation,[2] its first performance took place in Boston in December 1949. This chapter is concerned with two issues surrounding the work: Messiaen's own commentaries, in particular his remarks about the inspiration he drew from the Tristan myth; and the response of critics to the first performances in Boston, New York and elsewhere.

First, though, it is helpful to consider the works which make up the first and third parts of Messiaen's Tristan trilogy. This is an unusual triptych in that it includes works in strikingly contrasting genres; all three were composed in the five years following the end of World War Two. In his interviews with Claude Samuel, the composer was at pains to point out that he was not attempting to emulate either of the great musical precursors which drew on the Tristan myth: Wagner's *Tristan und Isolde* and Debussy's *Pelléas et Mélisande*. He admired both these operas enormously, but Messiaen's motivation in his own Tristan works was different: he sought to evoke the spirit of the legend, and to derive an intentionally remote and somewhat generalised inspiration from it: 'One might

---

[1] C. Samuel, *Conversations with Olivier Messiaen*, trans. F. Aprahamian (London, 1976), p. 8.
[2] Other works commissioned by the Koussevitzky Music Foundation include Bartók's *Concerto for Orchestra*, Britten's *Peter Grimes*, Copland's Symphony no. 3, Dutilleux's Symphony no. 2, Poulenc's Gloria, Schoenberg's *A Survivor from Warsaw*, Stockhausen's *Mixtur*, Stravinsky's *Ode*, Tippett's *King Priam* and Xenakis's *Akrata*. The autograph manuscripts of all the works commissioned by the Foundation, including the *Turangalîla-Symphonie*, are in the Koussevitzky Archives at the Library of Congress.

Une page du Manuscrit d'Olivier MESSIAEN.

Fig. 1. From the programme for the first night of the play *Tristan et Yseult* by Lucien Fabre

say that this legend is the symbol of all great loves and of all great love poems in literature or in music. But only the Tristan myth seemed worthy of attention.'[3] Moreover, Messiaen's works are not dramatic representations but symbolic ones. When Claude Samuel commented that Messiaen's 'Tristans' do not place characters on a stage, the composer's response was revealing:

> No, mine have absolutely no connection with the old Celtic legend, and even its essential idea of a love potion is brushed aside (except for some allusions in the *Cinq Rechants*). I've kept only the idea of a love that is fatal, irresistible and which, as a rule, leads to death; a love which, to some extent, invokes death, for it transcends the body – even the limits of the mind – and extends on a cosmic scale.[4]

Given that the overt inspiration for almost all his works before 1945 was specifically Christian, it is reasonable to ask why Messiaen felt so powerfully drawn to the Tristan myth at this point in his career. The explanation perhaps lies in the personal circumstances which surely motivated his contemplation of love during the immediately post-war years. From the early 1940s, his first wife,

[3] Samuel 1976, p. 9.
[4] Samuel 1976, p. 9.

Claire Delbos, or 'Mi' (Messiaen's pet-name for her), had been increasingly troubled by mental illness, and by 1945 Messiaen was gravely concerned about his beloved Mi's health (while friends were worried that her instability might make it difficult for him to devote his attention to composition).

Claire was a violinist and composer whom Messiaen had married in June 1932. The same year he composed the *Thème et Variations* for violin and piano and dedicated the work to her (using a musical representation of her pet-name 'Mi'); together they gave the première on 22 November 1932. She was, famously, the dedicatee of the *Poèmes pour Mi*, composed during the summer of 1936 at Petichet, and of the first of the *Chants de Terre de de Ciel* (1938), entitled 'Bail avec Mi'. *Harawi* – with its highly emotional exploration of love and death – could perhaps be seen as the darkest possible counterpart to the blissful rapture of the *Poèmes pour Mi*, standing not as a celebration of married love, as the earlier cycle did, but as a memorial to a love which was imperilled by Claire's declining health.

In January 1949, Claire was the victim of a medical accident during an operation, a tragedy about which Yvonne Loriod-Messiaen spoke in an interview with Peter Hill:

> Messiaen's wife became ill – she had to have an operation and following that she lost her memory. She had to be put into a home where everything was done for her. From that time Messiaen brought up his son by himself. He did all the housework and all the cooking and he would get up at 5 o'clock in the morning to make the coffee and get breakfast for his son before he went to school. Eventually, in 1959, his wife died.[5]

By the time *Harawi* was published on 15 February 1949, this hospital calamity had all but placed his beloved Mi beyond reach. Messiaen himself seldom discussed this traumatic episode, but he did so movingly in an iterview with Brigitte Massin:

> There was post-operative shock as a result of which she lost her memory, all her memory, and then, little by little, her sanity. It was dreadful for her above all, but more appalling still for my little boy who didn't understand what was happening. I loved my son Pascal very much.[6]

It is the great recurring love theme in *Harawi* which provides a direct and explicit connection, hitherto unremarked in the Messiaen literature, with the Tristan legend. Either at the end of 1944 or in the first few weeks of 1945, Messiaen was commissioned to compose music for a production of the play *Tristan et Yseult* by Lucien Fabre, which opened at the Théâtre Edouard VII in Paris on 22 February 1945. The original programme book states that 'Olivier Messiaen has composed the incidental music which he has recorded on the organ in the Théâtre National at the Palais de Chaillot.' According to Messiaen's unpublished diaries, he recorded his partly-improvised music on this very large instrument on 2 February 1945, between 5 p. m. and midnight.[7] The programme

[5] P. Hill, ed., *The Messiaen Companion* (London, 1995), p. 294.
[6] B. Massin, *Olivier Messiaen: une poétique du merveilleux* (Aix-en-Provence, 1989), p. 172.
[7] Extracts from Messiaen's diaries will be published for the first time in N. Simeone and P. Hill: *Messiaen in Words and Pictures* (New Haven and London, forthcoming).

for the first night of the play includes a facsimile of a manuscript page in Messiaen's hand headed 'Tristan et Yseult – Thème d'Amour', scored for organ (Fig. 1).[8] An explicit connection with the Tristan story was never mentioned by Messiaen, but this fragment provides just such a link: the theme which is such a pivotal force in *Harawi*, one of his most personal masterpieces, was first used in the incidental music for a play about Tristan and Yseult.

The third of Messiaen's Tristan pieces to be composed was an unusual and highly original choral work, *Cinq Rechants*, for twelve unaccompanied voices. Setting a text which is partly in French and partly in an invented language, it was inspired by, and drew its title from, Claude Le Jeune and other early French masters. The programme for the first public performance, in Paris on 15 June 1950, provides an explanatory subtitle: 'Rythmes vocaux sur des poèmes d'amour en langue inventée'. This work was pounced upon gleefully by Messiaen's detractors, especially those who had always doubted the sincerity of his religious inspiration. Antoine Goléa recalled the accusatory reaction after the première:

> Des yeux allumés de ceux qui ayant toujours mis en doute la sincérité des sentiments religieux de Messiaen, proclamèrent: "Le voici enfin, le vrai Messiaen! La même que tous les autres! Sa religion, pfutt! La voici, sa religion!" Il ne pense qu'à "ça"![9]

In his conversations with the composer, Goléa explored not only the Tristan analogies in the *Cinq Rechants* but also discussed the invented language used in much of the work. Messiaen's comments on this are fascinating:

> C'est pour essayer d'exprimer cet infini inexprimable que j'ai inventé des mots nouveaux. Nouveaux pas entièrement, car ils ressemblent pour certaines de leurs sonorités au sanscrit. Chaque syllabe a été choisie à la fois pour ses qualités phonétiques, sa tendresse ou sa force et ses aptitudes à mettre le rythme musical en valeur.[10]

Goléa also proposed an overall compositional concept for the whole trilogy, unrelated to any extra-musical source of inspiration:

> Pour [Messiaen], les *Cinq Rechants* sont l'aboutissement et la cime de sa trilogie de Tristan; personellement, je trouve que cela est vrai non seulement sur le plan humain, psychologique, mais aussi sur le plan d'écriture, à propos on l'a peut-être deviné, le schéma suivant peut être établi: *Turangalîla* = musique seule; *Harawi* = poème en premier, musique en second; *Cinq Rechants* = musique et poème confondus.[11]

---

[8] Copy of the programme in the author's collection.

[9] A. Goléa, *Rencontres avec Olivier Messiaen* (Paris, 1960), p. 184. 'The eyes lit up of those who had always had their doubts about Messiaen's religious sincerity. They proclaimed that "here, at last, is the real Messiaen! He's just the same as everyone else! So much for his religion – here is his religion! All he thinks about is 'It'!"'

[10] Goléa 1960, p. 180. 'It was in an attempt to express the infinitely inexpressible that I invented new words. Not entirely new, for they resemble some of the sonorities of Sanskrit. Each syllable has been chosen at once for its phonetic qualities, its tenderness or its strength, and its possibilities for exploiting the rhythms of the music.'

[11] Goléa 1960, p. 175. 'For him, the *Cinq Rechants* are the climax and the summit of his Tristan

Messiaen's Early Commentaries on the Turangalîla-Symphonie

The prehistory of *Turangalîla* consisted of performances in Paris, Vienna and Barcelona of three movements from the work. The earliest of these were in the Théâtre des Champs-Elysées on 14 and 15 February 1948. André Cluytens conducted the Orchestre de la Société des Concerts du Conservatoire, with Yvonne Loriod and Ginette Martenot as the piano and Ondes Martenot soloists, in a new work entitled *Trois Tâla*. These were to become the third, fourth and fifth movements of *Turangalîla*, though the programme makes no mention of the fact that the *Trois Tâla* were to form part of a larger work (as yet unfinished), nor is there any reference to a Tristan connection. Messiaen's (unsigned) note is extremely brief and opens with a straightforward explanation of the title: 'Tala est un mot hindou qui signifie rythme.'[12] A short report (signed 'Y.H.') appeared in the *Guide du Concert*:

> A la Sté des concerts, les 3 Tala de Messiaen ont soulevé une houle. C'est une oeuvre difficile avec ses rythmes complexes et enchevêtrés, ses timbres ultra-modernes, son extraordinaire science d'orchestration. Mais Messiaen est 'une force en marche'.[13]

The *Trois Tâla* were given in Vienna, at the Konzerthaus, by the Vienna Symphony Orchestra on 28 June 1948 (with the same conductor and soloists as the Paris première). Messiaen's note for this performance is much more fully developed and it opens with the short but resonant sentence which was to begin so many of his subsequent programme notes on *Turangalîla*, placing the *Trois Tâla* firmly in a Tristanesque world of love: 'Dieses Werk ist ein Liebesgesang.'[14] His programme note (in Spanish) for the Barcelona performance (25 February 1949, conducted by Eduardo Toldrá) opens in the same way.[15] By then, the whole symphony was complete: Messiaen finished the work on 28 November 1948.[16]

The première of the *Turangalîla-Symphonie* took place in Symphony Hall, Boston, on Friday 2 December 1949 at 2.30p.m., with Yvonne Loriod as the piano soloist, Ginette Martenot as the Ondes Martenot soloist (her brother, Maurice Martenot, the instrument's inventor, also came on this trip) and the Boston Symphony Orchestra, conducted by the thirty-one-year-old Leonard Bernstein.

---

trilogy. Personally, I find that to be true not only from a human and psychological standpoint, but also from a compositional standpoint: concerning this, it would perhaps be possible to construct the following plan: *Turangalîla* = music alone; *Harawi* = poem of first importance, music second; *Cinq Rechants* = music and poetry flowing together.'

[12] 'Tala is a Hindu word which denotes rhythm.' Copy of the programme in the author's collection. An identical note was printed in the *Guide du Concert*, vol. xxviii, nos. 19–20 (13 and 20 February 1948), p. 217.

[13] *Guide du Concert*, vol. xxviii, nos. 23–25 (12, 19 and 26 March 1948), p. 254. 'At the Société des Concerts, the *Trois Tâla* by Messiaen caused quite a stir. This is a difficult work, with its complex and confusing rhythms, its ultra-modern sounds, and its extraordinary orchestral writing. But Messiaen is a man on the move.'

[14] 'This work is a song of love.' Copy of the programme in the author's collection.

[15] 'Esta obra es un canto de amor.' Copy of the programme in the author's collection.

[16] Messiaen gives this date on the first edition of the score.

The concert was repeated in Symphony Hall the following evening (Saturday 3 December) and the same performers gave the work at Carnegie Hall, New York, exactly one week later, on 10 December. At all of these concerts, the *Turangalîla-Symphonie* was the only work on the programme, with an interval placed between the fifth and sixth movements. A few years later, when the score was first published, by Durand et Cie in March 1953, Messiaen declared in his prefatory note that the work should be performed with no break of this kind: 'L'auteur a conçu "Turangalîla-Symphonie" comme un *tout*. Il désire donc que les exécutions de l'oeuvre soient *intégrales et sans interruption*.'[17] To this, however, he has added a modification which appears more dutiful than enthusiastic: 'Si le chef désire cependant faire un entr'acte, celui-ci peut se placer entre le n° V et le n° VI.'

The programme for the Boston première includes a very substantial and well-informed note about Messiaen in general, and the *Turangalîla-Symphonie* in particular. It was written by John N. Burk, the Boston Symphony Orchestra's annotator of the time, but it quotes extensively from remarks by Messiaen. Nowhere in this note is there explicit reference to the Tristan legend, though the commentaries on individual movements (all in the composer's own words) mention love which is characterised as 'tender', 'carnal' and 'terrible'. Messiaen described the work here as 'almost a concerto for piano and orchestra', as he was often to do in later commentaries (and in at least one, quoted below, he went slightly further). The note also includes Messiaen's characteristic and oft-repeated remarks about the symphony's 'very special rhythmic language'.[18]

The work's first European performance took place at the Aix-en-Provence Festival, in the Théâtre de la Cour de l'Archevêché, on Tuesday 25 July 1950 at 9.30p.m., with Loriod, Martenot and the Orchestre National de la Radiodiffusion Française, conducted by Roger Désormière. The Festival programme book includes a note by Messiaen himself with similar commentaries on each movement to those in the Boston programme. Messiaen's introductory remarks are also largely familiar from the earlier Boston programme, apart from the addition of the arresting opening sentence which had first been used to describe the *Trois Tâla*: 'Cette oeuvre est un chant d'amour'[19] – words precisely echoed in many of his later notes, including the first concert performance in London (Royal Festival Hall, 12 April 1954, with Loriod, Martenot, and the London Symphony Orchestra, conducted by Walter Goehr): 'The whole work is a love-song.'

In a manuscript note on the work, dating from about 1953 (the latest date for any of the performances listed), and presumably intended for publication, Messiaen, writing in the third person, provides much more detail about the Tristan-related origins of all three works in the trilogy. After introductory

---

[17] The large-format full score of *Turangalîla-Symphonie (pour piano principal et grand orchestre)* was first published by Durand, Paris, in March 1953 with the plate number D. & F. 13498 on pp. 1 and 429. In April 1953 a study score was put on sale, with the plate number D. & F. 13666 on p. 1 and 13498 on p. 429. Both editions contain this note. See N. Simeone, *Olivier Messiaen: A Bibliographical Catalogue* (Tutzing, 1998), pp. 96–9.

[18] Boston Symphony Orchestra, Seventh Program of the Sixty-Ninth Season, 2 and 3 December 1949.

[19] IIIe Festival International de Musique, Aix-en-Provence, 15 Juillet–4 Août 1950. Programme des Concerts.

remarks about the commissioning of the symphony and its performance history
to date, Messiaen writes as follows:

> La "Turangalîla-Symphonie" est un chant d'amour. Elle se situe dans l'oeuvre
> de Messiaen entre "Harawi", chant d'amour et de mort, pour chant et piano, et
> les "Cinq Rechants" pour choeur a cappella, sur des poèmes d'amour en
> langue inventée.
>
> "Harawi", "Turangalîla-Symphonie" et les "Cinq Rechants" constituent
> chez Messiaen un bloc séparé, une sorte d'immense Tristan et Yseult en 3
> volets. "Turangalîla-Symphonie" nous offre à peu près constamment deux
> aspects violemment contrastés de l'amour humain: soit un amour passionné-
> ment corporel et charnel, soit un amour plus tendre, uniquement jailli du
> coeur. Les 2 aspects de l'amour sont présentés côte à côte dans la 2ᵉ et la 8ᵉ
> parties ("Chant d'amour I", "Développement de l'amour"), ou isolément:
> l'amour charnel dans la 5ᵉ partie ("Joie du sang des étoiles"), l'amour tendre
> dans la 6ᵉ partie ("Jardin du sommeil d'amour").[20]

Messiaen goes on in this commentary to make some interesting observations on
the work's genre. His ten-movement symphony is not all it seems, and here he
makes the clearest and most unequivocal statement of its dual purpose: part
symphony, part piano concerto:

> "Turangalîla-Symphonie" est en plus un concerto pour piano et orchestre. La
> partie de piano, d'une extrême difficulté, est destinée à "diamanter" l'orch-
> estre par des traits brillants, des grappes d'accords. Elle est aidée en cela par
> un petit orchestre dans l'orchestre: les 3 claviers: jeu de timbres, célesta,
> vibraphone, traités comme les "gamelang" de Bali (île de la Sonde).[21]

This note also includes a rather more developed account of the use of birdsong
in the work. In the Boston programme, 'bird songs' are listed as just one of the
characteristics of the solo piano part, but here the composer adds some details of
a kind that were to become a familiar feature of his later writings about birds.
Less typical of later Messiaen is that the birdsong here is that of an imaginary,
idealised bird, rather than a real one: an amalgam of several songbirds brought
together to create enchantment:

---

[20] O. Messiaen, autograph document, undated, headed 'Olivier Messiaen, Turangalîla-
Symphonie', 2ff., written in blue ink and signed 'Olivier Messiaen' at the end. Apparently
unpublished and written c.1953, in the author's collection. 'The *Turangalîla-Symphonie* is a
song of love. It is situated in Messiaen's output between *Harawi*, a song of love and death, for
voice and piano, and the *Cinq Rechants* for choir a capella, on love poems in an invented
language. *Harawi*, *Turangalîla-Symphonie* and the *Cinq Rechants* constitute a separate block in
Messiaen's works, a sort of immense Tristan and Isolde in three sections. *Turangalîla-
Symphonie* offers us almost constantly two violently contrasted aspects of human love:
either a passionate physical and carnal love, or a more tender love, bursting out from the
heart alone. The two aspects of love are presented side by side in the second and eighth
movements ("Chant d'amour I", "Développement de l'amour"), or alone: carnal love in the
fifth movement ("Joie du sang des étoiles"), and tender love in the sixth movement ("Jardin
du sommeil d'amour").'
[21] 'The *Turangalîla-Symphonie* is, moreover, a piano concerto. The piano part, of extreme
difficulty, is intended to clothe the orchestra in jewels, with brilliant virtuoso passages,
and with chord clusters. It is assisted in this by an orchestra-within-the-orchestra, consisting
of the three keyed instruments: jeu de timbres [keyed glockenspiel], celesta and vibraphone,
treated like a gamelan from Bali (Ile de Sonde).'

L'écriture mélodique de "Turangalîla-Symphonie" est souvent inspirée de chants d'oiseaux. Voir notamment la 6ᵉ partie: "Jardin du sommeil d'amour", où le piano déroule le chant d'un oiseau idéal, féérique, qui résume le rossignol, le merle, le rouge-gorge, et d'autres oiseaux chanteurs.[22]

Messiaen wrote his most extended commentary on the *Turangalîla-Symphonie* a few years after this, to accompany the work's first complete recording, made by Véga on 11 and 13 October 1961 with Yvonne and Jeanne Loriod as soloists, and the Orchestre National de la RTF, conducted by Maurice Le Roux. It was made in the unlikely and joyless surroundings of the Salle des Fêtes at Puteaux, a suburb to the west of Paris. Messiaen is credited with the 'direction artistique' of the whole project, and the producer was Claude Samuel who wrote of the difficulties of finding a suitable venue:

Mon souci majeur fut de trouver une salle libre et acoustiquement convenable pour l'enregistrement. Finalement, nous nous installâmes dans un lieu dénué du moindre charme: la salle des fêtes de Puteaux![23]

The set was issued the following year in a magnificent reddish purple silk box (according to Claude Samuel, the colour was chosen by Messiaen himself[24]), together with an extra 10-inch disc containing a discussion between Messiaen and Samuel, and extensive booklet notes by the composer, enhanced by hand-written musical examples.[25] There is a richer vocabulary of descriptive detail than in his earlier commentaries:

Turangalîla-Symphonie est un chant d'amour. *Turangalîla-Symphonie* est un hymne à la joie. Non pas la joie bourgeoise et tranquillement euphorique de quelque honnête homme du XVIIᵉ siècle, mais la joie telle que peut la concevoir celui qui ne l'a qu'entrevue au mileu du malheur, c'est à dire une joie surhumaine, débordante, aveuglante et démesurée. L'amour y est présenté sous le même aspect: c'est l'amour fatal, irrésistible, qui transcende tout, qui supprime tout hors lui, tel qu'il est symbolisé par le philtre de Tristan et Yseult.[26]

---

[22] 'The melodic writing in the *Turangalîla-Symphonie* is often inspired by birdsong. This can be seen especially in the sixth movement, "Garden of the Sleep of Love", where the piano unfolds the song of an ideal, magical bird, which embodies the nightingale, the blackbird, the robin, and other songbirds.'

[23] C. Samuel, *Permanences d'Olivier Messiaen: Dialogues et commentaires* (Arles, 1999), p. 259. 'My major concern was to find a hall which was available and acoustically suitable for the recording. Finally, we installed ourselves in a place devoid of the slightest charm: the salle des fêtes at Puteaux!'

[24] Samuel 1999, p. 259: 'Messiaen fut évidemment consulté pour la couleur de la soie qui entourait le coffret: de la pourpre cardinalice.' ['Messiaen was of course consulted about the colour of the silk which covered the box: the purple of cardinals.']

[25] Originally issued by Véga with the set number VAL 27, this performance, without the interview has been reissued on CD at least twice, most recently (in 2001) on Accord/Universal 465 802-2. The interview disc has been reissued as the bonus disc in the set *Le monde de Messiaen* (Accord/Universal 472 031-2). The lavish documentation described here was issued only with the original Véga LP set.

[26] 'The *Turangalîla-Symphonie* is a song of love. The *Turangalîla-Symphonie* is a hymn to joy. Not the comfortable, quietly euphoric pleasure of some honest man in the seventeenth-century, but joy of a kind which can only be conceived by one who has glimpsed it in the midst of adversity, in other words a superhuman joy, overflowing, blinding and limitless. Love is

Messiaen goes on in this note to write at length about the Tristan parallels in each of the components of his trilogy, drawing other similarities with Arthurian legend, with Edgar Allan Poe, and – an interesting contemporary link – with the paintings of Marc Chagall:

> Harawi, Turangalîla, Cinq Rechants, sont trois aspects – de matière instrumen-tale, d'intensité, d'importance et de style différents – d'un seul et même Tristan et Yseult. Dans les trois oeuvres – comme Viviane, bien-aimée de Merlin l'enchanteur, comme Yseult la belle, habile aux philtres, comme Ligeia d'Edgar Poe dominant la mort – l'héroïne est un peu magicienne. "Ses yeux voyagent . . . dans le passé . . . dans l'avenir . . ." Dans les trois oeuvres – comme dans les tableaux de Marc Chagall – les amoureux se dépassent eux-mêmes et s'envolent dans les nuages: "les amoureux s'envolent . . . Brangien, dans l'espace tu souffles". Dans les trois oeuvres enfin il s'agit d'un amour mortel – jeu de vie et de mort – et comme le résume cette dernière citation des Cinq Rechants: "l'explorateur Orphée trouve son coeur dans la mort."[27]

These disc notes constitute some of the most detailed and revealing remarks Messiaen ever published on the emotional range of each movement in the symphony, and he makes explicit reference to the Tristan story in several of them. For example, here is the opening of his commentary on the fifth movement ('Joie du sang des étoiles'):

> C'est une longue et frénétique danse de joie. Pour comprendre les excès de cette pièce, il faut se rappeler que l'union des vrais amants est pour eux une transformation, et une transformation à l'échelle cosmique. André Breton retrouve tous les éléments dans l'être aimé: "Ma femme, aux yeux de niveau d'eau, de niveau d'air, de terre, et de feu". Déjà l'amoureuse de Shakespeare disait: "Ma richesse est immense comme la mer . . ." (Roméo et Juliette). Et Tristan dit à Yseult: "Se tous li mondes estoit orendroit avec nous, je ne verroie fors vous seule." (Roman en prose de Tristan).[28]

The sixth movement ('Jardin du sommeil d'amour') is a rich seam of Tristan inspiration, with evident associations for Messiaen with the Act II love duet in

---

present here in the same way: it is a love which is fatal, irresistible, transcending everything, overwhelming everything outside itself, like the love which is symbolised by the love potion of Tristan and Isolde.'

[27] 'Harawi, Turangalîla and Cinq Rechants are three different aspects – in terms of instrumenta-tion, intensity, importance and style – of one single Tristan and Isolde. In all three works – like Viviane, beloved by the wizard Merlin, like the beautiful Isolde, adept at love potions, like Edgar Allan Poe's Ligeia ruling over death – the heroine is something of an enchantress. "Her eyes journey . . . into the past . . . into the future . . ." In all three works the lovers – as in the paintings of Marc Chagall – go beyond themselves and take wing into the clouds: "the lovers take flight . . . Brangäne, in the space you breathe". Finally, all three works are about mortal love – the game of life and death – summed up in this last quotation from the Cinq Rechants: "The explorer Orpheus found his heart in death." '

[28] 'This is a long and frenetic dance of joy. To understand the excesses in this movement, it must be remembered that the union of true lovers is for them a transformation, and a trans-formation on a cosmic scale. André Breton rediscovered all four elements in the loved one: "My wife, with eyes on a level with water, on a level with air, with earth and with fire." Already in Shakespeare, the young heroine declared: "my bounty is as boundless as the sea . . ." (in Romeo and Juliet). And Tristan said to Isolde: "If all the world were visible to us at once, I would see nothing but you" (in the roman en prose of Tristan).'

Wagner's *Tristan und Isolde*, as well as a magical evocation of nature at its most mysterious and bewitching:

> Cette pièce est en contraste absolu avec la précédente. Les deux amants sont enfermés dans le sommeil de l'amour. Un paysage est sorti d'eux. Le jardin qui les entoure s'appelle Tristan, le jardin qui les entoure s'appelle Yseult. Ce jardin est plein d'ombres et de lumières, de plantes et de fleurs nouvelles, d'oiseaux clairs et mélodieux. "Tous les oiseaux des étoiles . . ." disait Harawi. Le temps s'écoule, oublié. Les amoureux sont hors du temps: ne les réveillons pas . . .[29]

Turangalîla *in Boston and New York: An Anthology of Early Reviews*[30]

The reaction of critics at the work's first performances was a mixture of bafflement, hostility and, occasionally, admiration. The Boston première was widely reviewed in the local press the next day. In the *Boston Globe* (3 December 1949), Cyrus Durgin attempts to set out the case for the prosecution in a chatty, flippant style – a review more notable for its lumbering attempts at wit and sarcasm than for any musical insights:

> "Turangalîla" is a girl's name, and a poetic Indian word for love song, and it is also the title of a gigantic and ear-blasting new Symphony by Olivier Messiaen. This piece in 10 movements – count 'em – takes well over an hour to play and it was commissioned by the Koussevitzky Music Foundation. Yesterday it was given its world premiere by Leonard Bernstein and the Boston Symphony Orchestra. As music it isn't much, but it has focussed attention upon the subject of love in the East Indies, and that is something even in Boston.
>
> Among the titles of the individual movements are 'Joy in the Blood of the Stars', 'Gardens of the Sleep of Love', and 'Development of Love'. Upon reading these lines in the program book I was at once convinced they are inflammatory and searched for a nickel to call up the censor. But when the music began, it was quickly evident how wrong one can be.
>
> For in the two or three million notes that Mr. Messiaen put to paper with sublime persistence, the only offense is to the ears. This work, says Mr. Messiaen, "is written in a very special rhythmic language, and makes use of several new rhythmic principles – quantitative (note values), dynamic (intensity), cinematic (movement), phonetic (timbre), added values, non-reversible rhythms, asymmetric augmentations –," etc., etc. Even that "Development of Love" is only a "– canon in non-reversible rhythms, and lyric offshoots of the

---

[29] 'This movement is in total contrast to the preceding one. The two lovers are enclosed in the sleep of love. A landscape comes out of them. The garden which surrounds them is called Tristan; the garden which surrounds them is called Isolde. It is a garden full of light and shade, of new plants and flowers, of bright and melodious birdsong: "All the birds of the stars . . .", as Harawi described it. Time passes, forgotten. The lovers are outside time: do not wake them.'

[30] I am extremely grateful to Christopher Dingle for providing copies of several of these reviews. I am also grateful to Bridget Carr, Archivist of the Boston Symphony Orchestra, for her most helpful responses to my questions.

love theme –'' and ''– develops the three cyclic themes with a passion constantly increasing.''

No, nothing for the censor here. Evidently East Indian love consists only of walloping away at a large number of percussion instruments, which a full orchestra plus piano and the electronic ondes martenot industriously grind away at what sounds like 125 different compositions.

This, however, is not the most acrid music ever heard. Some of the sounds are nice, and the fifth and sixth movements actually have a couple of tunes. But it is the longest and most pointless music within memory, and some of the more extreme pages do have a suggestion of a tool and die works with a rush order. Mr. Messiaen's complicated adventures in rhythm may look wonderful on paper but they sound like – well, they sound like ''Turangalîla.''

At intermission the lobbies buzzed with rebellious and treasonous objections, and by the time the second half began a good many of the Friday afternoon subscribers had departed. But enough were left to applaud the composer when he appeared on stage at the end. The real heroes were Mr. Bernstein and the gentlemen of the orchestra, for they must have put in many hours of exhausting effort with this tricky and futile work.

In the *Boston Post* (3 December 1949), Warren Storey Smith at least took the work a little more seriously, though his judgement is scarcely any more positive than that of his colleague on the *Globe*. Smith's review deserves some sort of celebrity, or perhaps notoriety, for its unfortunate closing remarks: the *Turangalîla-Symphonie* may be massive and complex, but in the half century following the first performance, it has received several hundred concert performances[31] and been recorded on numerous occasions.

Yesterday afternoon's Symphony Concert was entirely given over to the world premiere of the ''Turangalîla-Symphony'' for piano, Onde Martenot and orchestra by Olivier Messiaen. Leonard Bernstein conducted this work, commissioned by the Koussevitzky Music Foundation and completed a year ago. Dr. Koussevitzky was to have presided over its first performance but there were delays, and Mr. Bernstein faced with a task of exceeding difficulty, made a worthy substitute. Incidentally, in Mr. Messiaen's effulgent sonorities one heard again the voluptuous Koussevitzkian tone.

Mr. Messiaen came from Paris for the performance, bringing with him an extraordinary pianist, Yvonne Loriod, for the taxing piano part. The Onde Martenot solo was played by Ginette Martenot, who came to the country for the double purpose of assisting in this premiere and playing the part for her brother's theremin-like instrument in the Concerto by Jolivet that a few weeks ago introduced it to Boston.

We must take Mr. Messiaen's word for it that turangalila is an East Indian word meaning love song, ''with connotations of rhythm'' though he admits that it is the sound of the word rather than its sense that has intrigued him. Love is the pervading motive of the symphony. Of its 10 sections two are called Love Song, another Garden of the Sleep of Love, a fourth Development of Love, and the fifth movement, Joy in the Blood of the Stars, is supposed to express the ''peak of carnal passion.'' Mr. Messiaen here used a motive that

[31] Almost two hundred of the most significant performances up to 1993 are listed in the 1994 Durand edition of the study score.

reminded listeners variously of Stephen Foster, a hillbilly tune and a popular song of the Gay Nineties.

The Symphony consumes about an hour and 10 minutes, and yesterday, fortunately for the ears of all and the sanity of some, there was an intermission in the middle.

This new work by a composer generally known as a religious mystic is remarkable for its rhythmic complexity, most of which cannot be taken in by the ear, for its alternations of frenzied excitement and idyllic – even obvious and slightly corny – passages and for its large array of percussion instruments: glockenspiel, celesta, vibraphone, temple blocks, wood blocks, small cymbal, suspended cymbal, Chinese cymbal, tam-tam, tambourine, maracas, side drum, snare drum, bass drum, tubular bells – and Mr. Bernstein's right foot, a gratuitous and perhaps necessary addition. No such tintinnabulation has been heard in Symphony Hall since Henry Eicheim gave us his "Java-Burma."[32]

Like certain Renaissance painters and modern composers of opera, Mr. Messiaen is concerned with the contrast between earthly and ideal love, his expression of the former being violent rather than sensuous and of the other decidedly soothing. The program notes dealt with strange concepts such as rhythmic diminution in "zigzag," rhythmic augmentation in "scissors," rhythms like a "spreading fan" and a canon in non-reversible rhythms. Several listeners left at the intermission, but those that remained applauded mightily at the end, especially when the composer came to the stage. Will we hear all this again, save for this evening's performance? I doubt it.

Rudolph Elie, writing in the *Boston Herald* (3 December 1949) presents a more open-minded position. He finds things to admire in the piece, while being troubled about a superficiality which he attributes largely to Messiaen's melodic invention:

How is one to write about this immense musical composition Olivier Messiaen has thrust upon us in his ten-movement, 70-minute symphony of love?

Are we to say, as the composer might well expect us to, that this is the most revolutionary and significant thing to appear since "The Rite of Spring?"

Are we to say that it points the way, in its formidable manipulation of rhythms in the contrapuntal sense that Bach manipulated melodies, to the music of the future?

Are we to say that it is a gigantic – and largely successful – attempt to marry the music of the east and the west?

Or are we to say that it is empty of real musical significance, that it is primarily the conceit of an idiosyncratic composer here striving, with apoplectic fury, to demonstrate himself a musical genius of almost abandoned creativeness?

At this moment I frankly do not know, but I suspect there is some measure of truth to all these queries, or I would if it weren't for one little thing –

But first of the symphony itself. The 37-year-old composer, inspired first by an absorption in the music of the east (and particularly in that of India, Java

[32] A reference to Henry Eichheim's *Java*, first performed in 1929, which employed 'a "gamelan" section, with 45 instruments' (N. Slonimsky, *Baker's Biographical Dictionary of Musicians*, 7th edn (New York, 1984), p. 649).

and Bali), in the second place by a profound interest in rhythm, in the third by the East Indian word "Turangalîla" which seems to mean love song, and fourth by a seeming determination to attract notice as an eccentric, has here assembled a strange medley of instruments and put them to work more feverishly than anyone else to this moment.

These instruments, besides the conventional symphony orchestra, include the piano, the ondes Martenot (a sort of Solovox with delusions of grandeur), the keyed glockenspiel, the celeste, the vibraphone and a vast gang of cymbals, maracas, gongs, chimes, bass drums, tambourines and temple blocks. For these instruments Messiaen has composed music evocating various aspects of love, which is a subject hard to go wrong on. He deals with ideal love, tender love, carnal love and delirious love, and with various levels of each, most of them accompanied by songs of the birds and all of them accompanied by anywhere from one to three rhythms simultaneously.

The prevailing sound of all this is distinctly eastern and often wonderfully exotic, wonderfully beautiful, wonderfully exciting. From the point of view of the technical listener its superimposed rhythms, its rhythms set canonically, in augmentation, in diminution and in reverse are astonishing, though few if any are the ears capable of holding the original rhythms in mind long enough to recognize them in variation. This fact, the human lack of memory for complex rhythms (as contrasted with the strong memory for melody) is one reason the basic vocabulary of the symphony is so baffling. That others will explore Messiaen's path in the future and produce better works than this is clear, and in this respect his symphony may be considered revolutionary.

But the "little thing" referred to above, the clue to the possible fundamental emptiness of this work, is the appalling melodic tawdriness of the three big cyclical themes heard throughout. Here Messiaen tips his hand. For the first is a motto of six notes Gershwin would have thought better of; the second might make the grade as a tune for Dorothy Lamour in a sarong, and the third, a dance of joy, might be ascribed to Hindu Hillbillies, if there be such. Had Messiaen's melodic inspiration been on a sublimer level, I should have unhesitatingly pronounced this a masterwork of revolutionary significance. As it is I cannot believe it to be very much more than the novelty of novelties – an interesting, exciting, almost frightening tour de force.

I cannot muster the words to sufficiently praise Leonard Bernstein, the pianist Yvonne Loriod (whose feat at the piano was electrifying) and every member of the orchestra. We can't realize what they all went through, preparing this fantastic piece, which was commissioned, incidentally, by the Koussevitzky Music Foundation. Although the audience thinned out a bit during the performance, a large audience was on hand at the end to applaud bravely when the composer appeared on the stage.

In the *Christian Science Monitor* of 3 December 1949, Harold Rogers wrote perhaps the most positive early review of the work. Though there are moments when Rogers rather over-simplifies Messiaen's methods, he is clearly deeply impressed by the piece. His article has two additional points of interest. First, he cites comments made about *Turangalîla* by Koussevitzky (who commissioned it) and Bernstein (who conducted it); second, Rogers detects audible parallels between passages in the eighth and tenth movements of the symphony with Wagner's *Tristan*. While the spotting of such allusions was speculative, Rogers

seems to be alone among the critics to suggest any Tristan connection, however
tenuous, before Messiaen himself wrote about his Tristan trilogy:

"Today will be a big day in music," Serge Koussevitzky said while
preparing to attend the concert in Symphony Hall yesterday afternoon.

He was referring to the world première of a work he commissioned – Olivier
Messiaen's ten-movement symphony, "Turangalîla," introduced by the
Boston Symphony Orchestra under Leonard Bernstein.

And Dr. Koussevitzky was right. It was a red-letter day, a new page in the
history of modern music. But whether future musicologists will refer to
"Turangalîla" as the dividing line of our century remains to be seen.

Koussevitzky, however, is convinced that "Turangalîla" is the first mile-
stone to appear on the musical horizon since Stravinsky's "Le Sacre du
Printemps." Time may confirm what he perceives.

As in the case of Bach and Wagner, Messiaen's music may be the summation
of an era, rather than the herald of a new school. It is certainly the synthesis of
all known techniques, as Koussevitzky has pointed out. It may be more
evolutionary than revolutionary.

The principal difference between "Le Sacre" and "Turangalîla," according
to Bernstein, is that Stravinsky had no system, whereas Messiaen has devised a
system basically simple, aurally complicated.

But yesterday afternoon his symphony did not create the storm of protest
that "Le Sacre" did when Pierre Monteux conducted it in Paris in 1913.
American audiences are not so volatile. If Bostonians suffer, they do so in
silence. They simply withhold their applause or leave the hall.

More than a few left yesterday; there was considerable applause withheld;
but the majority of the listeners remained to cheer. We have come a long way
since 1913. Boston may be conservative, but for new music it is the least
conservative city in America.

Messiaen speaks of his music thus: "It is a gleaming music that we seek,
bringing to the ordinary senses of the listener pleasures voluptuously
refined."

"Turangalîla" (an East Indian word meaning love song) contains some of
the most voluptuous music ever penned. Certain sweeping passages in the
eighth and tenth movements recall Wagner's "Liebestod" from "Tristan und
Isolde."

And there is the tender melody in the sixth movement, progressing in
consecutive sevenths on the strings and ornamented with bird calls played
on the piano. Whatever serves his purpose, be it the popular song or jazz
progressions, he employs unabashedly.

It would be interesting, if space allowed, to delve more deeply into
Messiaen's system. When explained, it is extremely comprehensible on paper.
Its main fault, however, lies in its incomprehensibility to the uninitiated listener.

But this symphony is not so cryptic that it cannot be appreciated by a
seasoned concertgoer. Many of its movements have strong popular appeal.
The composer makes brilliant use of percussion and the gamelan, an Oriental
gong orchestra consisting of glockenspiel, vibraphone, piano, and celesta. His
exotic rhythms are Hindu in origin, as are the modes he chooses for melody.

Yvonne Loriod, who came from Paris expressly to play the piano part, has
an incisive technique that glitters. She made the bird calls fluid and clear. Her
execution of the splattered cadenzas was almost unbelievable.

Messiaen's score also provides an integral role for the Onde Martenot, the electronic instrument played by Ginette Martenot, sister of its inventor. It added distinctive color to the tonal fabric and is more acceptable in ensemble than in solo.

Bernstein fulfilled this difficult assignment with distinction. "Le Sacre" would be child's play to what he accomplished yesterday.

Following the two Boston performances, the same musicians gave the symphony's New York première at Carnegie Hall on Saturday 10 December. This brought out two of the biggest names in American music criticism of the time: Olin Downes in the *New York Times* and Irving Kolodin in the *New York Sun*. Downes was a distinguished and influential figure whose enthusiasm for several twentieth century composers (notably Sibelius) did much to enhance their reputations in America. Messiaen, however, was plainly not for him:

Hollywood could have devised no more characteristic spectacle than Carnegie Hall yesterday afternoon when the Boston Symphony Orchestra, conducted by Leonard Bernstein, gave the first performance in this city of Messiaen's "Turangalîla" symphony, which takes an hour and a half in performance and is in ten movements. And no symphony that we can imagine would do better justice to a Hollywood spectacle and Hollywood apparatuses than this one.

It has every conceivable instrumental gadget in it, and it utilizes, as a set of gadgets, about all the discoverable devices of rhythm and counterpoint that have been placed at the composer's disposal by modern technicians of the art. Now the word "Turangalîla" mean[s] in the Indian language a love song, and love appears to be Mr. Messiaen's theme. It is heard in "non-reversible rhythms, asymmetric augmentations with several rhythmic identities (persons), rhythmic modes, and the combination of quantitative and sounding elements in reinforcing the values and timbres of each percussion instrument by chords which form the resonances of these timbres." And more of that quantatative and if you like, qualitative, characterization of his work by the composer in the program book.

The orchestra is the biggest, oddest and, on occasion, noisiest ever. It is noisiest, on the whole, in the fifth movement which yesterday came just before the intermission of the concert. It is a hoopla movement, one gathers, of unbridled passion, and "the piano solo, brilliant and vehement, participates in the dynamic exacerbation of this terrible love." Miss Yvonne Loriod played that piano with vehement exacerbation and abounding virtuoso, for which she deserved a hand. She was indeed the equal of the orchestra, also consumed and volcanic in the throes of passion.

The movement is indeed athletic. Nor did Mr. Bernstein lose the opportunity for effective gestures and eloquent calisthenics. The television man, plainly manipulating his lens and ducking about in his cupboard overlooking the stage, provided the final Hollywood touch of a piece palpably appropriate to that order of entertainment.

This, one would say, is the best movement and the most fun of the ten-movement symphonic circus. It is cunningly contrived to entertain and excite after much pretentious obscurity. The next best movement from the box office point of view would presumably be "Garden of the Sleep of Love." This is somnolent, as the title would imply, with a crooning ditty sweetly harmonized and many times repeated, in the strings, while the piano chirps and clucks in ornamentation of the slumber song. No doubt insects and feathered friends in the lover's retreat. O corn, where is thy sting?

But after this Mr. Messiaen was apparently not in the best position, creatively speaking. He had made about as much noise, exuded about as much syrup, and devised as many non-reversible rhythms and asymmetric augmentations as he was able to think of. So the last part of the symphony was anticlimax.

By the time the end was reached the audience was no longer in the amused frame of mind that it had been when it began to giggle at the queer and funny sounds of the first movement. For there is really very little growth in this music, aside from gadgetary manipulations, which are not the same thing.

At the end of the concert the soloists, orchestra, conductor, and composer assembled on the stage and Mr. Messiaen kissed Mr. Bernstein on the cheek, as they do in France when bestowing the medal of the Legion of Honor. And let it be said in all seriousness that Mr. Bernstein did a perfectly amazing job with an extremely difficult score, deserving any and all recognition that could be given him for his accomplishment.

He held the orchestra together as coolly and masterfully as if he had the whole of a most difficult and inconvenient score by heart. And if he did not have it by heart, apparently he didn't miss a trick. Or a gesture, either, at the right moment for the camera. Well what of it? Hasn't a conductor a right to something beside mere credit from such a piece? It was an amazing performance of a piece of most pretentious nonsense, and publicity is what it's for.

Irving Kolodin, writing in the *New York Sun* of 12 December, was more sympathetic to the work, and a great deal readier to accept the unexpected. His main reservations concerned the structure of the piece, but he also found plenty to enjoy:

A remarkable musical experience came and went on Saturday afternoon in Carnegie Hall in the space of an hour and a half required for the introductory performance of Olivier Messiaen's "Turangalîla-Symphony" by Leonard Bernstein and the Boston Symphony Orchestra. It was all a crescendo of interest till Bernstein decreed a halt midway in the ten sections; thereafter, it never re-established the same atmosphere.

"Turangalîla," the composer tells us, is derived from the Indian (Hindu) language, and means a love song. In this creation of 1948, Messiaen has taken the orchestra apart, and put it together in a way productive of extraordinary new sounds. The "ondes martenot" (the electronic instrument played with a keyboard) shrills higher than any piccolo, sighs more evenly than the clearest saxophone, blankets the strings with vibrato that puts a new wash of color on the bowed box.

With this spectrum of color, Messiaen combines a rhythmic detail and variety that made of the first five sections – in alternating phases of tension and release – a gaudy patchwork of pleasure and delight. The virtuosity of the playing, the burbling freshness of the tonal waves, the ever-changing panorama of smash, batter and tinkle, combined to extend musical sensation into a new dimension.

The cooling-off period, however, was something not decreed by the composer, and it put upon him a fresh burden of interest-quickening hardly possible. His melody is a patois of Scriabin, Ravel, Franck and even Ferde Grofe, his harmony varied but too much in a bright triadial vein to sustain a piece of such length. At last the whole structure began to impress one as top-heavy, leaning dangerously, Pisa-like, from the vertical. Bernstein did a prodigious work of recreation, with full authority and quickening imagination. Yvonne Loriod was the able pianist, Ginette Martenot the unrivalled (if only because unique) operator of her brother's invention. The orchestra shared in a really arousing experience.

Arthur Berger, in the *New York Herald Tribune* (12 December 1949), was evidently rather perturbed by the erotic nature of the work, and was also troubled by its sheer dimensions: he went so far as to suggest that Messiaen should salvage some of the best material from *Turangalîla* for a shorter, more tightly constructed work. However, Berger was not immune to enjoyment, and was clearly delighted by some of what he heard; the main problem, as he saw it, was that there was simply too much of this symphony, and that Messiaen should curb his grandiloquence. Berger is an interesting figure: born in 1912, he was a composer and critic who came to know Ives, Cowell and Varèse while a student in New York, and spent from 1937 to 1939 studying in Paris with Nadia Boulanger. He taught at Mills College (1939–42), and continued his composition studies there with Milhaud. It is likely that he became familiar with Messiaen's music during his sojourn in Paris, and it is possible that his apparent dislike of it was fostered by Nadia Boulanger, who never admired Messiaen. Berger was later the co-founder of *Perspectives of New Music*. In short, his credentials as an enthusiastic supporter of modernism are impeccable. Here is his verdict on the *Turagalîla Symphony*:

> Olivier Messiaen's seventy-five-minute-long symphony "Turangalîla," heard here Saturday afternoon for the first time, is based on high-sounding rhythmic theories over which erotic sentiments drip. The Hindu rubric of this ten-movement work means "love-song," and it is doubtless because this contemporary Frenchman is at bottom so much a romantic that he needs the intellectual peg to fasten together the impetuous inspirations evoked in him by such a theme. [. . .]
>
> In Messiaen's Symphony, as heard Saturday afternoon in Carnegie Hall with Leonard Bernstein brilliantly conducting the Boston Symphony Orchestra, intellectual claims seemed naive indeed. For much of it was like Hollywood atmosphere music or the grand finales of movie-house organs that impress by engulfing us in huge, sonorous cascades. The textures created by wide pitch range vibrating in the interior with glissandos, tremolos and Ondes Martenot, resulted in blending and obscuring the erudite rhythmic devices of "zigzag," "scissors," "non-reversibles," "personages" (terms coined by Messiaen), so that the effect was often arhythmic. Figures that emerged from the melee here and there, at times mercilessly repeated, had the common profile of our familiar popular song that kept curious company with bird-songs, and Hindu and mystic content.
>
> The jazzy bits seems to be Messiaen's way of painting earthly and carnal love. But even elsewhere he never kept away for very long from the sugary, sliding harmonies of popular music, and these fused surprisingly with his

ultra-chromatic texture and his Straussian climaxes. The suggestion of "Honky-tonk Train" in a bed of gamelan-like sounds in the introduction was one of the happier evocations of jazz – though I am sure Messiaen never heard Albert Ammons play boogie-woogie. A charming jazzy inspiration opened the scherzo, and throughout the symphony there were many bright touches that might have been salvaged for a shorter work.

Thus, Messiaen cannot be thrust aside, despite his bad taste and grandiloquence. A highly creative mechanism is somewhere at work. I was impressed at the beginning by the new sound-world opened up, but then the scenery did not change enough and was often cluttered up. The Oriental methods of pure color and rhythm, magnified on the screen of an enlarged orchestra, were intriguing, but after a while I became nostalgic for a work never given here, Igor Markevitch's "Flight of Icarus."

Symphonies the length of a concert have been made before, notably by Bruckner and Mahler. But the performance of a new one made Saturday's concert something of an occasion, and the U.N. flags and equipment set up for the television broadcast by the orchestra following the concert contributed their share to the audiences's expectant mood. So did the battery of percussion and keyboard instruments. After the first movement the odd sounds and their naive substructure provoked laughter. Indeed, if Messiaen had not taken himself quite so seriously, there would have been quite a bit of fun in this work. But as the afternoon wore on, the reception changed to a respectful and polite one, accompanied by no little boredom.

The other New York reviews included a widely syndicated article by W.G. Rogers (given as 'H.G. Rogers' on one review), an Associated Press arts reporter. The cuttings archive of the Boston Symphony Orchestra includes three versions of this article, all slightly different, and all with eye-catching headlines: the Waterbury *Republican* for 11 December 1949 has 'Audience Hisses New Symphony', while the same day's Louisville *Courier-Journal* opts for 'New Symphony Raises Snorts From Audience'. On 12 December the *Commercial* in Bangor, Maine, printed the article beneath the headline 'Odd Sounds Come From Carnegie Hall'. This article attempts both to report on the news aspect of the event, and the public's reaction, and also to give the critic's own, largely enthusiastic, response to the work. The following is the version of Rogers' article printed in the *Republican* of Waterbury, Connecticut:

Some extremely odd sounds from Carnegie Hall platform today matched the extremely rare sound of some hisses and snorts of laughter from the audience as the Boston Symphony Orchestra gave the New York premiere of Messiaen's "Turangalîla."

Described as a "symphony for piano, ondes martenot and orchestra," the hour-and-a-half-long work seemed so unsymphonic to a few listeners that they walked out on it.

"I wouldn't give a nickel for the whole blamed thing," said an angry Carnegie Hall employee who had to stay through it.

"If only it was bad enough to start a riot," a member of the audience complained.

Most of the audience, however, clearly found it good enough for generous applause.

Guest Conductor Leonard Bernstein, pianist Yvonne Loriod and Ondes Martenot soloist GInette Martenot were called back for several bows.

Ondes Martenot is an electronic musical instrument, invented by Maurice Martenot, a French radio technician. Ginette Martenot, today's ondes martenot soloist, is a sister of the inventor.

To this listener, the symphony seemed like one of the most radical extensions of orchestral range, color and expressivity contrived by any modern composer.

It was often exciting and moving, rarely repetitious.

Despite the climaxes of the various movements, Messiaen still had his big bolt to shoot in the grand climax of the finale.

Composed in 1946–48 by the Frenchman Olivier Messiaen on a commission from the Serge Koussevitzky Music Foundation, the work calls for an outsize orchestra and some unfamiliar instruments.

It is divided into 10 sections.

According to the composer, quoted in the program notes, the title "is a poetic word of the Indian language, meaning a love song, with connotations of rhythm. It is also known as a girl's name."

Praise for the performance itself is a constant theme in these reviews, but no recording has been published of the concerts in Boston or New York. However, a recording was made of a rehearsal of the sixth movement, 'Jardin du sommeil d'amour', on 28 November 1949 (issued in 2001 as part of a 12 CD set from the Boston Symphony Orchestra Broadcast Archives).

Epilogue: Turangalîla *returns to Europe*

Given the baffled and generally lukewarm reception which greeted the *Turangalîla-Symphonie* in the American press, it would be pleasing to be able to contrast this with a more enlightened recognition of the work's virtues in Europe. Regrettably, however, British and French critics were no more positive about it than their American counterparts, despite having greater familiarity with Messiaen's musical language. Two examples, by W.R. Anderson in 1953 and Ernest Newman in 1954, illustrate strikingly the hostility of most critics when the work reached London.[33] The first broadcast performance in London took place in June 1953, conducted by Walter Goehr. In the August 1953 issue of the *Musical Times*, W.R. Anderson ends his resolutely pompous report as follows:

> Messiaen's glorification of small ideas, and the use of so much fancy-percussion, make me doubt very much if there is anything really big in him. All this childish to-do sounds like yet another manifestation of the self-deceived infatuation which is so common in this neurotic age.

The first concert performance in London was given a year later, on 12 April 1954, and it was reviewed by the great Ernest Newman in the *Sunday Times*

---

[33] Both these reviews are reprinted complete in N. Simeone, ed., *Bien Cher Félix: Letters from Olivier Messiaen and Yvonne Loriod to Felix Aprahamian* (Cambridge, 1998), pp. 8–9.

(25 April 1954). His closing remarks on the symphony raise some interesting questions, though Newman admits to being puzzled by it:

> I am more conscious of trees than of a wood. It abounds in ingenious 'effects' of line, of rhythm, of colour, and of all three in combination; but for me they are mostly effects without causes. I see it all as a sort of masterly musical doodling, a stroke here automatically evoking an answering stroke there, without any controlling idea, any end foreseen, any organic structure, any composition in the sense we normally attach to that word.
>
> Is the trouble entirely with me, or, to some extent at any rate, with the composer? Has the language of music, perhaps, arrived at a stage of evolution at which the apparatus for saying things has outrun our supply of things worth saying?

In Messiaen's native France, the work had harboured some outspoken detractors from the outset. Pierre Boulez had attended the preliminary performance of the *Trois Tâla* in February 1948 (discussed above) and was famously revolted by what he heard, declaring that it made him want to 'vomit'.[34] In a letter of November 1949, he mentioned the work to John Cage, in fractured but unmistakably withering English:

> Have you seen Messiaen in New York? I believe it is actually at Boston for the first performance of Turangalîla (by a music composer and rhythmician!), this symphony being in many movements and being longer (increasing) in few years (until the people becomes whole crazy). Have you heard the famous (??!) concerto for Martenot by Jolivet? It is absolutely zero.[35]

Francis Poulenc was at the Aix Festival to give the first European performance of his Piano Concerto on 24 July 1950. As an inveterate enthusiast for new music by other composers, he went to hear the *Turangalîla-Symphonie* the following night, but did not enjoy the experience. On 1 August he wrote to Messiaen:

> On n'a certes pas du manquer de vous dire, à plusieurs reprises, que je n'aime pas votre *Symphonie*, ce qui est vrai, mais comme, par ailleurs, je pense que, Paul Rouart excepté, personne ne vous a dit combien vos *Rechants* m'avaient *ravi* ce printemps, je tiens à le faire pour vous assurer que mon comportement, dans le cas présent, est strictement épisodique et basé uniquement sur une divergence esthétique.[36]

In a letter of 6 September 1950 to Milhaud, Poulenc described the strong differences of opinion among those at the performance, while leaving his old friend in no doubt of his own view:

---

[34] See D. Jameux, *Pierre Boulez* (London, 1991), p. 31.

[35] J.-J. Nattiez, ed., *The Boulez–Cage Correspondence* (Cambridge, 1993), p. 36.

[36] M. Chimènes, ed., *Francis Poulenc: Correspondance 1910–1963* (Paris, 1994), p. 690. 'You can't have failed to have been told, many times over, that I don't like your Symphony, which is true. On the other hand, since nobody except Paul Rouart has told you how much your *Rechants delighted* me this spring, I want to reassure you that my behaviour, in the present case, is strictly temporary, based solely on an aesthetic disagreement.'

A la sortie de l'*atroce Turangalîla* de Messiaen, sur la place de l'Archevêché, devant une foule ahurie, Roland et Arthur se sont pris à partie; quant à Georges et moi, cela a été épique. Georges vert, encore indisposé d'un mélange de grippe et de melon glacé et moi rouge comme une pivoine nous sommes dit pendant 7 minutes les pires choses, Georges défendant Messiaen, moi à bout de nerfs de la malhonnêteté de cette oeuvre écrite pour la foule et l'élite, le bidet et le bénitier, tout ceci dans une affreuse tradition Dukas, Marcel Dupré. On nous entourait comme dans un combat de coqs.[37]

Poulenc usually such a generous and open-minded listener, could not accept what he saw as Messiaen's descent into a kind of hedonism for *Turangalîla*. However, in October 1961 he attended the concert performance given as a preparation for the Véga recording; he visited Claude Samuel the next day, a meeting at which he declared that he had been wrong about the work, and that he had written to Messiaen to express his newly discovered enthusiasm – and to admit to his earlier mistake. This letter has not been found, but Messiaen's reply, dated 28 October 1961, is moving evidence of the generosity and warmth of both composers:

J'ai été infiniment touché de votre lettre. Devant la noblesse, la franchise et l'affection, la probité artistique d'un tel geste, les mots sont impuissants . . . Je vous remercie de tout mon coeur et beaucoup plus que je ne sais le dire.[38]

[37] Chimènes 1994, p. 695. 'At the end of Messiaen's *atrocious Turangalîla-Symphonie*, in the place de l'Archevêché, in front of an astonished crowd, Roland [-Manuel] and Arthur [Honegger] set upon each other; as for Georges [Auric] and me, that was a real drama. Georges was green, still unwell from a mixture of flu and a frozen melon, and I was red as a beetroot. For seven minutes we said dreadful things, Georges defending Messiaen, while I was at the end of my tether about the dishonesty of this work, written to please the crowd and the élite, the bidet and the baptismal font, all in the awful tradition of Dukas and Marcel Dupré. People surrounded us as if they were at a cock-fight.'
[38] Chimènes 1994, p. 983. 'I was infinitely touched by your letter. Before the nobility of spirit, the frankness, the affection and the artistic integrity of such a gesture, words are powerless . . . I thank you with all my heart, and much more than I know how to say.'

'Good lodging': Harrison Birtwistle's Reception of Sir Gawain and the Green Knight

ROBERT ADLINGTON

Harrison Birtwistle's decision to write an opera based on the fourteenth-century romance *Sir Gawain and the Green Knight* will have surprised few people familiar with his compositional career. Although *Gawain* (1991, revised 1994) was the first of his works to be explicitly designated an 'opera' by the composer, it was preceded by a number of imposing music-theatre works whose dealings with myth and folk-tale prepared the ground for this later venture. English traditional stories feature prominently in a number of these earlier works. *Punch and Judy* (1967) and *Down by the Greenwood Side* (1969) are reinterpretations of the Punch and Judy show and the mummers' play, popular theatrical forms dating back several centuries. A later work, *Bow Down* (1977), incorporates numerous different versions of the traditional ballad of the 'Two Sisters'; Tony Harrison's text draws on English, American and Scandinavian traditional sources. Similarly, in *The Mask of Orpheus* (1973–1983) the focus is not so much on the story itself as on the various ways in which it has been told; variants of the myth are juxtaposed and combined in a presentation that gives an integral role to dance and mime as well as instrumental music and song. *Gawain*, by contrast, presents its narrative with a minimum of fuss, but its grappling with a time-honoured tale obviously represents a continuity.

The medieval world is also a recurrent presence in Birtwistle's music. This is most clearly evident in a number of musical homages to the fourteenth-century composer and poet Guillaume de Machaut. In 1969, Birtwistle made a rather gaudy instrumental arrangement of Machaut's motet 'Hoquetus David', a piece he had arranged for military band during his National Service some fourteen years earlier. Then in 1987 he brought a new, more drastically recomposed version of the 'Hoquetus' together with a similar treatment of another Machaut motet ('Fons tocius/O livoris feritas') to create the orchestral piece *Machaut à ma manière*. This work, in which Machaut's works are, as it were, refracted through a Birtwistlian rhythmic and textural prism, emphasised the affinities between Birtwistle's own musical language and that of this greatest of fourteenth-century composers. The multi-layered textures; the rhythmic asymmetry and complexity; the 'Focket' (or 'hiccup', in which a single musical line is dispersed between different voices or instruments); the consignment of melody to submerged registers: all these are central to both Machaut's and Birtwistle's music. Little surprise, then, that Birtwistle should also repeatedly alight on medieval texts as a basis for his vocal works. Birtwistle has set late medieval English verse (an anonymous carol in *Monody for Corpus Christi*, 1959), medieval Latin (Sedulius Scottus in *Carmen Paschale*, 1965; Boethius in *On the Sheer Threshold of the Night*, 1980), and Spenser's translations of Petrarch (*The Visions of Francesco Petrarca*, 1966). *Sir Gawain and the Green Knight* had itself received earlier attention in *Narration: A Description of the Passing of a Year* (1963), a short choral setting of two verses of Brian Stone's translation.[1]

In his opera Birtwistle sets a modern libretto rather than the original text. David Harsent's libretto generally follows the narrative sequence of the poem closely, but it neither borrows directly from the original nor attempts to emulate its distinctive alliterative and metrical style. Harsent also introduces a number of significant modifications to the tale as related by the *Gawain*-poet. The most prominent of these concerns Morgan le Fay. In the original, Morgan is a marginal figure whose ultimate responsibility for Gawain's travails is briskly revealed only at the very end of the poem. Harsent transforms her into the 'principal driving-force of the piece'; she is 'on stage as the drama opens and, thereafter, is rarely off it; her voice is the first we hear, and the last'.[2] The effect of this is to emphasise a sense of conflict from the very start of the opera. Morgan circles Arthur's court unseen; whenever she speaks, the court freezes. More subtly, Harsent shifts the moral perspective of the original verse to make Morgan's purposes seem 'essentially virtuous'.[3] Arthur's court, on the other hand, is beset by 'deceit, blindness and self-love',[4] a modern characterisation of the seat of power quite at odds with the 'attitude of praise' that predominates in the *Gawain*-poet's account of courtly life.[5] Where in the poem the Green Knight's arrival represents the culmination of a scene of colourful celebration and lively high spirits, in the opera it shatters the prevailing listlessness of a court lost in nostalgic reminiscence about a more glorious past. In Harsent's reading, Morgan's purpose is to puncture the complacency of Camelot by 'ushering in self-doubt, and therefore self-knowledge',[6] and in this she is joined from the very start by Bertilak's wife (Lady de Hautdesert), whose enthralment to Morgan is musically symbolised by recurrent, rather claustrophobic duetting textures. It is Morgan who lulls Gawain to sleep prior to Lady de Hautdesert's threefold temptation (and interestingly, Morgan's music here is far more sexy than that of the 'actual' seductress); it is Morgan, too, who reveals the true identity of the Green Knight at the work's denouement.

These alterations to Morgan's role within the story mark Harsent's version

---

[1] *Sir Gawain and the Green Knight*, translated with an introduction by Brian Stone (Harmondsworth, Middlesex: Penguin, 1974 [originally 1959]).

[2] David Harsent, 'Morgan le Fay', programme booklet to *Gawain* (London: Royal Opera House, 1994), p. 36.

[3] 'From page to stage' [David Harsent in conversation with Peter Porter], programme booklet to *Gawain*, p. 32.

[4] *Ibid.*

[5] Derek Brewer, 'Introduction', in Derek Brewer and Jonathan Gibson, eds., *A Companion to the Gawain-Poet* (Cambridge: D.S. Brewer, 1997), p. 13.

[6] 'From page to stage', p. 32.

with a new seriousness and cynicism. This shift in tone is apparent in other modifications to the original. Gawain's new self-awareness, concisely signalled in the very last verse of the poem, is joined in Harsent's libretto by a more conventionally realistic portrayal of the shifting feelings of the other characters: as Barry Windeatt has noted, 'the other dramatis personae variously gain kinds of awareness and tokens of motivation that their counterparts in the poem do not have'.[7] Lady de Hautdesert, for instance, actually falls in love with Gawain, and as she admits this she bitterly curses her bondage to the 'dingy, wild' Morgan. Bertilak for his part appears to devise the exchange of winnings largely in order to ensure that his wife remains faithful; jealousy tangibly colours his reception of Gawain's kisses. Gawain's return to the court is treated at greater length in the opera (particularly in the first, unrevised version), allowing him more expansive reflection on his failure, while the other members of the court, in place of the gently supportive reception offered in the poem, angrily abandon him when he refuses to 'prove his courage'.

A number of the alterations to the story as told in the poem have a more strictly formal rationale. In the opera the Green Knight's arrival occurs not once but three times, generating an accumulating sense of tension as the door is opened to find, firstly, no-one outside, then to admit the Green Knight who lays down his challenge, and then a third time for the beheading. Layers of additional formal complexity are similarly applied to two other key scenes to create the opera's principal set pieces. Act One closes with the 'Turning of the Seasons', in which the poem's description of the passing of a year and Gawain's preparation for his journey are superimposed to create a structure of multiple temporal levels that combines repetitive and developing textual and musical elements in a complex verse structure. This passage lasted forty minutes in the first version of *Gawain* but was replaced with a far shorter scene in the 1994 revision. Then in Act Two the *Gawain*-poet's already sophisticated intercutting of the temptation and hunt scenes is taken a stage further by interspersing episodes of the hunt *within* each of Lady de Hautdesert's amatory advances. The repetitive design of the original is in this way multiplied to create a more complex structure of alternating segments.

Both of these last two devices – the multiple temporal levels of the Turning of the Seasons, and the complex verse structure of the seduction scene – intersect with recurrent obsessions in Birtwistle's music. Rhian Samuel states that Birtwistle chose *Sir Gawain and the Green Knight* for setting as an opera principally for 'its wealth of formal patternings and its capacity for the inclusion of more';[8] in other words, Birtwistle sees these alterations to the narrative structure of the poem as being in an important sense consistent with it. In elucidating the relationship of *Gawain* to its principal source, the resonances of the form and sound of the fourteenth-century text in Birtwistle's twentieth-century musical idiom are just as significant as the

---

[7] Barry Windeatt, '*Sir Gawain* at the *fin de siècle*: Novel and Opera', in Brewer and Gibson, eds., *A Companion to the Gawain-Poet*, p. 380.

[8] Rhian Samuel, 'Birtwistle's *Gawain*: An Essay and a Diary', *Cambridge Opera Journal* 4/2 (1992), p. 166.

treatment meted out in libretto and scenario. The alterations made to the poem's narrative are to some degree compensated for by this relationship: at times the music connects with the poem almost 'over the head' of the libretto. This affinity is immediately suggested by evocative descriptions of the language of the *Gawain*-poet which could just as readily be applied to Birtwistle's music. In the eyes of John Spiers, for instance, medieval English alliterative poetry – of which the *Gawain*-poet was one of the last major practitioners – carries 'a certain massive native strength';[9] Derek Brewer, meanwhile, observes that 'harshness of experience' is a common theme to all of the *Gawain*-poet's works, and notes 'the poet's enjoyment in describing the violence and hostility of nature'.[10] 'Massive strength', 'harshness' and 'violence' are qualities widely discerned in much of Birtwistle's music, and nowhere more so than in *Gawain*. In part this is due to Birtwistle's tumultuous orchestral writing. Always vivid, sometimes strident and aggressive, even (in the eyes of some) unremitting, *Gawain*'s score revels in registral extremes, heightened volume and the heavy artillery of brass and percussion. One may perceive a consistency here with the poem, in which the 'crakkyng of trumpes' and the 'Newe nakryn noyse with the noble pipes,/ Wylde werbles and wight'[11] of Arthur's court are allowed to permeate out through the rest of the text. Sound and din are everywhere: the grotesque ensemble of noises marking the beheading of the Green Knight, as the axe slashes through the air, slices flesh and shatters bone, and then clatters to the ground followed quickly by the thud of the decapitated head; the sounds of icy stream and birdsong during Gawain's journey; the uproar of baying hounds, bugling horns, urgent shouting and noisy celebration accompanying the hunt; and the 'wonder breme noyse' that signals the Green Knight's presence at his chapel:

> What, hit clatered in the clyff as hit cleve schulde,
> As one upon a gryndelston had grounden a sythe;
> What, hit wharred and whette as water at a mulne;
> What, hit rusched and ronge, rawthe to here.[12]

However, it is not just the *Gawain*-poet's *descriptions* of sounds that establish a point of contact with Birtwistle's sound-world. Commentators have stressed the way in which it is the sound of the language itself – and specifically its dense alliteration – that gives a poem such as *Sir Gawain and the Green Knight* its particular impact. John Burrow, for instance, has spoken of the 'power of alliterative verse . . . to communicate physical reality with heightened

---

[9] John Spiers, 'A Survey of Medieval Verse and Drama', in Boris Ford, ed., *The New Pelican Guide to English Literature: 1. Medieval Literature, Part One* (Harmondsworth, Middlesex: Penguin Books, 1991), p. 56.

[10] Brewer, 'Introduction', p. 9 and p. 11.

[11] 'The fresh noise of the drums together with the noble pipes, wild and vigorous trillings'; translation by J.A. Burrow in his edition of *Sir Gawain and the Green Knight* (Harmondsworth, Middlesex: Penguin Books, 1972), p. 91.

[12] 'What! It clattered amid the cliffs fit to cleave them apart,/ As if a great scythe were being ground on a grindstone there./ What! It whirred and it whetted like water in a mill./ What! It made a rushing, ringing din, rueful to hear.' Lines 2202–5, from *Sir Gawain and the Green Knight*, translated by Brian Stone, p. 103.

intensity'.[13] Alliterative poetry may have had its origin in traditions of oral recitation;[14] as such, the repetitive deployment of sounds within each line held a more than purely abstract or formal significance. Rather, the language strives at times for an onomatopoeic reality. A similar reality – a physical immediacy – can be found in Birtwistle's equally highly-formalised music. Alliteration represents, I believe, one of a number of specific ways in which the poetry of *Sir Gawain* establishes an affinity with Birtwistle's music. Others concern formal design, and metre and rhythm. The remainder of this chapter is devoted to an exploration of these affinities.

I have noted the appeal that *Sir Gawain*'s formal qualities held for Birtwistle. It is indeed a closely organised poem, containing many elements that align it with Birtwistle's own music. Its 101 verses vary somewhat in length and are principally unrhymed, but each ends with a rhyming 'bob-and-wheel' made up of a two-syllable line that closes the main part of the verse plus four short lines with the rhyme scheme ABAB (the B rhyming with the 'bob'). Overall the poem has 2530 lines making for an average of 25 lines per verse (with 5 lines left over); this focus on multiples of 5, together with the 101 verses, has encouraged speculation that there is some sort of number symbolism at play.[15] In addition, the narrative has clear symmetrical and cyclical aspects. Michael Hall's summary of the structure of the plot reveals this symmetrical structure clearly: court – beheading – turning of the year / Gawain's preparation – journey – seduction – beheading – court.[16] This is reinforced by other elements suggesting the completion of a circle: the poem starts and ends at New Year; the first line reappears at the very end of the final verse (just before the bob-and-wheel); and the number of verses (101) itself suggests the completion of one cyclic journey and the beginning of another.

These various formal aspects of *Sir Gawain* find striking parallels in Birtwistle's music. The importance of verse structures to Birtwistle has already been mentioned. It is however *altered* repetition that has particularly attracted Birtwistle: he shies away from the predictability of verbatim reprisals. It is at this level that the parallel with the poem is particularly marked. The structure of the latter can be interpreted in different ways. At one level, it involves the regular alternation of changing verses (the series of long lines, of varying length) with the unchanging refrain of the bob-and-wheel (always five lines long, and with a fixed rhyme scheme). But of course, the bob-and-wheel is not unchanging: while the basic structure remains the same, the words are different on each occasion, and indeed often so is the metre. This ambiguity regarding the role of an element in a verse scheme is entirely characteristic of Birtwistle's own verse structures: a musical segment that appears to take a refrain-like function in fact contains elements of change. In works such as

[13] J.A. Burrow, 'Sir Gawain and the Green Knight', in Ford, ed., *The New Pelican Guide to English Literature*, p. 212. Thorlac Turville-Petre similarly points to 'the power of the [alliterative] line to describe scenes of violent action' in the Introduction to his *Alliterative Poetry of the Later Middle Ages: An Anthology* (London: Routledge, 1989), p. 1.
[14] See Spiers, 'A Survey of Medieval Verse and Drama', p. 57, and H.N. Duggan, 'Meter, Stanza, Vocabulary, Dialect', in Brewer and Gibson, eds., *A Companion to the Gawain-Poet*, pp. 229–30.
[15] H.N. Duggan, 'Meter, Stanza, Vocabulary, Dialect', p. 238.
[16] Michael Hall, *Harrison Birtwistle in Recent Years* (London: Robson Books, 1998), p. 55.

Verses for clarinet and piano (1965) and *Verses for Ensembles* Birtwistle juxtaposes a number of different types of material and subjects them to different degrees of varied repetition so that, to use Birtwistle's expression, 'there's an ambiguity about what the bread is and what the filling is'.[17] The same procedure lies behind the large-scale verse structures in *Gawain*. In the original version of the opera, each season of the Turning of the Seasons comprised no fewer than seven distinct sections, each of which was variously more or less related to the corresponding section in the other seasons. The revised version makes do with a simpler two-part structure for each season, but the principle of varied repetition remains the same. Gawain's return to the court in Act Two was occasion for a similarly elaborate verse structure in the original version, comprising five interleaved units repeated five times; sadly this was entirely cut in the 1994 revision. These revisions serve to throw the weight of attention onto the seduction scene. Here, each part of the poet's threefold construction is divided into up to eleven sections,[18] from Morgan's initial Lullaby to the exchange of winnings at the end of each day. Identifiable repetition is less apparent here than in the Turning of the Seasons, but the Lullaby and Morgan's spell on Gawain (just before the exchange of winnings) are repeated identically, and the music accompanying the killing of each animal is clearly related.

Symmetries and cyclic forms also loom large in Birtwistle's music. Loosely palindromic forms may be identified in two pieces from the mid-1960s, *Précis* for piano and *Tragoedia*. More characteristic of Birtwistle's music, however, are other ways of applying symmetrical principles: stage layout for instance (many of Birtwistle's instrumental works specify a strictly symmetrical seating plan), or textural organisation (where the starting point may take the form of a strictly symmetrical partitioning of registral space[19]). In *Gawain* it is cyclical organisation rather than symmetry that features most prominently. Verse structures with repetitive refrains have a cyclical aspect of course – the refrain can suggest a new beginning – but the metaphor is arguably stronger in the case of structures that, like *Sir Gawain and the Green Knight*, make one single cycle to end where they began. Such structures, instead of signalling a new episode or departure (as in most verse schemes), raise the expectation that the whole thing might repeat itself identically. Symmetrical forms such as those found in *Précis* and *Tragoedia* represent an example of this sort of cyclical design. Birtwistle's more recent orchestral work *Exody: '23:59:59'* (1997) also ends where it began (with soft pulsing at the registral extremes of the orchestra), but it is not a symmetrical design; the music takes a different route, so to speak, back to its starting point. In *Gawain*, the obvious example is the Turning of the Seasons scene. Both the original and revised versions deploy essentially the same music for the two Winters at the beginning and very end of the scene, thus giving the impression of a single, completed circle. The staging for the original Royal Opera House production, with its circular revolves demarcating the 'world indoors' and the

[17] Birtwistle, cited in Ross Lorraine, 'Territorial Rites 1', *Musical Times* (October 1997), p. 8.
[18] The second day comprises only nine distinct sections.
[19] See Robert Adlington, *The Music of Harrison Birtwistle* (Cambridge: Cambridge University Press, 2000), p. 184.

'world outside', played an important role in reinforcing the cyclical elements of the music and plot.

Verse structure and symmetrical and cyclic design are commonly found in poetry and music: they do not represent a particularly distinctive set of similarities between these particular poetic and musical styles even if they are undoubtedly significant ones. There are more individual areas of connection however. The first concerns an interest in time. Marie Denley has observed how the *Gawain*-poet manages to combine and control a number of different time-scales. Firstly of course there is the time-scale of the action, which covers a little over a year, from one New Year to the next. But in addition,

> other time-scales and time-patterns are invoked; the self-renewing natural cycle; the artificialities of human time-division in the day's social rituals; the linear and finite life of human beings; the ecclesiastical year; the Christian history of the redemption of the world; the ups and downs of secular history from the fall of Troy to the Arthurian present; and, above time, eternity.[20]

Birtwistle's fascination with time is well documented.[21] In the early 1970s he stated that 'new concepts of time are my main compositional preoccupation',[22] and the titles of a number of his works – *Chronometer*, *The Triumph of Time*, *Pulse Sampler*, *Harrison's Clocks*, *Exody: '23:59:59'* – explicitly allude to this interest. In the instrumental music, a concern for time may take the form of an exploration of pulse or a manipulation of a listener's formal awareness (that is to say, their sense of what the past held, and what the future might). In the stage works, Birtwistle's librettists have been given free reign to extend the narrator's traditional prerogative regarding the temporal manipulation of events. In the chamber opera *Yan Tan Tethera* for instance, certain actions performed by the main characters serve to accelerate the passing of time; Birtwistle says 'the whole thing is like a big clock mechanism, like one of those intricate clocks you get in Bavaria'.[23] The libretto to *The Mask of Orpheus* presents a more formidably complex temporal picture: here the desire to combine and juxtapose different versions of the Orpheus myth leads to all manner of temporal anticipations and echoes as well as the superimposition of different time scales – as when Orpheus relates his return from the underworld at the same time as the entire journey (including the loss of Euridice and Orpheus's own suicide) is enacted. *Gawain* tells a straightforward narrative by comparison. It is enlivened, however, by the reprisal of the Green Knight's entrance, and also by the recurrent image at the back of the stage of a knight crossing a landscape, anticipating both the Green Knight's arrival and Gawain's own journey to and from the Green Chapel. And in the combination of a number of different temporal levels in the Turning of the Seasons section – the dressing of Gawain, the passing of five nights and days, the passing of a

[20] Marie Denley, 'Sir Gawain and the Green Knight', in programme booklet to *Gawain*, p. 17.
[21] For a fuller description of Birtwistle's engagement with time and the temporal, see Adlington, *The Music of Harrison Birtwistle*, chapter 4.
[22] Birtwistle, cited in Michael Hall, *Harrison Birtwistle* (London: Robson Books, 1984), p. 74.
[23] Birtwistle, cited in *ibid.*, p. 144.

whole year – we may detect a clear point of contact with the poem's own multiple time scales.

A second point of formal connection concerns matters of local organisation. In the principal part of each verse of the poem (that is, the part preceding the bob-and-wheel) every line follows the same general metric pattern – four or five main stresses, divided by a caesura – and individual lines are not linked by rhyme or alliteration to any of their neighbours. There is nothing else in the way of internal formal patterning within the long line verses. This means that it is the single line that is the basic structural unit for the bulk of the poem: each line establishes no formal association with any other line, beyond the general metric consistency.[24] This approach to structure, which concentrates on the vividness of the local context rather than larger-scale patterning, finds a strong parallel in those stretches of Birtwistle's music not contained by some larger verse scheme – and that means the bulk of Birtwistle's music of the 1980s and 1990s. Birtwistle's style evolved during the 1970s so that the structural associations between individual sections of a piece went underground; much of Birtwistle's music since then appears to the listener as an almost improvisatory succession of vividly inventive and wildly contrasting but largely unconnected musical segments. Musical ideas are not by and large retained or developed and identifiable recurrence is reduced to a minimum. Architectural schemes, with their rather questionable relevance for a majority of listeners, are eschewed in favour of a confidence in the flow of moment-to-moment incident. In *Gawain*, this approach to musical form – in which, as Michael Hall has noted, 'the orchestration and texture change at every formal juncture'[25] – jostles with the imposing verse schemes of the set pieces. It is a tension that is arguably the defining feature of the work.

It is the internal organisation of individual lines, then, rather than the associations established between them, that carry the burden of structural interest in the poem. Two aspects of this organisation are particularly import-ant: alliteration and metre. I will consider each of these in turn. The principles of alliteration in *Sir Gawain and the Green Knight* are fairly easily summarised.[26] Each line of the poem is alliterative, and alliterating words principally fall upon stressed syllables. Every consonant alliterates only with itself while vowels may alliterate with each other or with [h]. In the long, non-rhyming lines, there are normally three or four alliterating words: two or three in the first half and one in the second half. In the shorter lines of the bob-and-wheel there may be two or three alliterating words. Alliteration was a standard structural device in Old English poetry, but the *Gawain*-poet was one of the last (alongside his contemporary William Langland, author of *Piers Plowman*) to utilise it so fully; the rhyming line endings of medieval French literature were by the fourteenth century becoming more usual in England, as attested

[24] Norman Davis, 'Appendix' to *Sir Gawain and the Green Knight*, edited by J.R.R. Tolkien and E.V. Gordon, second edition edited by Norman Davis (Oxford: Oxford University Press, 1967), pp. 147–8.
[25] Hall, *Harrison Birtwistle in Recent Years*, p. 147.
[26] For more detail, and comments on exceptions to these general principles, see Duggan, 'Metre, Stanza, Vocabulary, Dialect'.

by the poetry of Chaucer. Yet it is the more old-fashioned alliterative language of *Sir Gawain* that strikes the stronger chord with Birtwistle's very modern musical idiom. This is because end-rhyme is to alliteration rather as tonality is to atonality. Rhymed verse possesses certain qualities that align it with tonal harmony: the end-orientation that arises from the focus upon the final destination of each poetic or musical phrase; the structural connections and raising of expectations between adjacent or alternate phrases; the sense of closure that a careful adherence to patterns of rhyme or the principles of tonal harmony brings about. The alliterative line of the *Gawain*-poet, on the other hand, has rather different characteristics. It prioritises repetitive, iterative structure over linear goal-directedness; it provides no structural reference point by means of which surrounding lines may orientate themselves; and it consistently rather than intermittently foregrounds the material qualities of sound alongside the connotative ones. All this can also be said of Birtwistle's atonality. It is this parallel between alliteration and atonality which may explain Birtwistle's decision to omit the rhyming 'wheels' from his setting of the 'turning of the seasons' verses in his choral work *Narration: the Description of the Passing of a Year*. In spite of the potential that the bob-and-wheel held as an analogy for Birtwistle's verse schemes, he seems to have decided that its regular rhyme was out of place both with the rest of the verse and with his own thorny musical idiom.

I have suggested general parallels between the *Gawain*-poet's alliterative style and Birtwistle's music. In fact, Birtwistle's approach to musical texture some-times leads to a closer correspondence. Birtwistle tends to construct orchestral textures from strictly defined layers of instrumental sound. While each layer may have some connection to one or more of the others, as far as the musical surface is concerned it typically possesses its own distinctive timbral qualities, its own register, and its own rhythmic profile. On occasion, one of these textural layers may come to the fore to serve a particularly articulatory function. The result comes close to musical alliteration. The effect is strongest when the foregrounded layer consists of isolated, staccato attacks – forming repeated plosive consonants, as it were, against a more continuous musical stream. Such an effect is created by the solo trumpet, solo trombone, harp and marimba during Morgan and Lady de Hautdesert's duet shortly after the Green Knight is seen for the first time ('Now I shall test his strength with mine').[27] In this instance the musical 'consonant' occurs almost thirty times during the scene, which rather limits the parallel that can be drawn with the three or four repeated consonants of the *Gawain*-poet's line. Elsewhere, Birtwistle's use of the device is more appropriately parsimonious: Arthur's offer of food and wine to the Green Knight, for instance, is rhythmically 'alliterated' by four percussive attacks on harp, cimbalom and marimba.

As these two examples suggest, Birtwistle's distinctive percussion section, and particularly the jangling bite of the cimbalom, play an important role in projecting the work's alliterative qualities. On occasion the percussion

---

[27] Compact disc recording of *Gawain* (London: Collins Classics, 1996 [Collins 70412]), disc 1, track 10, 0'19". All subsequent timings refer to this recording.

instruments combine to form a more complex pattern, as if in imitation of a consonant cluster: Example 1 shows an example from the rich orchestral music that accompanies Gawain as he sets out on his journey at the start of Act Two.[28] The percussion does not carry all the music's alliterative responsibility however. Birtwistle's inclusion of two extra tubas in his brass section gives his brass writing an awesome weight, and trombones and tubas regularly punctuate the musical texture with belly-shaking interjections – providing voiced consonants ([g]s and [d]s), as it were, to complement the unvoiced plosives and fricatives ([c]s, [t]s and [s]s) of the percussion. A good example may be found as the Green Knight envisages Gawain's fate shortly before himself succumbing to the axe at Arthur's court.[29] It should be stressed that these moments of musical alliteration have no direct connection with the sounds of the sung text, which largely avoids alliteration. Rather, Birtwistle's music provides an analogy to the chief structuring principal of the *Gawain*-poet's lines, etching out a rhythmically projected sonic coherence in the short term, with the 'alliterating' sounds being changed at regular intervals.

The effective projection of alliteration in poetry naturally depends upon a close allegiance between alliterative syllable and rhythmic stress. In the view of H.N. Duggan, the alliteration in *Sir Gawain and the Green Knight* 'always falls on a stressed syllable'.[30] This view is not uncontested,[31] but there is no doubting the importance of a certain rhythmic pronouncedness to the effective functioning of alliteration. The vivid metric energy of the *Gawain*-poet finds a good match in Birtwistle's anxious pulses and rhythmic constructions. Indeed English poetic metre's foundational contrast of stressed and unstressed syllable is heard at prominent moments throughout the opera, in the form of an iambic rhythm. This rhythm is heard at the very opening of Act One in the three tubas (Ex. 2), and in this form it appears twice more in the opening scene. The Lullaby music and the hunting horns take up the same rhythm in Act Two, and the iamb plays a more subtle textural role in numerous other places throughout the work.

As far as the poem is concerned, iambic metre is most prominent in the wheels ending each verse, which typically comprise four iambic trimeter lines.[32] It is the rhythmic *irregularity* of the long lines that are the poem's lifeblood, however. In contrast to the regular alternation of stressed and unstressed syllables found in both medieval Latin and much later English verse, in *Sir Gawain* the gaps (or 'dips') between stressed syllables (or 'lifts') are varied in length. The metre of *Sir Gawain* is best understood, not in terms of an unvarying pattern reproduced from line to line, but as the product of permutated variants of a basic shape. The regularity is provided by the four or sometimes five stressed syllables of each line, whose prominence is often further heightened by

---

[28] Disc 2, track 8, 0'53".
[29] Disc 1, track 13, 1'19".
[30] Duggan, 'Metre, Stanza, Vocabulary, Dialect', p. 226.
[31] Marie Borroff elaborates an alternative interpretation in chapter 8 of her book *Sir Gawain and the Green Knight: A Stylistic and Metric Study* (New Haven: Yale University Press, 1962).
[32] For more detail see Duggan, 'Metre, Stanza, Vocabulary, Dialect', p. 237, and Borroff, *Sir Gawain and the Green Knight*, p. 158.

Ex. 1. *Gawain*, Act Two, [30]+2 (harp and percussion only). Brackets show 'consonant cluster'.

alliteration; the variation takes the form of the varying lengths, from none to seven syllables, of the dips separating these syllables.[33]

Ex. 2. *Gawain*, Act One, b. 5 (tubas only)

Viewed as such, the poem's metre provides a further striking intersection with Birtwistle's music. There is, to begin with, the question of the lack of a regular pulse. The varied lengths of dips, and the intermittent occurrence of pentameters amongst the prevailing tetrameters, present a severe challenge to an evenly-pulsing recitation. The sort of disturbed pulse that might result is highly characteristic of Birtwistle's music. Unlike many post-war modernist composers, Birtwistle has always retained a faith in the power of pulse. For Michael Nyman, writing in 1971, pulse was one of the defining characteristics of Birtwistle's style – one of the crucial respects in which Birtwistle's music retrieved 'elements forgotten by atonality and post-Webern serialism'.[34] But Birtwistle generally rejects the unchanging, regular pulse of much classical and popular music in favour of a pulse which is, in his own words, 'always reassessing itself'.[35] A simple example of this basic principle can be found in *Gawain* during the decapitated Green Knight's injunction to Gawain to 'Ride north.' Here, a temple block accompanies the characters' exchanges with a pulse that repeatedly jumps out of alignment with itself (Ex. 3). Earlier, as the Green Knight first proclaims 'Here is the challenge', the low brass intone a rhythmic pattern more closely akin to the pronounced lifts and varying-length dips of the poem (Ex. 4).[36] In this last example it is as if the stressed syllables of the poetic line have been isolated, and the unstressed syllables replaced by silence.

Underlying the rhythmic similarities of the poem and Birtwistle's music is the idea of varied repetition. The importance of varied repetition to Birtwistle's music has already been noted, with particular reference to the verse structures that inform the progress of his music over the medium to long term. Such varied repetition is also apparent at the smallest level of compositional detail. Birtwistle has said that 'at the root of my music is ostinato, varied ostinato'.[37] By this, he is referring to the way in which the textural layers of his music are typically built out

[33] See Duggan, 'Metre, Stanza, Vocabulary, Dialect', pp. 224–32.
[34] Nyman, 'Harrison Birtwistle', *London Magazine* 11/4 (October–November 1971), p. 122.
[35] Birtwistle, cited in *The Harrison Birtwistle Site*, 'Reinventing Music',
     http://www.braunarts.com/birtwistle/basics.html
[36] Ex. 3: disc 1, track 17, 2'37". Ex. 4: disc 1, track 12, 2'45".
[37] Birtwistle, cited in Hall, *Harrison Birtwistle*, p. 149.

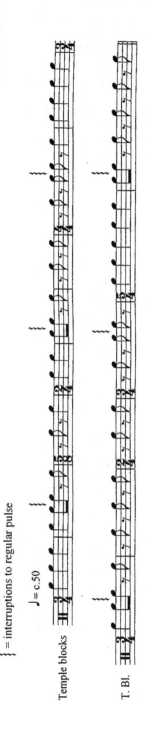

Ex. 3. *Gawain*, Act One, [87]+2 (temple block only)

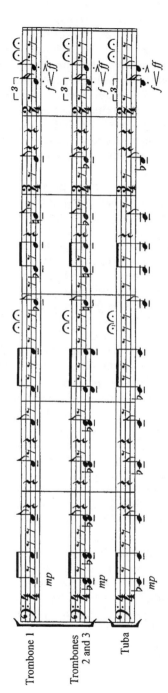

Ex. 4. *Gawain*, Act One, [50]+1 (trombones and tuba 1 only)

of ostinato patterns (that is, a short musical figure repeated many times), which instead of being repeated identically undergo continual slight modification. Ex. 5 shows a simple example of this strategy, from the music accompanying Gawain's journey.[38] Here the trumpets and horns form one of the music's textural layers; their two-chord figure is in certain respects the same on each occasion, but notes and rhythmic placement are slightly altered. The more complex varied ostinatos shown in Examples 6 and 7 present a somewhat closer analogy to the *Gawain*-poet's rhythmic practice. Example 6 shows the dance rhythm accompanying Morgan and Lady de Hautdesert's duet 'This is the moment that waited for you' which occurs twice in Act One.[39] The vertical wiggly lines mark out the repeated units which, while retaining a recognisable shape throughout, are slightly different on each occasion. The units have between two and four principal accents, rather as the *Gawain*-poet alternates between four and five in his long lines, and the durational gap between these principal accents varies, as in the poem. Example 7 appears in the low strings in the middle of the Green Knight's challenge, as Baldwin strikes up his fervent prayer 'Custodi me, Domine.'[40] The extract is laid out so as to reveal the individual metric 'lines' of the music. In this case, the pitch material is repeated almost identically from one 'line' to the next, but rhythmic placement is altered on each occasion. Notes that were well separated on one appearance are yoked together on a second one, just as the first and second stress in lines of the poem may be separated on one line and 'clashing' (brought abruptly together) in the next. Such varied rhythmic treatment of an identifiable basic shape (in this case a seven-'syllable' line) is entirely characteristic of the local construction of Birtwistle's music. One may readily imagine that Birtwistle perceived in *Sir Gawain and the Green Knight* a rhythmic style akin to that of his own music.

I have noted some ways in which Birtwistle's *Gawain* departs from the original poem: the newly important role accorded to Morgan; the gloomy assessment of life at Arthur's court; the ascription of motives and character traits previously absent. The relationship between the opera and the poem is strengthened, on the other hand, by aspects of Birtwistle's musical style that offer strong connections with the *Gawain*-poet's technique. It is these connections – to do with form, sound and rhythm – that I have been concerned to establish here. It would of course be incorrect to imply that the medieval source was uppermost in Birtwistle's mind when writing the music for *Gawain*. The influence of Wagner is as readily detected, for instance; rather as the *Gawain*-poet was composing in the context of earlier generations of Romance poets (including those who wrote about Tristan and Perceval),[41] so Birtwistle embarked on an intensive study of *The Ring* in preparation for the composition of his own Arthurian opera.[42] *Gawain*'s repeating 'leitmotivs', rich orchestral texture and practically unbroken continuity of invention, as well as a host of more specific parallels, may be traced back to the towering figure of late musical

[38] Disc 2, track 4, 0'53".
[39] Disc 1, track 15.
[40] Disc 1, track 12, 4'45".
[41] See Elisabeth Brewer, *Sir Gawain and the Green Knight: Sources and Analogues* (Cambridge: D.S. Brewer, 1992) and Ad Putter, *Sir Gawain and the Green Knight and French Arthurian Romance* (Oxford: Clarendon Press, 1995).
[42] Hall, *Harrison Birtwistle in Recent Years*, p. 78.

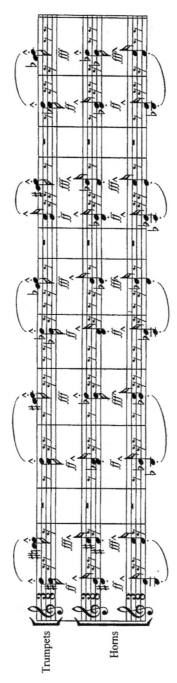

Ex. 5. *Gawain*, Act Two, [18]+2 (trumpets and horns only)

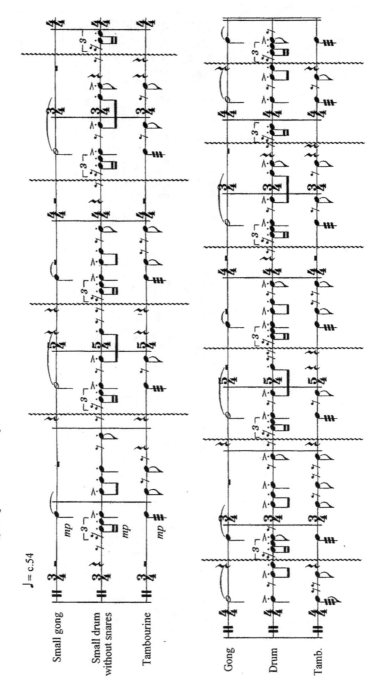

Ex. 6. *Gawain*, Act One, [32] (percussion only)

Ex. 7. *Gawain*, Act One, [54]–2 (cellos and double basses only). Shows repeating pitch pattern and rhythmic modification; dynamics and articulation omitted.

Romanticism. However, these debts counterpoint rather than eradicate the qualities of Birtwistle's distinctive idiom that strike the clearest correspondences with the language of the *Gawain*-poet. I hope to have shown why Birtwistle should have found this particular poem compellingly attractive, and ways in which Birtwistle's musical language provides singularly appropriate accommodation – truly a 'bone hostel' – for the story of Sir Gawain and the Green Knight.

King Arthur in Popular Musical Theatre and Musical Film

While the focus of this book has been on images of King Arthur in concert music and opera, the legend also provided the basis for several twentieth-century American musicals and musical films. The two most successful stage incarnations are Richard Rodgers and Lorenz Hart's *A Connecticut Yankee* (1927, revived with additional material 1943) and Alan Jay Lerner and Frederick Loewe's *Camelot* (1960). Musical films – that is, films with distinctive songs that are sung on-screen – based on the Arthurian legend also exist. Film versions include *A Connecticut Yankee in King Arthur's Court* (1949), though with a score by James Van Heusen and Johnny Burke rather than Rodgers and Hart, and *Camelot* (1967), with Lerner and Loewe's music and words. Original Arthurian musical films appeared as well: *The Sword in the Stone* (1963), *Monty Python and the Holy Grail* (1974), and *Quest for Camelot* (1998). In each of these manifestations, the creators, in their musical numbers, emphasized the juxtaposition of old and new – or historic and modern – in order to create effective musical numbers. While this is certainly the norm for literary retoolings of the Arthurian legend, the anachronistic conflations in text-music relationships made the tale accessible to twentieth-century musical theatre and film audiences. Furthermore, each creative team used Arthurian Britain as the basis for a work in which either their own unique artistic personalities or stock aspects of a particular genre (e.g. musical comedy, musical film) were clearly evident. Adherence to a faithful rendering of King Arthur was secondary to a personal or generic conception of the legend.

A Connecticut Yankee

Mark Twain, in *A Connecticut Yankee in King Arthur's Court* (1889), used the time of Arthur as a backdrop for social commentary on the nineteenth century. The novel's comic tone with its socially conscious underpinning made it a solid choice for a 1920s musical comedy, a genre that had as its central characters everyday people who become entangled in various sorts of amusing misadventures.

Special thanks to Drs. Luke Howard, Lynda Payne and Ann Sears for their helpful comments and suggestions regarding this article.

Musical comedies, as opposed to operettas or musicals (as a noun, also known as musical plays), were meant to be upbeat and fast-paced, with distinctive musical numbers in a popular style (verse-refrain form). The emphasis was on comedy and individual songs – character development was not paramount. Among the major contributors to the genre were composer Richard Rodgers (1902–79) and lyricist Lorenz Hart (1895–1943). Prior to their Arthurian musical comedy, the team had created eleven shows, including *Poor Little Ritz Girl* (1920) and two versions of *The Garrick Gaieties* (1925, 1926). They were certainly experienced in the workings of the musical theatre when they embarked upon their musical version of Twain's tale.

It was actually not the novel, but rather a film version from 1921, that served as inspiration for the musical comedy. According to Richard Rodgers:

> Back in 1921, Herb Fields and I wandered into the Capitol Theatre to see a silent picture called "A Connecticut Yankee," with Harry C. Myers in the lead. We laughed for nearly two hours and walking home decided that there, by cracky, was the perfect idea for a musical comedy. Mr. Hart thought so too, so a couple of days later I walked into the office of the lawyer for the Mark Twain estate to try to get the necessary permission to make a musical version of the novel.[1]

In the musical version of Twain's book which opened at New York's Vanderbilt Theatre on 3 November 1927, and ran for 418 performances, librettist Herbert Fields transformed several aspects of the novel for the stage. The tale opens in the grand ballroom of a hotel in Hartford, Connecticut in 1927, and Hank Martin is about to marry Fay when his ex-fiancee Alice arrives on the scene. Fay discovers Hank and Alice, and hits Hank over the head with a champagne bottle. In a *Wizard of Oz*-like dream, Hank awakens during the time of King Arthur, ca. 528 A.D. Alice becomes the Demoiselle Alisande Le Carterloise (nicknamed Sandy), his love interest, while Fay is none other than the enchantress Morgan le Fay. After he is threatened with being burned at the stake, Hank recalls his knowledge of astronomy and, as in the novel, correctly predicts an eclipse. Also, following the basic premise of Twain's tale, Hank then proceeds to modernize King Arthur's court. But Morgan Le Fay wants to cause trouble, and the only way Hank can escape is to awaken from his dream. He does so, and finds himself back in 1927, in the gardens of the Hartford hotel. Hank's dream was not without its lessons, however, for the Yankee learns that it is Alisande's real-life double, Alice, who he really loves and decides to marry.

William Gaxton and Constance Carpenter played the romantic leads, and Nina Bryant appeared as Morgan le Fay. The production included spectacular sets and the eclipse was accomplished through special effects that were considered marvels for the time.[2] Roy Webb and Robert Russell Bennett were the orchestrators, and Busby Berkeley was the choreographer.

The musical appeared in London under the title *A Yankee at the Court of King*

---

[1] 'Mr. Rodgers' Yankee', *New York Times*, 21 November 1943.
[2] William G. Hyland, *Richard Rodgers* (New Haven and London: Yale University Press, 1998), p. 67.

Arthur. It did not fare well, playing for a scant forty-three performances (10 October to 16 November 1929) at Daly's Theatre. Harry Fox starred as 'The Yankee' and Constance Carpenter reprised her role as Alisande. The opening duet, 'My Heart Stood Still,' was replaced by 'I Don't Know How,' with music and lyrics by Vivian Ellis and Desmond Carter. Ellis and Carter also wrote 'I Never Thought of That,' a song for Merlin, for the London production.[3] Critics were pleased with the songs and the performances, but as is so often the case, blamed the book for the show's problems.

In the original New York production, Hank and Sandy, the romantic leads, had two primary love songs, sung immediately one after the other early in the show: the aforementioned 'My Heart Stood Still' and 'Thou Swell.' 'My Heart Stood Still' appears in the prologue, set in 1927, while 'Thou Swell' is the first musical number sung on the road to Camelot.

'My Heart Stood Still' first appeared in the London revue *One Dam Thing after Another*.[4] The show opened at the London Pavilion on 19 May 1927, where it played for 237 performances. It was typical for musical comedy creators of the era to interpolate songs from one show into another, and the case of 'My Heart Stood Still' was certainly no exception. The song had been heard on the London stage, but not in New York. Therefore it had a sense of 'newness' for American audiences. Similarly, because it had already been heard in London, it was removed from the British production and replaced with a new song. Because the number appeared in the prologue, set in 1927, the lyric did not have to contain Arthurian references in order to be relevant to the show (not that this was necessarily a steadfast requirement for any musical comedy number). A reprise of the song takes place before the first-act finale, in King Arthur's castle, where it serves a dramatic purpose as a link between Martin's two worlds. The musical setting is a typical Tin Pan Alley verse-refrain structure with the refrain in the standard AABA form. Hart's brilliance at creating lyrics that enjoin disparate elements is clearly evident in the song. In the verse, Hart melds literary references to classical philosophy (Plato) and the romantic novellas of Elinor Glyn, popular in the 1920s.

This integration of dissimilar elements is central to both Hart's approach to lyric writing and many nineteenth- and twentieth-century interpretations of the Arthurian legend, including that of Twain. Hart's genius at achieving dichotomatic juxtaposition made him an ideal creator of specific lyrics that would amplify the ideology of Twain's novel.

Perhaps nowhere is this more obvious than in 'Thou Swell,' where Hart effectively combined antiquated English expressions (Elizabethan, as in the novel) with contemporary slang. The anachronistic simultaneity that pervades the entire musical is epitomized in this number. The title itself encapsulates the conflation of eras that is present throughout the text. The well-constructed lyric coupled with a ballad-like setting that included plenty of jazz-influenced syncopations made the song one of the show's biggest hits.

Sir Galahad and Mistress Evelyn LaRondell, the secondary leads, have two

[3] Stanley Green, ed., *Rodgers and Hammerstein Fact Book* (New York: Lynn Farnol Group, 1980), p. 75.
[4] Hyland, p. 67.

significant musical numbers, 'On a Desert Island with Thee!' and 'I Feel at Home with You.' The former is a lyrical ballad while the latter is a jazz-influenced syncopated number replete with slithering melodic chromaticisms. Since neither Galahad nor Evelyn had any prior knowledge of 1920s musical style, the number is purely anachronistic. It is in fact the most daring musical number in the score in terms of melody, harmony and rhythm. Furthermore there are no references to any sort of English past, either Elizabethan or Arthurian, in the lyric. In typical musical comedy fashion, this was a pleasant tune that had no real relevance to the plot or its setting.

The legacy of *A Connecticut Yankee* certainly did not end in the 1920s. A revival of the show in the early 1940s was the result of creative differences on the part of Rodgers and Hart and their subsequent attempt at reconciliation. In 1942, Rodgers announced his decision to end his partnership with his longtime lyricist.[5] Rodgers' action was based on several factors, including Hart's unwillingness to work on a show for the Theatre Guild based on *Green Grow the Lilacs* (the result of which was *Oklahoma!*) and Hart's alcohol problems.[6] Rodgers decided to collaborate with veteran lyricist Oscar Hammerstein II (1895–1960), and when *Oklahoma!*, their first musical, appeared in 1943, it entered the annals of Broadway history. Although Rodgers had found a new collaborator, he did not forget his long-time relationship with Lorenz Hart nor his respect for him.

In 1943, the same year as the premiere of *Oklahoma!*, Rodgers and Herbert Fields decided to try to do something to help Hart and proposed a revival and reworking of *A Connecticut Yankee*. The idea seemed to please Hart, for he would not have to create an entirely new set of lyrics – a daunting task – and he would be working with people he already knew.[7]

The revised *A Connecticut Yankee* opened on 17 November 1943, at the Martin Beck Theater and played for 135 performances. The show was to be Hart's last contribution to Broadway, for he died on 22 November 1943, five days after it opened. The book was altered so that the three principals were in the military. In this way, homage was paid to the then-current war effort. Typical for refashionings of the Arthurian legend, contemporary issues and mores were grafted onto the basic text.

In the revival, the legendary Vivienne Segal played Morgan. Rodgers and Hart created the wonderfully morbid 'To Keep My Love Alive' especially for her. Hart's trademark textual dichotomy is clearly evident in the song, the disparate topics being marriage and murder. In the number, Morgan describes in colourful detail how she caused the deaths of her husbands. The lyrics, considered to be Hart's last, are replete with the techniques that made the lyricist famous. Who else could think of rhyming 'possibilities,' 'ill at ease' and 'kill at ease,' or 'fratricide,' 'patricide,' and 'mattress side'? Here again is a classic Hart combination of chivalric references and twentieth-century verbiage.

Two other new numbers, 'The Camelot Samba' and 'You Always Love the

[5] Hyland, p. 136.
[6] Hyland, p. 136.
[7] Hyland, p. 151.

Same Girl,' evinced advances in the musical theatre from the 1920s to the 1940s. 'The Camelot Samba' integrated Arthurian Britain with the then-current Afro-Brazilian dance craze. A lavish diversion at Morgana's palace, the number included the line 'all the way from Camelot to Rio' and combined Tin Pan Alley steadfastness with samba rhythms and instrumentation.

'You Always Love the Same Girl,' a duet sung by Arthur and Martin after their Jeep breaks down, is significant in the musical comedy because it was a song that advanced the dramatic plot. Although it did not contain any overt Arthurian references, the lyric extolled the truth of loving the same girl in whatever world one lives – whether it be sixth-century Britain or twentieth-century Connecticut. It was therefore directly related to the show's romantic plot, Martin's love for Sandy. This integration of songs with plot was atypical in the Rodgers and Hart canon from the 1920s. The nearly two decades that separated the original 1927 Connecticut Yankee from the 1943 revival included shows such as Show Boat (1927) and Oklahoma!, musicals in which drama was central. Expectations and norms had changed. Rodgers and Hart were certainly aware of contemporary developments in musical theatre and incorporated these ideas into their later work, as in 'You Always Love the Same Girl.'

In A Connecticut Yankee, Rodgers and Hart made the time of King Arthur accessible and likeable to audiences in the 1920s and again in the 1940s. The musical style made the era suddenly quite modern. Similarly Hank took with him to the sixth century the musical comedy idioms of the 1920s and 1940s. Rodgers and Hart, therefore, working through Hank, were twentieth-century equivalents of the hero – they introduced American slang and Broadway musical language to the sixth century just as the time-travelling Yankee had introduced nineteenth-century technology to the same era.

Paramount Studios released a film version of A Connecticut Yankee in King Arthur's Court (with full title) in 1949. When the idea of the film was proposed, Rodgers and Hammerstein were asked to write additional songs to complement the Rodgers and Hart selections. However, they were working on Allegro at the time, and Hammerstein did not think he would have time for the cinematic project. The team subsequently decided that they would have time, but other factors intervened, and it was ultimately decided that they would not be involved with the project. Hence Paramount jettisoned the Rodgers and Hart score and hired Johnny Burke and James Van Heusen, already under contract to Paramount, to write an entirely new set of songs for the film [8]

A Connecticut Yankee in King Arthur's Court starred Bing Crosby and Rhonda Fleming. Edmund Beloin's original screenplay set the 'present day' portions of the film in 1912 England as Hank Martin is touring Pendragon Castle. He remembers artifacts on display in the castle's museum and tells his tale of life in the sixth century to Lord Pendragon, the modern incarnation of King Arthur. Four songs appeared in the film:

[8] Ken Bloom, Hollywood Song: The Complete Musical Companion, vol. 1 (New York: Facts on File, 1995), p. 1158.

If You Stub Your Toe on the Moon
When Is Sometime?
Once and for Always
Busy Doing Nothing[9]

As was typical for many musical films of the era, the songs were conceived to showcase the vocal talents of the stars. None of the songs in *A Connecticut Yankee in King Arthur's Court* are related to the Arthurian plot. Three of the film's four songs feature the singing talents of the romantic leads. Hank Martin (Bing Crosby), as an early twentieth-century mechanic, tells a group of adoring children about various gadgets and inventions in 'If You Stub Your Toe on the Moon.' Alisande (Rhonda Fleming) makes her entrance in the film singing the wishful 'When Is Sometime?' as entertainment for the King's dinner. In the ballad, she sings about waiting for her true love just as Hank is brought into the hall. The romantic style continues in Hank and Alisande's duet 'Once and For Always,' the film's primary love song. The couple reprises the number later in the film.

The only song that is not a sentimental ballad is the comic trio 'Busy Doing Nothing.' Hank, King Arthur (Sir Cedric Hardwicke) and Sir Sagamore (William Bendix) sing the upbeat diversion with a 'La, la, la' refrain as they travel through the country *incognito*.

Victor Young composed the film's musical score.[10] While an analysis of the score is beyond the scope of this essay, the musical underscoring that holds the film together includes both material derived from the songs and original music.

Two self-references to musical comedy appear in the film, one musical and the other textual. The musical reference appears before and during the Turkey Trot sequence. Hank teaches Arthur's court how to do the American dancestep. Beforehand, he instructs the minstrels in a vamp, creating a different part for each instrumentalist. When he arrives at the dulcimer player, Hank changes the meter from 3/4 to 4/4. The tempo increases at this point as syncopations also enter the soundworld. Hank thus shows his preference for musical comedy (as opposed to operetta) styles by replacing the leisurely outmoded 3/4 (associated with operetta) with a fast-paced modern 4/4.

The second self-reference occurs in the scene where Hank encourages the King to get to know his people. When Arthur remarks that he already does, Hank responds 'I don't mean these musical comedy personalities.' With this remark, the Yankee describes the fun-loving and humourous court characters as stereotypical musical comedy stock.

Scenes from Rodgers and Hart's *A Connecticut Yankee* did make it to the silver screen, however. The pseudo-biographical film of the team, *Words and Music* (1948), included a *Connecticut Yankee* sequence that included excerpts from 'Someone Should Tell Them,' 'Thou Swell,' and 'My Heart Stood Still.' Because

---

[9] Bloom, vol. 1, p. 182. An additional song, ''Twixt Myself and Me', was written for the film but was not used.

[10] In this essay, musical score refers to the music in the film that does not include lyrics nor is part of a song. It includes the opening and closing titles, underscoring for dialogue and music to accompany transitions such as scene changes.

Paramount controlled the rights to the Rodgers and Hart score (although they didn't use it in their film), they were reticent to allow MGM, the studio that produced *Words and Music*, to include songs from the stage musical in their release.[11]

The *Connecticut Yankee* sequence begins with an introductory march, after which the Blackburn Twins, costumed as lute-playing knights (although a harp in heard in the orchestration), sing the verse of 'Someone Should Tell Them.' June Allyson, as Sandy, responds with the second verse of 'Thou Swell' in a *molto rubato* rendition, followed by the refrain. Two instrumental repetitions of the refrain performed to Robert Alton's choreography conclude the scene. As was typical for the filmographies of musical theatre creators, songs were taken out of context in the cinematic offerings, and allegiance to original vocal scoring (recalling that 'Thou Swell' was a duet for the romantic leads) was certainly not obligatory. A section of the refrain appears in the 'Tribute to Lorenz Hart' sequence that concludes the film.

In the penultimate section of the film, the chronicle of Lorenz Hart's decline, the lyricist journeys to the Martin Beck Theatre in the pouring rain for the opening night of the revival of *A Connecticut Yankee*. The tumultuous underscoring is based on motifs from 'My Heart Stood Still,' and a disembodied, barely distinguishable chorus can be heard singing the final phrase of the refrain as Hart enters the back of the house and leaves almost immediately.

Camelot

While Mark Twain's literary work provided inspiration for the major musical versions of the Arthurian legend in the 1920s and 40s, it was T.H. White's *The Once and Future King* that would provide the inspiration for the classic Arthurian musical of the second half of the century, Lerner and Loewe's *Camelot*. In the late 1950s, after the successes of the stage musical *My Fair Lady* (1956) and the film *Gigi* (1958), lyricist Alan Jay Lerner (1918–88) and composer Frederick Loewe (1901–88) embarked upon a new project: the musicalization of T.H. White's epic retelling of the Arthurian legend, *The Once and Future King* (1939–1958). White's novel consisted of four distinct parts: *The Sword in the Stone, The Queen of Air and Darkness, The Ill-Made Knight*, and *The Candle in the Wind*. In securing rights for the show, Irving Cohen, on behalf of Lerner and Loewe, ran into difficulties because of Walt Disney, who had purchased the rights to make an animated film of *The Sword in the Stone* in 1939, the year in which the book appeared.[12] Cohen did succeed in gaining permission to adapt the remaining three books for the new show, however. Hence Arthur's boyhood, the subject of *The Sword in the Stone*, is told only in the form of memories in *Camelot*.

Bringing the novel to the musical stage was no easy task. The trek was beset with health ailments (and death) for several people associated with the show.[13]

[11] Bloom vol. 1, p. 1168.
[12] Leonard Maltin, *The Disney Films* (New York: Crown, 1973), p. 17.
[13] Among the problems were the death of costume director Adrian, Lerner's hemorrhaging ulcer and director Moss Hart's heart attack.

Furthermore, the show ran four and a half hours at its Toronto premiere.[14] This was, of course, exceedingly long for a musical headed for Broadway. Subsequently over one and a half hours of music and dialogue had to be cut, including a ballet sequence and a jousting scene. The musical opened on 3 December 1960 at the Majestic Theater, where it played for 873 performances in its initial run.

Richard Burton, in his musical debut, starred as King Arthur, and Julie Andrews, whom Lerner and Loewe knew from her work as the star of *My Fair Lady* and who was friends with T.H. White, played Guenevere. Robert Goulet made his New York debut in the role of Lancelot, and veteran actor Roddy McDowell played Arthur's illegitimate son Mordred.

In London, *Camelot* played at the Drury Lane Theatre, where it opened on 19 August 1964, and received 518 performances. The production featured Laurence Harvey as Arthur and Elizabeth Larner as Guenevere.

The musical opens as Arthur expresses his nervousness about his upcoming arranged marriage to Guenevere, whom he has never met ('I Wonder What the King Is Doing Tonight'). He spies a young maiden who is bemoaning the loss of 'The Simple Joys of Maidenhood.' It is none other than Guenevere. They meet, but he keeps his identity secret as he sings of the glories of Camelot ('Camelot'). His identity is revealed as his entourage approaches. Following Arthur's marriage to Guenevere, the King begins to assemble his Round Table. Lancelot du Lac arrives from France to join the Table, but falls in love with Guenevere and leaves, so as not to embarrass Camelot. He cannot stay away, however, and returns to woo Guenevere in the show-stopping 'If Ever I Would Leave You.' Mordred appears on the scene and exposes the lovers, who are then, according to Arthur's own law, condemned to death. Lancelot rescues his lover from the stake, and they escape to France, where Arthur meets the couple and forgives them. He finds hope for the future in a young boy, Tom of Warwick (Thomas Mallory, author of *Morte d'Arthur*, even though Mallory lived in the fifteenth century and Arthur in either the fifth or sixth century), and implores him to remember the glory days of Camelot and to tell the tale to future generations.

In constructing their show, Lerner and Loewe followed the plan established by Rodgers and Hammerstein in their musical plays – a long first act leading to a dramatic finale and a short second act. Character development was now paramount, and music and musical style were essential and integral to the telling of the story, rather than peripheral as they were in *A Connecticut Yankee*. Songs were no longer entertaining diversions but rather had to be central parts of the drama.

Loewe's musical score contains a number of distinctive features: (1) speech-singing for dramatic effect; (2) different musical styles for different characters; (3) the use of song to accentuate a character's dramatic development; (4) a precise use of underscoring, and (5) an accessible musical style.

Speech-singing is cardinal to the musical characterization of Arthur. The King does not really 'sing' his songs in *Camelot*, but rather 'intones' them. Speech and song are melded into one in Loewe's score. Arthur appears to be singing because his melodic lines are always doubled in the orchestra. The actor

[14] Alan Jay Lerner, *The Street Where I Live* (New York and London: W.W. Norton, 1978), p. 214.

portraying the King, while having to follow the natural vocal rises and falls of the musical line, does not really have to produce each note with a well-focused vocal technique. This is the obligation of the actor who plays Lancelot.

Loewe developed this musical idiom with Rex Harrison for *My Fair Lady*, where the character of Henry Higgins was never supposed to *really* sing, since he lacked the humanity necessary to do so.[15] Rodgers and Hammerstein utilized a similar technique in *The King and I* (1951) for the King of Siam's music.[16] In both *My Fair Lady* and *The King and I*, the male protagonist's specific vocal style is in direct contrast to that of the female lead, showcased in such numbers as 'I Could Have Danced All Night' in *My Fair Lady* and 'Getting to Know You' and 'Hello Young Lovers' in *The King and I*. In *Camelot* however, it is not Guenevere but rather Lancelot who is the vocal foil for Arthur.

In 'I Wonder What the King is Doing Tonight,' Loewe indicates Arthur's opening passage with 'x's, recalling the notation of Arnold Schoenberg's *Sprechstimme*. Approximate pitches are noted in the vocal line with precise rhythms. The orchestra doubles Arthur's line, creating the aural illusion that Arthur is singing. At the last line of the verse ('Whenever the wind blows this way'), the indication 'He sings' appears in the score. Thus, Loewe creates a subtle change between pure speech and the speech-singing style. Loewe begins 'How to Handle a Woman' and the Finale Ultimo (a reprise of 'Camelot') in similar fashion.

What does this stylized setting say about Arthur? He is the king; he is dashing; he is the supreme leader of his people. But he lacks something – that very thing which Guenevere desires and cannot find – that thing which Guenevere finds in Lancelot and sacrifices everything to obtain. What is this quality? Is it intimacy? Perhaps. Is it the desire to be loved above all else, including one's country and ideals? Or is the answer to this question found in the very concept of courtly love, where a queen must love down? Noted theatre historian Lehman Engel poses a related question:

> Why was Guenevere disenchanted with Arthur, a kind, loving and attractive husband, and so carried away by Lancelot, a second-rate romantic superman? It is not a lack of fidelity that makes for our dissatisfaction but an unmotivated, rather arbitrary choice that seemed to make no sense. (I am referring to the musical and not to the novel on which it was based.)[17]

Whatever the answer to this mystery may be, Lerner and Loewe offer a musical explanation: Lancelot can sing and does so, while Arthur does not. Guenevere is captivated, at least in the musical, by Lancelot's soaring baritone. From the opening of 'C'est Moi,' Lancelot's anthem of self-deification, when the Frenchman intones the Camelot motif and lingers on the final syllable if for no other reason than he can, we know that Lancelot possesses something that

---

[15] Kurt Gänzl, *The Musical: A Concise History* (Boston: Northeastern University Press, 1997), pp. 289–90.

[16] In both instances, the idiom also had something to do with Rex Harrison and Yul Brynner, the stars of the shows, both being primarily non-singing actors.

[17] Lehman Engel, *Words with Music: The Broadway Musical Libretto* (New York: Schirmer, 1972), p. 87.

Arthur does not. And how could Guenevere resist Lancelot's ballad 'If Ever I Would Leave You'? Whatever is lacking in Arthur's persona, represented by his inability to truly sing, exists in Lancelot, for the French knight can sing, and does so marvelously.In drastic contrast to Lancelot is Mordred, the catalyst for the fall of Camelot. In Loewe's musical depiction, Mordred is so diabolic that he cannot (and does not) sing at all, not even in the speech-singing style of Arthur. The non-singing villain is common in German opera and a convention with which Loewe, with his Berlin roots, would have been familiar. In Carl Maria von Weber's *Der Freischütz* for example, Samiel, the evil character, does not sing. The technique is also evident in American music; for example, in Gershwin's *Porgy and Bess*, the police officers speak rather than sing their lines.

Mordred's solo number, 'The Seven Deadly Virtues,' typifies the style. The fast-paced accompaniment and the nearly melodramatic musical presentation (the melodic material appears in the orchestra) set Mordred apart from both Arthur and Lancelot. Although notated in standard fashion, the frequent rests and consistent use of short rhythmic values (crochets and quavers) prohibit the actor who portrays Mordred from creating legato musical lines.

Loewe resorts to pure melodrama, both as a musical style (speech over music) and as a dramatic form associated with villainy and evil plotting, in 'The Persuasion.' In this number, Mordred implores Morgan le Fay to use her magic to capture Arthur. Both vocal lines utilize the cross-stem notation described above. The characters intone their lines in precise rhythm but without the musical doubling seen in Arthur's music and 'The Seven Deadly Virtues.' True deceit is apparent through the unmistakable lack of singing.

Loewe was a master of musical characterization, as his portrayals of the two sympathetic male leads, Arthur and Lancelot, and the malevolent Mordred so ably demonstrates. But he was also able to musically depict the psychological growth of an individual character – Guenevere. Here is the central personality in the drama, the woman who betrays the King. Her transformation from a young maiden to a mature woman is evident in her music. It becomes increasingly refined and cultured as the show progresses. Her opening numbers, 'Genevieve' and 'Where Are the Simple Joys of Maidenhood?' (separated by a brief dialogue with musical underscoring) display her innocence and naivete. Near the end of the first act, she sings 'Before I Gaze at You Again.'[18] In this number, Guenevere expresses her love and admiration for Lancelot as he is about to depart on a series of quests. By the time the Queen confesses her complete love and devotion to Lancelot during the second act in 'I Loved You Once in Silence,' she has matured. Guenevere realizes the impact her decision to betray Arthur has had upon the court of Camelot. Lerner himself describes the number:

> The music is more sophisticated, more harmonically complex, and the lyric a sad reflection of a woman whose guilt and grief has aged. We intentionally wrote it 'unpassionate.'[19]

---

[18] This number was added to the score just days before the show opened in New York (Lerner, pp. 231–35). It was subsequently cut from the film.

[19] Lerner, pp. 192–93.

As Jerome Kern and Oscar Hammerstein II had done with Magnolia Hawks's music in *Show Boat*, Lerner and Loewe's songs for Guenevere show through musical means the dramatic development of the heroine. It is this sort of musical characterization that defines the musical of the era – songs were not merely excuses for tuneful numbers but rather were central to the audience's perception of the drama and its protagonists.

Loewe was concerned about every aspect of the well-integrated dramatic musical score, including underscoring. His choice of musical material for the underscoring of dialogue was not haphazard, but well planned. One of the most memorable moments in *Camelot* is Arthur's monologue at the end of Act 1. During his soliloquy, Arthur ponders current events in his household; he knows that something is happening between Guenevere and Lancelot, yet he idolizes them both. He resolves that it *is* the time of King Arthur, a time of ideals and dreams that must rise above any problems in the realm. Music used for this section begins with 'How to Handle a Woman.' At this point in the dialogue, Arthur is bemoaning the impending fate of Guenevere and Lancelot. When he finds resolve, the musical underscoring changes to a ceremonial version of 'I Wonder What the King Is Doing Tonight,' Arthur's opening number. Through a reprise of this music, the audience is reminded of Arthur's strong character and his ability to do what needs to be done for the greater good despite his own personal fears and insecurities. Just as Arthur resolves himself to marriage when he sings the song at the beginning of the show, the choice of this number for underscoring at this point reiterates the King's inner strength and determination that allow him to rise above his personal concerns.

Finally, it is the accessible musical style which contributed so significantly to the success of *Camelot*. 'If Ever I would Leave You,' Lancelot's big number, became one of the great love ballads of the 1960s, particularly through its association with the singer who introduced it, Robert Goulet. One of the most phenomenal aspects of the overtly romantic song is that the word 'love' never appears in Lerner's lyric. Lancelot and Guenevere's love is a secret one, and as such, the word that specifically names it could not be uttered.[20]

Camelot became a symbol for President John F. Kennedy and his administration, an administration whose days, like those of Arthur's Camelot, were cut tragically short. Arthur's Camelot and Kennedy's presidency both represented a utopian ideal – a world filled with hope and dreams. Lerner himself relates what happened at a performance of *Camelot* in Chicago on the day Kennedy was assassinated, 22 November 1963:

Louis Hayward was playing King Arthur. When he came to those lines ['one brief shining moment'], there was a sudden wail from the audience. It was not a muffled sob; it was a loud, almost primitive cry of pain. The play stopped, and for almost five minutes everyone in the theater – on stage, in the wings, in the pit, and in the audience – wept without restraint. Then the play continued.[21]

[20] Stephen Citron, *The Wordsmiths: Oscar Hammerstein 2nd & Alan Jay Lerner* (New York: Oxford University Press, 1995), p. 327.
[21] Lerner, p. 252.

The next day, after Lerner returned home to New York City devastated by the news of Kennedy's assassination, he was even more shocked when he saw his lyrics as the banner headline of the *New York Journal–American*: 'Don't let it be forgot that once there was a spot, for one brief shining moment that was known as Camelot.' Apparently he was so dazed when he saw his lyric that he not only did not buy a copy of the newspaper but also walked ten blocks beyond his destination before he realized what had happened.[22]

Camelot continued as a popular allusion to the Kennedy presidency. Even the *Oxford History of the American People*, which covers the history of the United States to the end of the Kennedy era, cites Lerner and Loewe, for the chronology ends with the final lines of the show as a cultural reference to the Kennedy years.[23]

A film version of Lerner and Loewe's musical appeared in 1967. Produced by Jack L. Warner and directed by Joshua Logan, the Warner Brothers release starred Richard Harris as Arthur, Vanessa Redgrave as Guenevere, and Franco Nero, whose singing was dubbed by Gene Merlina, as Lancelot. The fifteen-million-dollar production was a full-blown Hollywood extravaganza shot in Spain with all the fashionable visual effects of the late 1960s but in a Gothic atmosphere. Lerner wrote the screenplay and maximized the possibilities of the cinematic medium. The visual spectacle of the knighting of Lancelot included lavish costumes and sets, and the jousting scene, cut from the stage version, was restored and presented in a manner not possible in live theatre. Finally, the visual cues for 'If Ever I Would Leave You' featured ten shifts of scene that narrated the history of the relationship.

Camelot, in both its stage and screen versions, became the iconic Arthurian musical. Through a combination of its accessible musical style, integrated musical score, and musical characterization, the musical continues to entertain audiences and remains in the standard musical theatre repertory.

The Arthurian Musical Film: The Sword in the Stone, Monty Python and the Holy Grail, *and* Quest for Camelot

Three original films (as opposed to adaptations of stage works), *The Sword in the Stone* (1963), *Monty Python and the Holy Grail* (1974), and *Quest for Camelot* (1998), included songs that advanced the Arthurian plot. But in all three films, the Arthurian legend was not as important as the manner in which is was told. The *Sword in the Stone* and *Monty Python and the Holy Grail* were Disney and Monty Python films at least as much as they were Arthurian retellings, and *Quest for Camelot* took an approach to the Arthurian legend that promoted women and the disabled.

[22] Citron, p. 328.
[23] Samuel Eliot Morison, *The Oxford History of the American People* (New York: Oxford University Press, 1965), p. 1122. Musical examples are included throughout the volume to enhance discussions of various epochs in American history. One curious and perhaps even bizarre coincidence exists regarding the date 22 November and Arthurian musicals. Lorenz Hart, lyricist for *A Connecticut Yankee*, passed away on 22 November 1943, and John F. Kennedy, with whom *Camelot* became closely associated, died exactly twenty years later on 22 November 1963.

As discussed above, when Lerner and Loewe were creating *Camelot*, they could not stage the first book of White's *The Once and Future King*, *The Sword in the Stone*, because Disney had already acquired its film rights. The resulting animated feature appeared in 1963, three years after *Camelot*. According to Kathy Merlock Jackson, 'stylization replaced realism' in the film, akin to *101 Dalmatians*.[24] Richard M. Sherman and Robert B. Sherman composed the songs, and George Bruns provided the musical score. As was typical for animated feature films of the era, nearly all of the action included musical underscoring. In *The Sword in the Stone*, the songs, all of which are quite brief, emerge out of the underscore texture and return to it immediately afterwards. Thus the musical fabric of the film is continuous and quite distinctive from that of a stage play.[25] The feature's six songs are as follows, in their order of appearance:

The Legend of the Sword in the Stone
Higitus Figitus (Merlin's Magic Song)
That What Makes the World Go 'Round
A Most Befuddling Thing
Mad Madam Mim
Blue Oak Tree[26]

'The Legend of the Sword in the Stone' is a 60s-style folk ballad for solo singer and guitar. Lyrics appear on screen in an illuminated manuscript, telescoping the time difference between medieval England and the 1960s through the amalgam of visual and aural imagery.

Merlin performs the fast-paced march 'Higitus Figitus' as he 'conducts' material objects around the room after casting a spell on them. The number is reprised as an instrumental version later in the film as Merlin helps Wart (young Arthur) clean the kitchen. Dancing broomsticks and the parade of inanimate objects recall the *Sorcerer's Apprentice* sequence from *Fantasia* (1940) in an obvious self-reference to the Disney animated film tradition.

Merlin sings 'That's What Makes the World Go 'Round' and 'A Most Befuddling Thing' as he turns Arthur into a fish and then a squirrel. The intoned vocal style is reminiscent of that of the verse of 'How to Handle a Woman' in *Camelot*, where Arthur recalls how Merlin taught him about life by changing him into various creatures. The songs amplify the verse of 'How to Handle a Woman' through both textual references and the *Sprechstimme* style of Arthur's music in the Lerner and Loewe musical.

'Mad Madam Mim', sung by the character of the same name, is a waltz, evoking the cliched musical depiction of women in triple meter and men in duple meter. (Merlin's songs are all in 2/4.) The lyrical waltz is apt for Mim's whimsical flying scenes.

Sir Kay and his family sing 'Blue Oak Tree,' a short drinking song, in their castle the night before the tournament. It is not much longer than the single-couplet choral fanfare 'Hail King Arthur, Long Live the King' that concludes the film.

[24] Kathy Merlock Jackson, *Walt Disney: A Bio-Bibliography* (Westport, CT, and London: Greenwood, 1993), pp. 63–64.
[25] This was common for the misnamed 'silent films,' where live music was a constant.
[26] Bloom, vol. 2, p. 936. Bloom lists the songs in alphabetical order.

The musical numbers in *The Sword in the Stone* are typical of those in other Disney animated feature films. They are relatively brief, but are related to the plot. Their decidedly accessible musical style is geared toward the intended family audiences who, because of the familiar style of the music, could experience the time and magic of Camelot.

Just as *The Sword in the Stone* reflected the Disney animated genre, *Monty Python and the Holy Grail* demonstrated the aesthetics of its creators. While the treatment of the Arthurian legend according to Monty Python is not the focus here, the film included three musical numbers by Neil Innes that are relevant to this discussion:

Knights of the Round Table
Pie Jesu Domine
Bravely Bold Sir Robin

None of the musical numbers in the film are in the same style – each is a pastiche of a different musical genre, accentuating the film's postmodern juxtaposition of disparate temporal elements.

'Knights of the Round Table' begins as Arthur and his band of knights approach Camelot castle, the visual image a model of Segovia's Alcazar Castle from the *Camelot* film. The number itself, sung inside the castle as a choreographic fantasy, is a fast-paced comic romp for male chorus, complete with can-can and tap dancing. Visual images recall the classic Errol Flynn film *The Adventures of Robin Hood* (1938) in the replication of the staircase and the banquet and sword-fighting scenes, thus conjoining the cinematic images of the castles of Camelot and Nottingham. At the end of the song the knights decide not to visit Camelot, calling it 'a silly place' – perhaps an overt reference to the musical film of the same name.

The two other principal musical numbers, 'Pie Jesu Domine' and 'Bravely Bold Sir Robin,' evoke medieval and Renaissance musical styles. 'Pie Jesu Domine' parodies Gregorian chant and ninth-century parallel polyphony (of the Continental as opposed to the English variety). The number is reprised several times throughout the film. 'Bravely Bold Sir Robin' is a pastiche of a Tudor-era madrigal for solo voice and instrumental ensemble.[27]

It is not recreations of past musical idioms but rather 1990s popular styles that form the basis of the songs in *Quest for Camelot*. Notable performers such as Celine Dion, Steve Perry, Leann Rimes and The Corrs appear on the soundtrack. It is largely through the modern sound world that late twentieth-century references are made in the family-orientated moral tale.

Vera Chapman's book *The King's Damosel* (1985) formed the basis of the Warner Brothers animated feature. The film related the saga of Kasey, Sir

---

[27] While much of the humor of the film overall is derived from its anachronistic juxtapositions, this particular pastiche has deeper roots in historic reality than may be immediately obvious. The Welsh Tudors were great fans of the Arthurian legend, and both Henry VII and Henry VIII made use of the propagandist and patriotic dimensions of the legend, Henry VII even naming his eldest son Arthur (Arthur B. Ferguson, *Utter Antiquity: Perceptions of Prehistory in Renaissance England* (Durham and London: Duke University Press, 1993), p. 86). Furthermore, Henry VIII drew upon the Arthurian legend as justification for his break with the Roman church (Keith Thomas, *Religion and the Decline of Magic* (New York: Charles Scribner's Sons, 1971), p. 416).

Lionel's daughter, who rescues Excalibur after it has been stolen by Lord Ruber and returns it to Camelot with the assistance of the blind hermit Garrett and the two-headed dragon Cornwall and Devon. In addition to the basic storyline, there is a romantic sub-plot between Kasey and Garrett as well as one that concerns Cornwall and Devon overcoming their differences to achieve things thought impossible. Women and people with disabilities are affirmed in the principal characters of Kasey and Garrett, both of whom become Knights of the Round Table at the end of the film.

Carole Bayer Sager and David Foster wrote the film's songs, all of which are in a soft-rock style with the notable exception of 'If I Didn't Have You,' a comic number for Cornwall and Devon. Celtic instruments such as Irish fiddle, bodhrain, Uillean pipes and penny whistle are used in the film's orchestration, giving it a folk-like feel rooted in both the past and the present. Patrick Doyle composed the soundtrack's instrumental numbers. The film's songs, in order of appearance, are as follows:

United We Stand
On My Father's Wings
Ruber
The Prayer
I Stand All Alone
If I Didn't Have You
Looking through Your Eyes
I Stand All Alone (reprise)

Arthurian references are scant in the songs: most textual references are of a more general nature, keeping with the popular nature of the score and its performers. The songs do tell something about the characters who sing them, however, whether it be Kaley's memory of her knightly parent in 'On My Father's Wings,' Ruber's evil intent in the number that bears his name, Julianna's hope and care for her daughter in 'The Prayer,' Garrett's self-reliance in 'I Stand All Alone,' the perils of over-togetherness between Cornwall and Devon in 'If I Didn't Have You,' or Kaley and Garrett's eventual symbiosis in 'Looking through Your Eyes.' Arthurian ideals are celebrated in the film's opening number, 'United We Stand.'

'United We Stand,' an anthem calling for justice in the spirit of 'Do You Hear the People Sing?' from *Les Misérables*, emerges during the opening titles. The Gaelic sound transports the listener to the fantastic domain of King Arthur, emphasizing its Celtic roots through contemporary sounds. The number ends abruptly as Ruber interrupts the knights' recitation of virtues with the sardonic remark 'charming singalong.'

'Ruber' is the villain's song of self-identification. As a musical number for the evil character (Gary Oldman), it is performed in a dramatic intoned style that lies somewhere between speech and song, freely including and oscillating between the two types of vocal production. As with *Camelot*'s Mordred, Ruber's evil character is depicted through musical means. The soliloquy concludes in a primitivistic dance sequence with low-pitched chants as Ruber creates his mechanical army.

In the film, Canadian superstar Celine Dion sings 'The Prayer,' Julianna's supplication for her daughter's safety. A rendition by tenor Andrea Bocelli, in Italian, appears in the end credits. The lyrical melody is of the type associated with both the pop singer and the Italian tenor. As with the numbers that showcased the vocal style of Bing Crosby in *A Connecticut Yankee in King Arthur's Court*, this song accentuates the élan of its performers. In 'If I Didn't Have You,' Cornwall and Devon, the two heads of the conjoined dragon, assert how much better their lives would be without each other. A self-reference to the Arthurian musical genre surfaces in the line 'I'd be the star of *Camelot* . . . if I didn't have you.' The song typifies the classic musical theatre comic duet and recalls numbers such as 'Together' from *Gypsy* (1959) and 'Bosom Buddies' from *Mame* (1966). Disparate visual images appear on-screen, ranging from lava lamps, Gilbert and Sullivan's *The Mikado*, Picasso-esque cubism, Sonny and Cher, to Elvis. Aurally and visually, therefore, this number exhibits the anachronistic-based humour and unexpected juxtapositions common to several of the Arthurian retellings discussed in this essay.[28]

Quest for Camelot includes musical numbers in a 1990s popular vein and is strongly influenced by Celtic styles. The numbers are basically lyrical and lack overt textual references. In *Monty Python and the Holy Grail*, the plot-related musical numbers are comic, taking the basis of their humour from anachronisms. The songs in *The Sword in the Stone*, the earliest of the three films, lie somewhere between the two latter ones. The songs are related to the plot and are in a style typical of Disney animated feature films. The music for the three films are as much products of their creators as attempts to create a particular aural image of Arthurian Britain.

Similarly, the stage musicals *Camelot* and *A Connecticut Yankee* are tell-tale products of their creators. *Camelot* is a musical play in the Rodgers and Hammerstein mold, where songs advance the plot and characters are defined through their musical styles. *A Connecticut Yankee* typifies the musical comedy of the 1920s through its light-hearted score that focuses on individual musical numbers.

Anachronisms, shifting popular music styles, individual creative personalities, performers, and generic conventions: these parameters define much of the musical theatre and musical film in the twentieth century, including Arthurian ones. Creators were not as concerned with providing a faithful rendering of any particular Arthurian text as they were in using the mythical era as a backdrop for their own artistic visions.

---

[28] Other anachronisms appear in the film as well, most notably the mechanical army of Ruber, references to airline travel and the musical quotation of John Williams' 'Superman' theme in the battle sequence near the end of the film.

A Listing of Arthurian Music

JEROME V. REEL

This listing is based on the research by Professor Jerome V. Reel, Jr., of Clemson University, which is posted on the Camelot project at the University of Rochester Professor Reel's full listing can be accessed at
http://www.lib.rochester.edu/camelot/acpbibs/reel.htm
The editor of the present volume is most grateful to him for allowing the use of his material in a shortened and reformatted version.

This list does not include arrangements or excerpts (either by the composer or others) from major works; ballads for which no tune is known; music which is only tangentially Arthurian, such as operas based on *Amadis de Gaule*; and music which contains Arthurian references, but of which the plot is not Arthurian (*L'elisir d'amore*, *Francesca da Rimini*). It is intended to represent only those works which are (as far as can be determined) genuinely based on Arthurian stories or excerpts from them.

Sources of information are given in brackets at the end of the entry; the full bibliographical details are at the end of the list. 'Source' indicates that it is personal information.

Adair, James. *Isolde and the Shortstop*. Librettist: Thomas K. Baker. (Gillis, 23.)
Adam, Leon. 'Deux Aires de Ballet: Liselotte et Lancelot.' 1912. (British Library.)
Adam, Leon. 'Liselotte et Lancelot.' (Piano Duet.) 1911. (British Library.)
Adams, John. *Harmonielehre Symphony*. (Includes movement entitled 'Amfortas' wound'.) Première March 1, 1985, Davies Hall, San Francisco.
Addi, Renée di. *Isolda*. Librettist: Signora Addi. Première: Bellagio, 10 January 1881. (Tower, 342.)
Ager, Laurence. 'King Arthur'. Traditional. Published: London, B. Feldman, 1969.
Aguilar, Emanuel. *The Bridal of Triermain*. Words: Walter Scott (adapted). Published: London, 1884.
Akers, Howard E. *Enid*. Published: Carl Fischer, 1921.
Akhurst, William M. *Arthur the King, or the Knights of the Round Table*. Published: London, T.H. Lacy, 1871.
Akhurst, William M. *King Arthur, or Lancelot the Loose, Gin-Ever the Square etc.* Published: Melbourne, R. Bell, 1868.
Albeniz, Isaac Manuel. *Merlin* (the first of a projected trilogy: *Guinevere* and *Lancelot* were not set to music). Librettist: Francis Money-Coutts. Première: Paris 1906. Published: Paris, Editions Mutuelle, 1906 (text and piano score).
Allwood, Peter. *Pendragon*. Librettist: Allwood; Joanna Horton, Jeremy James Taylor,

and Frank Whatley. Première: Horsham Arts Centre, Horsham, Sussex, 6 April 1994. (Source: Kevin Harty).

Alter, J. *King Arthur's Night Out*. Librettists: S. Perlin and L. Naftalison. (Library of Congress).

Amegarn, Benedictus. *Lancelot*. Words: Benedictus Amegarn. Published: Paris, Editions Meronani, 1975.

Amicone, A. *La Grotta del Mago, Merlin*. Librettist: unknown. Première: Teatro Valle, Rome, 7 January, 1786. (Tower, 427 and 694; Mellen, I, 32, gives première as 1780.)

Amorphis. *Karelian Isthmus*. Includes: 'Grail Mysteries' and 'Sign from the North'. 1995. (Source: Keir Howell.)

Anderson, Angelee Sailer. *Horns of Elfland: An Arthurian Symphony*. (Not finished.) (Source: Keir Howell.)

Andrade, Auguste. 'Viens, Arthur'. Words: Louis de Crevel. (British Library.)

Anonymous. *The Magic Sword*. Librettist: Ken Hill and Alan Klein. Première: Newcastle-upon-Tyne, 10 December 1982. (Ganzl, II, 1103.)

Arlanc, Sylvain. *Tristan et Yseut*. Librettist: Paul Gautier. Published: Rodez, France, Berger, 1943.

Arne, Thomas. *King Arthur* (a revision of Purcell). Librettist: John Dryden. Première: Covent Garden, London, 1771. Published: London, Longman Lukey, 1770.

Arne, Thomas. *Opera of Operas, or Tom Thumb the Great*. Librettist: Henry Fielding (revisions and additions by W. Hatchett and E. Haywood). Première: Little Theatre, London, 31 May 1733. (Library of Congress.)

Arne, Thomas. *The Fairy Prince*. Librettist: George Colman. Première: Covent Garden, London, November 12, 1771.

Arnedo, Luis. *Lorenzín*. Librettist: Salvador María Granés. Published: Madrid, Velasco, 1910.

Arnold, Samuel. *The Cambro-Britons*. Librettist: James Boaden. Première: Theatre Royal, Haymarket, London, 1798. Published: London, G.G. & J. Robinson, 1798 (text).

Arthur, Robert. 'A Chance to Live in Camelot'. Words: Robert Arthur. Published: New York, Chroma Music, 1968.

Asher, Peter. 'The Quest for the Holy Grail'. Published: P & P Music Ltd., n.p.,1968.

Assmus, Karl. *Merlin*. Libretto: Albert von Puttkamer. Première: Stadttheater, Baden-Baden, 11 September 1919. (Stieger, II, 804.)

Astarita, Gennaro. *La Tomba di Merlino*. (Tower 426 and 700.)

Aston, Sue. *Sacred Landscapes: King Arthur's Kingdom* CD, no number given (www.geniusloci.co.uk)

Audran, Edmond. *Monsieur Lohengrin*. Librettist: Fabrice Carre. Première: Bouffes-Parisiens, Paris, 30 November 1896. Published: Paris, Choudens, 1896.

Auric, Georges. *L'Eternel Retour* . Film score. Book by Jean Cocteau, based on story of Tristan and Isolt. 1943.

Auton, John (arranger). *Folk Songs for Strings*. Published: London, Oxford University Press, 1985.

Avalon. *Second Sight*. Includes 'Tintagel'. 1998. (Source: Keir Howell.)

Averkamp, Anton. 'Elaine and Lancelot' (Symphonische Ballade). (Library of Congress.)

Ayreon. *Final Experiment*. Includes: 'Prologue'; 'Drawing'; 'King Arthur's Court'; 'Visual Echoes'; 'Merlin's Will and Ayreon's Fate'. 1995. (Source: Keir Howell.)

Bacewicz, Grazyna. *Przygoda Krola Arthura*. Librettist: Edward Fiszer. Première: 9 December 1959, over Polish Radio.

Bacharach, Burt. 'Arthur's Theme'. Words: Sager, Cross & Allen. Published: Warner Brothers.

Bad News. *Bad News*. [includes 'Excalibur'] Published: Santa Monica, CA, Rampage Records, 1989. (Source: Keir Howell.)

Baez, Joan. 'Sweet Sir Galahad'. Published: New York, Robbins, 1970.

Bainton, Edgar Leslie. 'Merlin's Apple Trees'. Words: Thomas Love Peacock. Published: London, Oxford University Press, 1934.

Baker, A.C. 'Sir Galahad: My Good Blade Carves the Casques of Men'. Words: Alfred, Lord Tennyson. Published: London, 1875.

Baldwin, Ralph. 'Song of Arthur's Knights'. Words: Abbie Farwell Brown. Published: Boston, MA, Ginn, 1927.

Balfe, Michael. *Fortune and Her Wheel*. Words: Alfred, Lord Tennyson. Published: London, Boosey and Hawkes, 1865.

Balfe, Michael. *Song of Love and Death*. Words: Alfred, Lord Tennyson. Published: London, Boosey and Hawkes, 1860.

Ballentine, Edward. 'Queen Iseult'.

Bantock, Granville. 'Morgan le Fey'. Words: S. Kaye-Smith. Published: London, J.B. Cramer, 1927.

Barbiere, V.U. *Lohengrin*. Librettist: unknown. Première: Naples, 1881. (Tower, 705, and Mellen, I, 120.)

Barkworth, Arthur. 'Vivien's Song'. Words: Alfred, Lord Tennyson. Published: Liverpool.

Barnett, John. *Love and Death*. Words: Alfred, Lord Tennyson. Published: London, Leader and Cock, 1859.

Barnett, John. *The Song of Fortune*. Words: Alfred, Lord Tennyson. Published: London, Leader and Cock, 1859.

Barnett, John. *Too Late*. Words: Alfred, Lord Tennyson. Published: London, Leader and Cock, 1859.

Bax, Arnold. *Picnic at Tintagel* (Ballet). Choreographer: Frederick Ashton. Première: New York City Center, New York, 28 February 1952. [from *Garden of Fand*]

Bax, Arnold. *Tintagel* (Symphonic Poem). Première: London 1919. Published: London, Murdoch, Murdoch & Co., 1923.

Beauchamp, B. *Song of Love and Death*. Words: Alfred, Lord Tennyson. Published: Brighton, JWC, 1879.

Becerra Schmidt, Gustavo. *Parsifae*. Librettist: T. Barrios. (Mellen, I, 140).

Becker, John Joseph. *The Queen of Cornwall*. Text: Thomas Hardy. (Slonimsky, *Twentieth Century*.)

Becker, Konrad. *Parzifal*. Librettist: Konrad Becker. Première: Vienna, 1984. (Lacy, *New Arthurian Encyclopedia*, 33.)

Bedford, David. 'Ronde for Isolde'. Published: London, Novello, 1988.

Bedford, David. *Toccata for Tristan*. 1989.

Béjart, Maurice. *Les Vainquerers* (Ballet). Composed: 1959. (Lacy and Ashe, 273.)

Bemberg, Herman. *Elaine*. Librettist: Paul Ferrier. Première: Covent Garden, London, 5 July 1892. Published: Paris, Huegel, 1892.

Bendall, W.E. *The Lady of Shalott*. Words: W.G. McNaught. Première: London, 1891. (Stieger, III, 693.)

Benedictus, Louis. *Mystère du Graal*. Librettist: Josephin Péladan. Composed 1893.

Bennet, Charles. *The Lady of Shalott*. Words: Alfred, Lord Tennyson. Published: Boston, MA, O. Ditson, 1925.

Bennett, F.J.W. *King Arthur*. Librettist: unknown. Première: Cadbury, England 1884. (Stieger, II, 672.)

Bergeron, Sylvain. *Perceval: La Quête du Graal*. Text: Chrétien de Troyes. Published: Troy, NY, Dorian, 1999.

Berghout, Johann. 'Tristan and Isolde' (Fantasia for Violin and Pianoforte. Opus 41). 1907. (British Library.)

Bergsma, William. 'Fantastic variations on a theme from *Tristan*.' Published: New York, Galaxy Music, 1963.

Berner, Frederick Wilhelm. *Der Zaubermantel*. Librettist: Carl Franz Van der Velde. Published: Dresden, Arnoldische Buchhandlung, 1827 (libretto).

Bernstein, Elmer. *Merlin*. Librettist: Don Black. Première: Mark Hellinger Theater, New York, 13 February 1983. Published: New York, Hal Leonard Corp., 1983.

Bertail, Inez. 'King Arthur'. Words: Traditional. Published: New York, Lothrop, Lee and Sheperd, 1947.

Bertoni, Ferdinando. *Ginevra*. Librettist: A. Salvi. Première: Teatro di San Samuele, Venice, 1753.

Bichel, Earl. 'Good King Arthur'. Words: Traditional. Published: Chicago, Follett, 1969.

Birch, Edward Henry. 'Sing Ye the Land'. (Chorus) 1910. (British Library.)

Birtwistle, Harrison. *Gawain*. Librettist: David Harsent. Première: Royal Opera House, Covent Garden, London, 30 May 1991. Published: London, Universal Editions, 1991.

Blacher, B. *Tristan* (Ballet). Book: Tatjana Gsovsky. Première: Berlin, October 10, 1965. Published: Berlin, Bote und Bock.

Blackford, Richard. *Gawain and Ragnall*. Librettist: Ian Barnett. Première: Cannon Hill Arts Centre, Birmingham, 4 April 1984.

Blackford, Richard. *Sir Gawain and the Green Knight*. Librettist: John Emlyn Edwards. Première: Blewbury, Oxford, 1978. Published: New York, Oxford University Press, 1982.

Blackmore, Richie. *Under a Violet Moon*. Includes 'Avalon' 1999. (Source: Keir Howell.)

Blackwood, Helen S. 'Selection of Songs'. Première: 1895. Published: London, John Murray, 1895. [In the series: *The Galway Resource for Anglo-Irish Literature*, Book 5.]

Blewitt, Jonathan. *Harlequin and Mother Red-Cap; or Merlin and Fairy Snowdrop*. Librettist: Richard Nelson Lee. Première: Adelphi Theatre, London, 1839.

Blind Guardian. *Imaginations from the Other Side*. Includes: 'Imaginations from the Other Side'; 'A Past and Future Secret'; 'Mordred's Song'; 'Bright Eyes'. 1995. (Source: Keir Howell.)

Bliss, Arthur. *The Lady of Shalott* (Ballet). Scenario by Bliss and Christopher Hassell. Première: University of California, Berkeley, CA, May 2 1958. (Lacy and Ashe, 273.)

Blockley, John. 'Fortune and Her Wheel'. Words: Alfred, Lord Tennyson. 1892.

Blockley, John. 'Late, Late, so Late'. Words: Alfred, Lord Tennyson. 1892.

Blockley, John. 'Sweet is True Love'. Words: Alfred, Lord Tennyson. 1879.

Blumenroder, Karl. *Die Kurze Mantel*. Librettist: unknown. Première: Theatre an der Wien, Vienna, 6 November 1824.

Blumenthal, Jacob. 'Elaine: Funeral March'. Published: San Francisco, CA, Sherman and Hyde, 1875.

Blumenthal, Jacob. 'Sweet is True Love'. Words: Alfred, Lord Tennyson. Published: London, Boosey and Hawkes, 1880.

Borano, Daniel. *Lancelot du Lac*. Première: 1977. (British Library.)

Borcese, Luigi. *Le Pecheur Roi*. Librettist: unknown. (Stieger, III, 933.)

Borders, William. 'Elaine' (Elegy for Violin and Pianoforte). Published: London, Opus Music, 1913.

Bornschein, Franz. *The Vision of Sir Launfal* (Cantata). Words: J.R. Lowell. Published: New York, J. Fischer, 1927.

Bosio, Aldo. *Parsifal*. Librettist: Giovanni Sala. Première: Teatro dell'Espozione, Genoa, 15 August 1914. (Stieger, III, 922; Mellen, I, 230.)

Boughton, Rutland. 'Avalon'. (in *Hour of Beauty*). Words: 'Fiona McLeod' [i.e. William Sharp]. Published: London, Stainer and Bell, 1924.

Boughton, Rutland. 'Chapel of Lyonness' (Song for Three Voices). Words: William Morris. 1905.

Boughton, Rutland. 'Isolt'. Words: Antonia Bevan Williams. 1935.

Boughton, Rutland. 'King Arthur Had Three Sons'. Traditional. Published: London, William Reeves, 1907. [from *Barkshire Tragedy*]

Boughton, Rutland. 'Mystic Dance of the Grail'. Words: Margaret Morris. 1913. Lost.

Boughton, Rutland. 'Sir Galahad' (March). Words: Alfred, Lord Tennyson. Published in *Choral Handbook*, London, J. Curwen, 1910.

Boughton, Rutland. *Avalon*. Librettist: Rutland Boughton. Never performed. (British Library) 1945.

Boughton, Rutland. *Birth of Arthur* (originally *Uther and Igraine*). Librettist: Reginald Buckley. Première: Assembly Hall, Glastonbury, 16 August 1920. (British Library.)

Boughton, Rutland. *Galahad*. Librettist: Rutland Boughton. Never performed. (British Library.) 1934.

Boughton, Rutland. *The Lily Maid*. Librettist: Rutland Boughton. Première: Church Room, Stroud, England, 10 September 1934. (British Library).

Boughton, Rutland. *The Queen of Cornwall*. Librettist: Thomas Hardy. Concert première: Assembly Hall, Glastonbury, 21 August 1924. Published: London, Joseph Williams, 1926.

Boughton, Rutland. *The Round Table*. Librettist: Reginald Buckley. Première: Assembly Hall, Glastonbury, 14 August 1916. (British Library.)

Bourgault-Ducoudray, L.A. *Myrdhin*. Librettist: Simone Arnaud. Première: Grande Théâtre, Nantes, 28 April 1912. Published: Paris, Delanchy et Fils, 1919.

Bradley, Marion Zimmer. Avalon Rising. *The Starlit Jewel*. Words: J.R.R. Tolkien. Published: Flowinglass Music. (Source: Keir Howell.)

Brauer, M. *Morgiane*. Librettist: Lemey. Première: Hoftheater, Karlsruhe, 11 April 1899.

Brenner, Walter. 'Vivien's Song'. (Library of Congress (missing).)

Bridgewater, Ernest Leslie. 'Legend of Lancelot' from *Train of Events*. Ealing Studios Production, 1949.

Britten, Benjamin (arr. Paul Hindmarsh). *King Arthur Suite for Orchestra: 1937*. Première: Aldeburgh Festival, 21 October 1995. Published: London, Oxford University Press, 1996.

Britten, Benjamin. *The Sword in the Stone*. Text: adapted from T.H. White. Première: 1939 British Broadcasting Corporation radio play. 'Suite from *Sword in the Stone*'. Concert première: Aldeburgh Festival, 14 June 1983.

Broadwood, L.E. & Maitland, 'King Arthur'. Traditional. Published: in *English Country Songs*, London, Leadenhall Press, 1893.

Brown, N.H. 'Avalon Town'. 1928. (British Library.)

Browne, John Lewis. 'Elaine, the Troubador's Song'. Words: R.E. Dormer. Published: Philadelphia, PA, Presser, 1908.

Budgen, L. 'Good King Arthur'. Traditional. Published: in *Songs for Children*, London, Joseph Williams, 1906.

Buechner, Emil. *Lanzelot vom See*. Librettist: Adolf Bottger. (Tower 371 and 718; Mellen, I, 263.)

Bullard, Frederic Field. 'King Arthur: A Hunting Song'. Words: R. Hovey. Published: Boston, MA, O. Ditson, Co., 1900.

Bullard, Frederic Field. 'Oh, Who Would Stay Indoor, Indoor'. Words: R. Hovey. Published: Boston, MA, O. Ditson, 1907.

Bullard, Frederick Field. *King Arthur*. Librettist: Richard Hovey. Première: 1900. Published: Boston, MA, O. Ditson.

Bunning, Herbert. *Sir Lancelot and Queen Guinevere*. Words: Alfred, Lord Tennyson. Published: London, Enoch and Sons, 1906.

Burghauser, J. 'Tristam a Izalda'. (Ballet). (Slonimsky, *Twentieth Century*.)

Burnassi, Ugo. *La Grotta di Merlino*. Librettist: Ugo Burnassi. Première: Teatro Mariani, Ravenna, April 1889. (Mellen, I, 269.)

Burt, Francis. 'Morgana'. Published: Vienna, Universal, 1985.

Busch, Carl. 'Prolog zu Tennyson's "The Passing of King Arthur" '. Words: Alfred, Lord Tennyson. Published: Leipzig, Boosey and Hawkes, 1899.

Busch, Carl. 'Sir Galahad'. Library of Congress. Words: Alfred, Lord Tennyson. Published: Boston, MA, O. Ditson, 1921.

Bush, Geoffrey. 'Legends: Joseph of Arimathea'. Words: Charles Causley. 1985. (British Library.)

Byron, Henry James. *Jack the Giant Killer, or, Harlequin King Arthur*. Librettist: Henry James Byron. Published: London, T. Lacy, 1859.

Cadman, Charles W. *The Vision of Sir Launfal* (Cantata). Words: J.R. Lowell. Published: New York, G. Schirmer, 1910.

Caldesoni, ——. *Merlino de Patone*. Librettist unknown. Première: Rovereto, 6 October 1875. (Clement and Larousse; Mellen, I, 289.)

Callcott, John Wall. *When Arthur First at Court Began; or Sir Lancelot Du Lake*. Words: traditional. Première: Covent Garden, London, 2 May 1800. Published: London, Novello, 1847.

Canthal, August M. *Morgana*. Librettist unknown. Première: Stadttheater, Hamburg, 1869. (Stieger II, 829; Mellen, I, 300.)

Capel, J.M. 'Song of Love and Death'. Words: Alfred, Lord Tennyson. Published: London, Ascherberg, 1902.

Carpenter, S. 'Avalon is Calling'. Words: C. Boyle. 1907. (British Library.)

Carr, Lily. 'Excalibur' (Waltz). 1892. (British Library.) Published: London, R. Cocke, 1892.

Casirola, ——. *Les Trucs d'Arthur*. Librettist: Dalvelle. Première: 1899. (Stieger III, 1237.)

Catelinet, Philip Bramwell. 'The Isle of Avalon' (Suite for Brass Band). 1978. (British Library.)

Caudel, Stephen. *The Earth in Turquoise*. Words: Caudel.

Chabrier, Alexis Emmanuel. 'Souvenirs de Munich'. (Fantasie en Forme De Quadrille sur les Thèmes Favorites de *Tristan et Isolde* de Richard Wagner, Piano à 4 Mains.) 1930. (British Library.)

Chamberlain, Philip Bramwell. 'The Isle of Avalon' (Suite for Brass Band). 1978. (British Library.)

Chaminade, Cécile. 'A Piano Study of Enid'. Published: New York, G. Schirmer, 1899.

Champein, Stanislaus. *Lanval et Viviane, ou les fées et les chevaliers*. Libretto: André Murville. Première: Théâtre Français, Paris, 13 September 1788. Excerpts published: Paris, Imbault, 1788.

Chapí y Torento, Ruperto. *El Cisne de Lohengrin*. Librettist: Miguel Echegaray. Première: Teatro Apolo, Madrid, 16 February 1905. Published: Madrid, R. Velasco, 1905.

Chausson, Ernest. *Le Roi Arthus*. Librettist: Ernest Chausson. Première: Théâtre de la Monnaie, Brussels, 30 November 1903. Published: Paris, Choudens, 1900.

Chausson, Ernest. *Viviane* (Poem symphonique pour orchestre). 1882.

Chauvet, J.J.V. *Arthus de Bretagne*. Librettist: Etienne Aignan. (*Archives de l'Opéra*.)

Cherney, J. 'The Bells of Avalon'. 1927. (British Library.)

Cheve, Emile. *Merlin*. (Ballet) Book: L. Bonnemere. Première: Brussels, 11 February 1894. (Stieger, II, 804.)

Christou, Jani. 'Death by Water' in *Six Songs for Mezzo-Soprano and Orchestra*. Words: T.S. Eliot. Published: Wiesbaden, Impero Verlag, 1957.

Clark, June. 'King Arthur and the Knights of the Round Table' (Piano Suite). Published: London, Ascherberg, 1963.

Clendon, Hugh. *Little Lohengrin; or The Lover and the Bird*. Librettist: Frederick Bowyer. Première: Plymouth, 2 March 1881.

Close, Alan Parker. *The Bridal of Triermain*. Librettist: John Joscelyn Coghill. Published: London, G. Drought, 1862.

Clutsam, George H. *The Lady of Shalott*. (symphonic idyll).

Coerne, Louis Adolphe. 'Excalibur: Symphonic Poem'. Opus 180. Published: Boston, MA: O. Ditson, 1931.

Cohen, Joel. *Tristan and Iseult*. Text from poems in the prose romance *Tristan* in Österreichisches Nationalbibliothek, Vienna, MS 2542. The score is Cohen's arrangement and realization of the music in the manuscript.

Collins, J. *Harlequin and Good King Arthur; or the Enchanter Merlin and the Queen of Fairyland*. Librettist: Greenwood. Première: Sadler's Wells, London, 26 December 1842.

Cook, Ernest. 'Sweet is True Love'. Words: Alfred, Lord Tennyson. 1892.

Cooke, Thomas Simpson. *King Arthur and the Knights of the Round Table*. Librettist: Isaac Pocock. Première: Drury Lane, London, 26 December 1834. (San Marino, California: Huntington Library.)

Coombes, Douglas. *Choral Symphony No. 1. Merlin, Magician of the Universe*. Words: John Emlyn Edwards. Première: Warwick University, 1985.

Coombes, Douglas. *Choral Symphony No. 2. Merlin the Starmaker*. Words: John Emlyn Edwards. 1988.

Coombes, Douglas. *Scatterflock and the Glastonbury Thorn*. Librettist: John Emlyn Edwards. Première: St. Albans, 11 December 1980. Published: Lindsay Music.

Corder, Frederick. 'O Sun, that Wakenest'. Words: Alfred, Lord Tennyson. Published: London, SLW, 1880.

Corder, Frederick. *The Bridal of Triermain* (Cantata). Words: Scott, Sir Walter. Published: London, 1886.

Corder, Frederick. *Morte d'Arthur*. Librettist: Frederick Corder. Première: London, 1877. (Slonimsky, 359.)

Courvoisier, Walter. *Lanzelot und Elaine*. Librettist: Walter Bergh. Première: Hof- und National Theater, Munich, 3 November 1917. Published: Munich: Masken Verlag, 1916.

Coward, Henry. *Gareth and Linet* (Cantata). Words: Frank Kirk. Published: London, Novello, 1902.

Cowles, Colin. 'The Legends of Avalon'. Published: London, Ricordi, 1995.

Cradle of Filth. *Dusk and Her Embrace*. New York, Fierce Recordings, 1997. (Source: Keir Howell.)

Cramer, Henry. 'Phantasiesück über Motive aus *Tristan und Isolde*'. 1876. (British Library.)

Crawley, Christopher. *Sir Gawain Carols*. Words: John Weeks. Published: Oxford: Oxford University Press, 1973.

Crook, John. *Lancelot the Lovely*. Librettist: Richard Henry. Première: Avenue Theatre, London, 22 April 1889. Excerpts published: London, C. Jefferys, 1892.

Crosby, David. 'Guinevere'. Recording: *Crosby, Stills, and Nash*. 1969. (Source: Keir Howell.)

Crosse, Gordon. *Potter Thompson*. Librettist: Alan Gardner. Première: 1975. Published: London, Oxford University Press, 1985.

Curtis-Smith, Curtis. *Tristana Variation*. (Slonimsky, *Twentieth Century*).

Cusins, William G. 'The Song of King Arthur's Knights'. Words: Alfred, Lord Tennyson. Published: London, SLW, 1880.

Dalayrac, Nicolas. *Urgande et Merlin*. Librettist: Monvel. Première: Théâtre Feydeau, Paris, 14 October 1793. (Clement et Larousse, 686.)

Dana, William H. *Elaine's Waltz*. 1875.

Dana, William H. *Lancelot's March*. Published: Warren, OH, Dana's.

Danner, Wilfred Maria. *Merlin in Soho*. Première: Berlin. (Source: Alan and Barbara Tepa Lupack.)

Darcy, Thomas F., Jr. 'King Arthur' (A March). Published: New York, Bourne, Inc., 1949.

Davies, Hugh. *Arthur* (Cantata). Librettist: W.G. Williams. Première: 1890. Published: Yr Awdwr: Rhosymedre, 1890.

Davies, Peter Maxwell. *Journey to Avalon* (Ballet). Choreography Barry Moreland.

Davis, J.D. 'The Maid of Astolat'. Words: Alfred, Lord Tennyson. Published: London, Novello, 1910.

Deacon, H.C. 'Too Late'. Words: Alfred, Lord Tennyson. 1864.

Debussy, Claude. *L'Histoire de Tristan*. Proposed librettist: Gabriel Mourey. Only one twelve bar theme was sketched. It was to be based on Joseph Bédier's work.

Delerue, George. *Le Chevalier de Neige*. Librettist: Boris Vian. Première: Nancy, 1957. Published: Paris, Union Générale d'Editions, 1974.

Deliverance. *Camelot in Smithereens*. (Source: Keir Howell.)

Dempster, William R. 'Late, Late, So Late'. Words: Alfred, Lord Tennyson. Published: New York, Wm. A. Pond and Co., 1864.

Dempster, William R. 'The Song of Love and Death'. Words: Alfred, Lord Tennyson, 1868. Published: London, Composer, 1868.

Dempster, William R. 'Turn Fortune, Turn'. Words: Alfred, Lord Tennyson. Published: London, Composer, 1864.

Dessau, Paul. *Lanzelot und Sanderein*. Librettist unknown. Première: Hamburg, 1918. Published: Frankfurt, Insel-Verlag, 1962. (Slonimsky, 424–425.)

Dessau, Paul. *Lanzelot*. Librettist: Herman Muller. Première: Staatsoper, Berlin, 19 December 1969. Published: Berlin, Henschelverlag Kunst und Gesellschaft, 1970.

Dibdin, Charles. *Jack the Giant Killer*. Published: London, 1803.

Dibdin, Charles. *The Institution of the Garter; or Arthur's Roundtable Restored*. Librettist: David Garrick. Première: Drury Lane, London, 1771.

Dibdin, Charles. *Tom Thumb*. Librettist unknown. Première: London, 1782.

Dibdin, C.I.M. *Wizard's Wake; or Harlequin and Merlin*. Première: Sadler's Wells, London, 23 August 1802. Published: London, Glendinning, 1803.

Dibdin, Thomas J. *Merlin's Mount; or Harlequin Cymraeg and the Living Leek*. Première: Sadler's Wells, London, 26 December 1825.

Dinn, Freda. 'Sir Eglamore'. Published: London, Schott and Son, 1956.

Dobbs, J.P.B. 'King Arthur's Servants'. Words: W.G. Whittaker. Published: London, J. Curwen. 1953.

Dodgson, Stephen. 'Merlin' (arranged for guitar by Philip Thorne). Published: Celle, Moeck Verlag, 1988.

'Dolores', [Elizabeth Dickson] 'Turn Fortune, Turn'. Words: Alfred, Lord Tennyson. Published: London, Jeffreys, 1861.

Donostia, Jose. 'La Quête Heroique du Graal'. (Slonimsky, *Twentieth Century.*)

Donati, Pino. *Lancilotto del Lago.* Librettist: Arturo Rossato. Première: Bergamo, 2 October 1938. Published: Milan, Sonzogno, 1943.

Donovan. 'Guinevere' in *Sunshine Superman.* Peer Records, 1967. (Source: Keir Howell.)

Doss, Adolphe. *Percival.* Librettist: L. Bailly. Première: Liège, 8 March 1908. Published: Liège, Belgium: Muraille, n.d.

Douglas, Sallie Hume (Composer). 'Follow the Gleam'. Words: Helen Hill Miller. Published: Philadelphia, Westminster Press, 1920.

Draeseke, Felix. *Merlin.* Librettist: Felix Draeseke after Carl Immermann. Première: Gotha, 1913. Published: Dresden, by the composer, n.d.

Dunstan, Ralph. 'Merlin the Diviner' for soprano solo. Première: Royal Institute of Cornwall, Truro, 1924. (Lacy, *New Arthurian Encyclopedia*, 338.)

Eastman, Donna Kelly. 'Sir Gawain and the Green Knight'. Published: Ann Arbor, MI, University Microforms, 1992.

Edmunds, Christopher. 'The Lady of Shalott'. Words: Alfred, Lord Tennyson. Published: London, Stainer and Bell, 1926.

Edwards, Edwin. 'Late, Late, So Late'. Words: Alfred, Lord Tennyson. Published: London. Novello, 1870.

Edwards, Edwin. 'Sweet is True Love'. Words: Alfred, Lord Tennyson. 1892.

Edwards, Michael (arr.). 'Dream of Olwen'. Published: London, Lawrence Wright, 1949.

Edwards, Sherman. 'A Whistlin' Tune'. 1962. [from *Kid Galahad*]. (British Library.)

Edwards, Sherman. 'Home is Where the Heart Is'. 1962. [from *Kid Galahad*]. (British Library.)

Ehler, Ursula. *Merlin oder das wüste Land.* Librettist: Tankred Dorst. Première: 1984. Published: Frankfurt am Main, Suhrkamp, 1984.

Eitner, Robert. 'Phantaisie über Motive aus Tristan und Isolde von R. Wagner' (Pianoforte). 1862.

Elend. (name of group). *Les Ténèbres du Dehors.* 1966. (Source: Keir Howell.)

Elgar, Edward. *Arthur.* Incidental music to play by Laurence Binyon. Première: Old Vic, London, 3 December 1923. Text published: London, W. Heinemann, 1923. Arranged as suite 'King Arthur'.

Ellerton, John Lodge. *Bridal of Triermain.* Librettist unknown. Never performed or published. (Boston, MA, Boston Public Library.)

Ellis, Vivian. 'I Don't Know How'. Words: Desmond Carter. 1929. (British Library.)

Enid. *Enid.* 1997. 5 parts: Satan und Candida; An Myrrdhin; Broseliawnd; Enid; Nahe Avalon. (Source: Keir Howell.)

Erb, M.J. *Der Zaubermantel.* Librettist: A. Beres. Première: Strasbourg, 1902. (Stieger, III, 1330.)

Erwin, Gail. 'Arthur the Orphan King'. Words: Kate Schrader. Published: Melville, New York, Pro Art, 1992.

Esipoff, S. 'Tristan und Isolde'. (Fantasia for Piano). 1904. (British Library.)

Evans, David. 'The Coming of Arthur'. Words: Robert Bryan. Published: Oxford University Press, 1932.

Evans, David. 'The Bells of Cantrer Gwaelod'. Published: Oxford University Press, 1932.

Evans, George T. 'Lancelot's Lament for Elaine'. Words: 'Caxton'. Published: San Francisco, S. Eaton, 1875.

Evans, T. 'Wandering on to Avalon'. (British Library.)

Eversole, Rose Mansfield. 'Lynette'. Words: Anna Swan Reynolds. Published: W.H. Willis Co., 1904.

Ewing, A. 'Song of Love and Death'. Words: Alfred, Lord Tennyson. Published: London, Boosey and Hawkes, 1872.

Excalibur 2000. *Excalibur 2000*. (Source: Keir Howell.)

Facchinetti, C. *Parsifal*. Words: V. Negrini. Published: Canzoni Moderne, 1973.

Farigoul, Joseph. 'Broceliande'. Published: Paris, 1899.

Fates Warning. *Awaken the Guardian*. El Segundo, CA, Enigma, 1986. (Source: Keir Howell.)

Favara, A. Two Lyrics by Tennyson (Lancelot). Words: Alfred, Lord Tennyson. Published: New York, G. Schirmer, 1919.

Felciano, Richard. *Sir Gawain and the Green Knight*. Librettist: Robert Fahrner. Première: Lone Mountain College, San Francisco, CA, 4 April 1964. (Northouse, 102 and Mellen, II, 570.)

Ferguson, Douglas. 'Elaine'. 1940. (British Library.)

Fervant, Thierry. 'Legends of Avalon'. Sausalito, CA, Real Music, 1988.

Fielitz, Alexander von. 'The Lily Maid'. Words: Gertrude Rogers. Published: Cincinnati, OH, John Church Co., 1906.

Fišer, Luboš. *Lancelot*. Librettist: E. Bezdekova. Première: Prague, 19 May 1961. (Slonimsky, 546.)

Fletcher, Percy. 'Song of the Apple Trees'. Words: 'Fiona McLeod' [William Sharp]. Published: London, Novella, 1924.

Foerster, Adolph Martin. 'Tristram and Iseult' (Song). Published: Boston, MA, O. Ditson, 1904.

Foote, Arthur. 'Elaine's Song'. Words: Alfred, Lord Tennyson. Published: Boston, MA, Arthur P. Schmidt, 1890.

Forbush, William Byron. 'Songs of the Knights of King Arthur'. Words: W.B. Forbush. Published: Detroit, MI, 1911.

Foster, Dave (arr.). 'Dream of Olwen'. Published: London, Lawrence Wright, 1947. [from Charles Williams: 'Dream of Olwen'].

Fothergill, Helen. 'Sweet is True Love'. Words: Alfred, Lord Tennyson. Published: New York, A. 1920.

Fricker, Peter Racine. *Morte d' Arthur*. Première: 1952, British Broadcasting Corporation, radio play.

Fricker, Peter Racine. *The Quest for the Holy Grail*. Première: n.d., British Broadcasting Corporation, radio play.

Fromings, Kevin and Duboski. *Shadows: The Life of Joseph of Arimathea*. Librettist: Kevin Fromings. Première: 1992. (British Library.)

Gallatly, James M. 'Guinevere' (Waltz for Pianoforte). Published: London, Francis, Day, and Hunter, 1913.

Galliard, John. *Merlin, or the Devil of Stonehenge*. Librettist: Lewis Theobald. Première: Drury Lane Theatre, London, 12 December 1734. Songs published: London, Watts, 1734.

Gambogi, Elvira. 'Coronation Song'. Words: Alfred, Lord Tennyson. Published: London, 1902.

Gardiner, Henry Balfour. 'Sir Eglamore'. Published: London, Novello, 1924.

Gaul, Alfred R. 'Too Late'. Words: Alfred, Lord Tennyson. Published: London, Novello, 1890.

Gazzaniga, Giuseppe. *La Tomba di Merlino*. Librettist: Giovanni Bertati. Première: Teatro di S. Moise, Venice, c. 1772. (Tower, 426 and 476.)

Gersheim, Friedrick. 'Der Zaubermantel'. Words: Felix Dahn. Published: Ries and Erler, 1889.

Gibbs, Cecil Armstrong. 'King Arthur' (in *Suite of Songs from the British Isles*). Published: London, Oxford University Press, 1960.

Gibbs, Cecil Armstrong. *The Lady of Shalott*. Words: Alfred, Lord Tennyson. Published London, J. Curwen, 1916.

Giffard, William. *Merlin, or the British Enchanter*. Librettist. Dryden's text was the base for Giffard's work. Most of Purcell's music was kept. Première: Lincoln's Inn Fields, London, 28 September 1736. (Avery, pt 3, II, 601; three other dates are given for the première: December 1735 (Fiske, p. 144); 1736 at Goodman's Field Theatre (Nicoll, II, 332); Edinburgh, 6 December 1750 (Stieger II, 804).) Published: London, 1736, with a note of a production at Goodman's Field Theatre.

Gilbert, Ernest Thomas. 'Guinevere' (Idylle musicale pour Piano). Published: London, n.p., 1860.

Gillette, James R. *Joseph of Arimathea*. (Easter Cantata for Choir and Narrator). Published: 1963.

Gillier, J.Cl. *Les Eaux de Merlin*. Librettist: LeSage. Première: Foire St. Laurent, Paris, 25 July 1715. (Stieger, I, 368.)

Glover, Stephen. 'The Song of Love and Death'. Words: Alfred, Lord Tennyson, 1892.

Gluck, Christoph W. *L'Isle de Merlin, ou le Monde Renversé*. Librettist: L. Anseaume. Première Schönbrunn Palace, Vienna, 3 October 1758. (New York, New York Public Library: Library of Performing Arts.)

Goldblatt, Maurice. 'Elaine' (Melody for Violin and Piano). Published: Boston, A.P. Schmitt, 1914.

Goldmark, Karl. *Merlin*. Librettist: Siegfried von Lipiner after Carl Immermann. Première: Vienna, 19 November 1886. Published: Leipzig, J. Schuberth, 1886.

Goodall, Medwyn. *Druid*. (Source: Keir Howell.)

Goodall, Medwyn. *Excalibur*. (Source: Keir Howell.)

Goodall, Medwyn. *Gift of Excalibur*. (Source: Keir Howell.)

Goodall, Medwyn. *Merlin*. (Source: Keir Howell.)

Grady, Don and Ted King. *EFX*. Words: Christopher, Crawford and Vilanch. Première: MGM Grand, Las Vegas, NE, 22 March 1995.

Grainger, Percy Alexander. 'Sir Eglamore'. Published: London, Vincent, 1904.

Gram, Peder. 'Avalon'. Words: Erik Stokkebye. Published: Copenhagen, Borups, 1928.

Grave Digger. *Excalibur*. 1999. (Source: Keir Howell.)

Graves, B 'King Arthur's Knights'. Words: B. James. Published: Bluebonnet Publications, No. 60, no date.

Gray, Louisa. 'Lynette's Song: O Sun that Wakenest All'. Words: Alfred, Lord Tennyson. 1873. (British Library.)

Griffiths, George Richard. 'Avalon Quadrille'. Published: London, 1860.

Guenther O. *Der Herr von Lohengrin*. (Tower, 315.)

Guest, J. 'Too Late'. Words: Alfred, Lord Tennyson. Published: London, Composer, 1876.

Gullin, Lars. 'Merlin'. Published: Stockholm: Ehrling and Lov, 1959.

Gullin, Lars. 'The Holy Grail of Joy and Jazz'. Première: Styrie, 1985.

Hadley, Henry. *Merlin and Vivian*. Librettist: Ethel Watts Mumford. Première: New York City, 1907. Published: New York, Schirmer, 1907.

Hale, Glyn. 'Arthur, King of the Celts'. Words: Glyn Hale. Published: Nightingale Music, 1990.

Haley, Bill. *Twistin' Knights of the Round Table*. 1962. (Source: Keir Howell.)

Hamilton, Iain Ellis. *Lancelot*. Librettist: Iain Ellis Hamilton. Première: Arundel Festival, Sussex, 24 August 1985. Published: London, Theodore Presser Co.

Harrison, Julius A.G. *Near Avalon*. Published: London, J. Williams.

Hay, Walter C. 'Sweet is True Love'. Words: Alfred, Lord Tennyson. 1861.

Heap, Charles S. *The Maid of Astolat* (Cantata). Words: Desmond L. Ryan. (British Library.) Premiere: Wolverhampton, 16 September, 1886.

Heber, Reginald. *The Masque of Gwendolyn*. Librettist: Reginald Heber. Published in part in Amelia Heber's *The Life of Reginald Heber*. London, Murray, 1830.

Heine, Carl. 'Lynette's Song: Oh! Morning Star'. Words: Alfred, Lord Tennyson. 1874. (British Library.)

Hemel, Oscar Van. *Viviane*.

Henry, John. 'Marchogion Arthur'. Words: Bryfdir. English words 'Arthur's Knights' by T. Gwynn Jones. (Lacy, *New Arthurian Encyclopedia*, 338.)

Hentschel, Theodore. *Lancelot*. Librettist: M. Franz Bittong. Première: Bremen, 31 October 1878. Published: Bremen, Cranz, 1878.

Henze, Hans Werner. 'Tristan' (Prelude für klavier, tonbänder, and orchester). Published: Munich, n.p., 1976.

Herbert, Victor. *The Magic Knight*. Librettist: Edgar Smith. Published: New York, Charles K. Harris, 1907.

Herman, Reinhold L. *Lanzelot*. Librettist: Ernst Wolfram. Première: Hoftheater, Braunschweig, 25 October 1891. (Tower, 371 and 774.)

Hermosos, Mariano. *Lohengrin*. Librettist: J. Veyan and R. Battaler. Published: Casa Dotesiol, 1903.

Herreshoff, C.M. 'Elaine'. 1931. (British Library.)

Hertel, P.L. *Morgana* (Ballet in Four Acts). Book: Philippe Faglioni. Première: Königliche Theater, Berlin, 25 May 1857. (Stieger, II, 829.)

Hervé (Florimond Ronger). *Les Chevaliers de la Table Ronde*. Librettists: Chivot and Duru. Première: Bouffes-Parisiens, Paris, 17 November 1866. Published: Paris, Benoit, 1866.

Hier, E.G. 'Avalon'. 1938. (British Library.)

Hildreth, Richard E. 'Sir Galahad Overture'. Published: Cleveland, OH, Ludwig, 1973.

Hill, Edward Burlington. 'Parting of Lancelot and Guinevere' (Symphonic Poem). 1915. (Slonimsky, 772.)

Hill, Mabel Wood. 'The Song of the Grail Seekers'. Words: H. Hagedorn. 1914. (British Library.)

Hiller, Johann Adam. *Lisuart und Dariolette, oder Die Frage und die Antwort*. Librettist: D. Schiebeler. Première: Leipzig, 25 November 1766. Published: Leipzig, Bernhard Christoph Breitkopf und Sohn, 1768.

Hinze, Chris. *Parzifal*. Librettist: James Batton. Première: Holland Festival, 1976. (Lacy, *New Arthurian Encyclopedia*, 237.)

Hodge, M.T. 'Tristram to Iseult'. Published: 1935. (British Library.)

Hoffman, Richard. 'Elaine'. Words: Alfred, Lord Tennyson. Published: New York, William A. Pond & Company, 1865.

Hofman, Heinrich, K.J. 'Tristan und Isolde' (song from *Minnelieder* No. 4). Published: London, n.p., 1887.

Holbrooke, Josef. 'Follow the Gleam'. Words: Alfred, Lord Tennyson. Published: London, Boosey and Hawkes.

Holbrooke, Josef. *Choral Symphony*. Words: Josef Holbrooke. Published: London, J. & W. Chester, 1908.

Hollins, Dorothea. *The Quest: A Drama of Deliverance*. Published: London, Williams and Norgate, 1910.

Holloway, Robin. 'Souvenirs de Monsalvat: Waltz-Synthesis on Themes from Wagner's *Parsifal*'. Published: London, Boosey & Hawkes, 1990.

Holmes, Augusta. *Lancelot du Lac*. Librettist: Augusta Holmes. Unfinished. (Paris, Bibliothèque Nationale.)

Homer, Sidney. 'Enid's Song'. Words: Alfred, Lord Tennyson. Published: New York, G. Schirmer, 1901.

Hoppin, S.B. *Yuletide at the Court of King Arthur*. Librettist: L.F. Merriam. Published: Boston, C.C. Birchard, 1934.

Horrocks, Amy. 'The Lady of Shalott'. Words: Alfred, Lord Tennyson. Published: London, Boosey and Hawkes, 1899. Première: Sheffield, 1918.

Hughes, Arwel. 'Draw Dros y Don'. 1975. (Lacy, *New Arthurian Encyclopedia*, 338.)

Hughes, Arwel. 'The Song of Enid'. Words: Alfred, Lord Tennyson. c.1972.

Hullah, John. 'Fortune and Her Wheel'. Words: Alfred, Lord Tennyson. Published: London, Addison, Hollier & Lucas, 1860.

Hutchinson, William M. *The Story of Elaine*. Words: H.L.D. Jaxone. Published: London, 1883.

Hutter, Herman. *Lanzelot*. Librettist: Wilhelm Hertz. Published: Leipzig, Gebrüder Hug, 1898.

Hyde, Lewis. 'A Dark Month' (in *Tristram of Lyonnesse and other Songs*). Words: A.C. Swinburne, 1950. (Gooch.)

Hyde, Lewis. 'What is Death' (in *Tristram of Lyonnesse and other Songs*). Words: A.C. Swinburne, 1950. (Gooch.)

Imig, W. and Simon, B. 'King Arthur (Had Three Sons)'. Words: Traditional. Published: New York, C. Fischer, 1958.

Ireland, John. 'We are No Knights of Lyonesse'. Words: John Drinkwater. Published: London, J. Curwen, 1926.

Jackson, Arthur Herbert. 'Elaine' (Idyll for Pianoforte). 1879. (British Library.)

Jacobson, Maurice. 'The Lady of Shalott'. Words: Alfred, Lord Tennyson. Published: London, J. Curwen, 1942.

Jag Panzer. 'The Moors' in *Age of Mastery*. 1998. (Source: Keir Howell.)

Jasienski, J. de. 'The Wheel of Fortune'. Words: Alfred, Lord Tennyson. Published: New York, William Hall & Son, 1866.

Jennings, Carolyn. 'A Feast of Lanterns'. Words: Carolyn Jennings. Published: New York, Lawson Gould, n.d.

Jerome, M.K. 'The Moon is in Tears Tonight'. Published: New York, Harms, 1937. (British Library.)

Joachim, Joseph. 'Merlin's Song'. Words: Alfred, Lord Tennyson. Published: London, CKP, 1880.

Johnson, Clair W. *King Arthur*. Librettist: Clair W. Johnson. (Library of Congress.)

Joncières, Victorien de. *Lancelot*. Librettist: Blau and Gallet. Première: 7 February 1900. Published: Paris, L. Grus, 1900.

Kafka, Heinrich. *König Arthur*. Librettist: Heinrich Kafka. (Stieger II, 680.)

Kalmaroff, Martin. *Half Magic in King Arthur's Court*. Librettist: Ernest Eager. Première: New York, 17 May 1963. (Northouse, 99.)

Kamelot. *Siege Perilous*. 1998. (Source: Keir Howell.)

Kapp, Paul. 'Good King Arthur' in *Cock-A-Doodle Doo; Cock-A Doodle Dandy*. Words: Traditional. Published: New York, Harper and Row, 1966.

Kay, Ulysses. 'King Arthur'. Traditional. Published: Pembroke Music Co., 1978.

Kayak. *Merlin*. 1981. (Source: Keir Howell.)

Keighley, T. 'King Arthur Had Three Sons'. Traditional. Published: London, Stainer and Bell, 1917.

Keller, Albert. 'Court of King Arthur Quadrilles' (selected from *English Melodies*). Published: London, n.p., 1843.

Kemp, Molly. 'To Every Season a Song'. 1980. (British Library.)

Kerr, James A. 'Lily Maid, Elaine'. Words: Bessie Girard. Published: San Francisco, Charles E. Eaton, 1875.

Kesling, Adolphe. 'Elaine' (Idyll musicale pour piano). Published: London, n.p., 1860.

Kidson, F. and Shaw, M.F. 'Sir Eglamore'. Published: London, Boosey & Hawkes, 1913.

Kirchner, Volker David. 'Nachtstuck: Varianten über eine Wagnersche Akkordverbindung'. Published: Mainz: B. Schott's Sohne, 1981. [from *Tristan und Isolde*].

Kleinsinger, George. *Tommy Pitcher*. Librettist: Paul Tripp. Première: Stockbridge, MA, 1952. Published: London, Chappell, 1954.

Klughardt, August F.M. *Iwein*. Librettist: Carl Niemann. Première: Hoftheater, Neustrelitz, 28 March 1879. Published: Leipzig, Fritzsch, 1881.

Kochiss, Joseph. *The Kids from Camelot*. Librettist: Joseph Kochiss. Published: Venice, FL, Eldridge Publishing, 1973.

Kogel, Gustave. *Fantasien über Motive der Richard Wagnerschen Opern: Tristan*. Published: Peters, 187?.

Kogen, H. 'Merlin'. Composed c.1929. (British Library.)

Koshkin, Nikita. 'Avalon'. Published: Berlin, Edit. Margaux, 1993.

Kotyczka, Stanislaw. 'In Time'. Published: Krakow, 1980.

Kralik, Richard von. *Der Heilige Gral*. Librettist unknown. Published: Trier, Petrus, 1912.

Krauer, Ferdinand. *Der Loewenritter*. Four of four libretti. Libretti: Hensler, Al. Gleich. Premières: Leopoldstadt Theatre, Vienna, 5 May 1799; 17 September 1801; 8 August 1807; 17 August 1807.

Kreymann, Louis. *Lohengrun*. Librettist unknown. Published: Leipzig, Conrad Glasser, n.d.

Krug, D. 'Schwanenlied'. Published: Vienna, Universal, 1930.

Ksawery, Josef. *The Wizard*. (Mellen.) Librettist: Wezyk. Premiere: Warsaw, 1813.

Kuzuu, Chinatsu, 'The Lady of Shalott'. Words: Alfred, Lord Tennyson. Composed 1985. (Lacy, *New Arthurian Encyclopedia*, 264.)

Kuzuu, Chinatsu. 'Elaine the Fair'. Words: Alfred, Lord Tennyson. (*New Arthurian Encyclopedia*, 264.) Composed 1986.

Ladmirault, Paul Emile. *Myrdhin*. Librettist: A. Fleury and L. Ladmirault. Première: 1908.

Ladmirault, Paul Emile. *Tristan et Iseult*. Librettist: Louis Artus, based on Joseph Bédier. Première: Nice. Published: (libretto) Paris, Impr. de L' Illustration, 1929.

Ladmirault, Paul. 'Deux Danses Bretonnes'. Published: Paris, Henri Lemoine Et Cie, 1957.

Ladmirault, Paul. 'Suite Bretonne'. Published: Paris, A. Rouart Et Cie, 1908.

Lambert, Lucien. *Broceliande*. Librettist: André Alexander. Première: Théâtre des Arts, Rouen, 25 February 1893. Published: Paris, Huegel et Cie., 1861.

Lampe, John Frederick. *Opera of Operas, or Tom Thumb the Great*. Librettist: Henry

Fielding. Première: Little Theatre, London, 10 May 1733. Published: London, J. Roberts 1733.

Latham, William. 'The Lady of Shalott'. Words: Alfred, Lord Tennyson. Première: Cincinnati Symphony, 3 July 1941.

Laurendeau, L.P. *Wheel of Fortune*. 1901.

Lawson, Peter. *Wizard*. Words: Katherine Hayes. Published: Malvern Music, 1986.

Lear, Edward. 'Late, Late, so Late'. Words: Alfred, Lord Tennyson. Published: London, Cramer, Beale & Chappell, c.1860.

Lear, Edward. 'Song of Love and Death'. Words: Alfred, Lord Tennyson. Published: London, Cramer, Beale & Wood, 1860.

Lear, Edward. 'Turn Fortune, Turn'. Words: Alfred, Lord Tennyson. Published: London, Cramer, Beale & Chappell, 1860.

Led Zeppelin. 'Battle of Evermore' in *Led Zeppelin IV*. 1971. (Source: Keir Howell.)

Legg, James. *The Wife of Bath's Tale*. Librettist: Melvin Freedman. Première: Aspen, CO, 1986.

Leitch, W. and Donovan, M. 'Guinevere'. Published: New York, Peer International, 1967.

Lemare, Edwin, Tr. 'Organ Music of Edwin Lemare'. Published: Boston, Wayne Leupold. 1992. [from *Lohengrin* and *Parsifal*].

Lennard, Emma. 'Tristram's Song'. Words: Alfred, Lord Tennyson. Published: London, Novello, 1894.

Leon, Laurent. *Tristan de Leonis*. Librettist: A. Silvestri. 1897.

Leveridge, Richard. 'The Gallant Days of King Arthur'. (Avery, pt. 3, v. 2, 771.)

Levien, E. 'Song of Love and Death'. Words: Alfred, Lord Tennyson. Published: London, Cramer, Beale & Wood, 1863.

Lewis, Anthony. 'O Merlin in Your Crystal Cave'. Words: Edwin Muir. 1944 (Gooch.)

Lindsay, Maria. 'Song of Love and Death'. Words: Alfred, Lord Tennyson. Published: London, Cocks, also Franklin, 1861.

Linley, William. 'Last Whitsunday They Brought Me'. Words: W.H. Ireland. 1796. (British Library.)

Linley, William. 'She Sung Whilst from Her Eye Ran Down'. Words: W.H. Ireland. 1796. (British Library.)

Lister, Anne. 'La Folie Tristan'. in *Spreading Rings*. 1993. (Source: Keir Howell.)

Lister, Anne. 'The Lady of Shallott'. in *Spreading Rings*. 1993. (Source: Keir Howell.)

Lister, Anne. *A Flame in Avalon*. (Source: Keir Howell.)

Loewe, Frederick. *Camelot*. Librettist: Alan J. Lerner. Première: Majestic Theatre, New York, 4 December 1960. Published: New York, Random House, 1961.

Loggins, Kenny. 'Back to Avalon'. New York, Columbia, 1988.

Lomax, Alan. 'Ballad of Sir Lancelot'. Ridgefield Music, 1956.

Longhurst, Herbert. *King Arthur*. Librettist: H.E. Turner. Première: London, 1896. Published: London, J. Curwen, 1896.

Lora, Antonio. *Lancelot and Elaine*. Librettist: Josephine Fetter Royle. Première: Cologne State Opera.

Lucassen, Arjen Anthony. *The Final Experiment*. 1995.

Lushington, C. 'Elaine's Song'. Words: Alfred, Lord Tennyson. 1881.

Lyle, Carlyon. *Idylls of the King*: 1. 'Avalon', 2. 'Elaine', 3. 'Camelot', 4. 'Tintagel' (for Pianoforte). Published: Swan and Co., 1920.

MacAlpin, Colin. *King Arthur*. Librettist: Colin MacAlpin. Première: London, 1896. Published: London, Bosworth and Co., 1897.

MacDowell, Edward A. 'Lancelot and Elaine' (Symphonic poem after Tennyson). 1886.

MacDowell, Edward A. Piano Sonata No. 2: 'Sonata Eroica: Flos regum Arthurus'. 1885. Published: Leipzig, Breitkopf und Hartel, 1894.

MacFarren, George A. 'Sir Eglamore'. Words: N. MacFarren. Published: London, n.p., 1882.

MacFarren, George A. 'Sir Lionel: My Only Thought at War's Alarms'. Words: A. Braham. Published: London, n.p., 1859.

MacFarren, George A. 'Fortune and Her Wheel'. Words: Alfred, Lord Tennyson. London, 1892.

MacFarren, George A. 'Late, Late, so Late'. Words: Alfred, Lord Tennyson. Published: London, CKP, 1880.

MacFarren, George A. 'Love and Death'. Words: Alfred, Lord Tennyson. Published: London, Novello, 1892.

MacFarren, Walter Cecil. 'Elaine' (Idyll for Pianoforte). Published: London, 1863.

MacKenzie, A.C. 'The Song of Love and Death'. Words: Alfred, Lord Tennyson. (British Library.)

MacKenzie, A.C. 'Turn Fortune, Turn'. Words: Alfred, Lord Tennyson, 1873. (British Library.)

Maes, Jef. *Tristan*. (A Ballet). (Slonimsky, *Twentieth Century*).

Maguire, Michael C. 'Tristan and Geraldo'. Première: Vancouver, B.C., 1992.

Mahen, André. *Viviane*. Librettist: Marthe Frontard. Published: Rouen, Lecerf Fils, 1912.

Malipiero, Gian F. *Lancelotto del Lago*. Librettist: A. de Stefani. Begun in 1914–15. Never completed.

Malipiero, Gian F. *Merlin, Maestro d'Organi*. Published: Vienna, Universal Editions, 1928.

Malipiero, Gian Francesco. *I Sonetti della Fate*. (Number 1 is 'Eliana' and 5 is 'Morgana'.) Words: Gabriele d'Annunzio. Published: Milan, Carisch e Janichen, n.d.

Mallandaine, John E. 'Elaine' (Romance for Pianoforte). Published: London, n.p., 1867.

Mark, Jon. *Land of Merlin*. 1992. (Source: Keir Howell.)

Markordt, J. *Tom Thumb*. Librettist: Kane O'Hara after Henry Fielding. Première: Covent Garden Theatre, London, 10 March 1780. Published: London, J. Preston, 1781.

Martin, Frank. *Le Vin herbé*. Librettist: adapted from Joseph Bédier by Frank Martin. Première: Zurich, 26 March 1942. Presented as an opera: Landestheater, Salzburg, 15 August 1948. Published: Vienna, Universal Editions, n.d.

Martin, Gilbert. 'More Things are Wrought by Prayer'. Words: Alfred, Lord Tennyson. Published: Dayton, Ohio, Temple.

Marx, Joseph. 'Isolde [from *Lieder und Gesang*]'. Words: Bruno Frank. Published: Leipzig, Schuberthaus, n.d.

Maryon, Edward. *Sangraal*. Librettist: Edward Maryon. One of seven operas in the Cycle of Life. (Boston Public Library.)

Mason, William. 'Elaine'. Published: London, n.p., 1872.

Massine, Leonide. *Mad Tristan* (Ballet). Music by Richard Wagner, scenery by Salvador Dali. Première: New York, 15 December 1944.

Mathias, William. *Culhwch and Olwen*. Librettist: Gwyn Thomas. Published: Cardiff, Wales, University of Wales, 1971.

Matthews, David. 'The Sleeping Lord'. Words: David Jones. Published: London, Faber, 1992.

Maurice, Pierre. *Lanval*. Librettist: Madeleine Maurice. Première: Weimar, 1913. Published: Munich, Maurice, 1913.

Mayerl, Billy. 'Marigold: Legends of King Arthur' (6 Impressions for Pianoforte. Op. 64). Published: London, Keith Prowse and Co., 1929.

Mayhew, Ralph. 'Good King Arthur'. Published: New York, Harper-Columbia, 1919.

Mayo, Jane. 'Lynette's Song'. Words: Alfred, Lord Tennyson. Published: London, WK, 1873.

McArthur, Douglas. *Merlin*. 1999. (Source: Keir Howell.)

McCabe, John. *Arthur Pendragon*. Suite 1. Première: Budapest, 28 October 2000.

McCabe, John. *Arthur*. (Ballet) Première: Birmingham, UK, 25 May 2000.

McCormick, Clifford. 'More Things are Wrought by Prayer'. Words: Alfred, Lord Tennyson. Published: Philadelphia, Shawnee Press, 1964.

McGlynn, Michael. 'Sir Gawain and the Green Knight'. Published: London, n.p.; Dublin, Century Composers Music, 1990; revised, 1993.

McGurty, Mark. 'Oisin and the Gwragedd'. (for orchestra). (Slonimsky, *Twentieth Century*.)

McKennitt, Lorena. 'All Souls' Night' in *The Visit*. Recorded: Warner Brothers, 1992.

McKennitt, Lorena. 'Lady of Shalott' in *The Visit*. Words: Lorena McKennitt. 1992. (Source: Joy Blanche Wilson.)

McPhee, Colin. Mort d'Arthur. (for orchestra). (Slonimsky, *Twentieth Century*.)

Meiniche, D.L. *Parzival*. Librettist: Wilhelm Hanze. Première: Stadttheater, Leibniz, 2 February 1910. (Stieger, III, 922.)

Merrill, Wilson P. 'Sir Morven's Hunt'. Words: W.R. Thayer. Published: Boston, MA, O. Ditson, 1896.

Messiaen, Olivier. 'Cinq Rechants' for choir. Words: Olivier Messiaen. Première: Paris, 15 June 1950.

Messiaen, Olivier. 'La Dame de Shalott' (for pianoforte). Composed, 1917.

Messiaen, Olivier. *Tristan et Yseult*. Incidental music for play by Lucien Fabre. Première: Théâtre Edouard VII, Paris, 22 February 1945.

Messiaen, Olivier. *Turangalîla-Symphonie*. 1948. Première: Boston, 2 December 1949.

Messiaen, Olivier. *Harawi*. Song cycle for voice and piano.1949.

Miero, Raffelo de. *Morgana*. Librettist: Antonio Colanetti. Première: Turin, 16 February 1922.

Mihalovich, Oden Peter. *Eliana*. Librettist: Hans Herrig. Première: Budapest, 16 February 1909. Published: Privately by the composer Oden Peter Mihalovich.

Mist of Avalon. *Belthana*. 1999. (Source: Keir Howell.)

Mitchell, Chris. 'The Quest'. Words: Alfred, Lord Tennyson. Première: St. George's Hall, Bradford, June 1975.

Mitchell, R.E. 'I'll go to Camelot' (for women's voices). Composed c.1937.

Moign, Pierre-Yves. 'Iseult Seconde'. Words P.J. Helian. 1979. (Bellaing.)

Moign, Pierre-Yves. 'Legendaire Pour le Roi Arthur'. 1978. (Bellaing.)

Mojsisovich, Roderich. *Merlin*. Librettist: Edward Hoffer. Première: Graz, 1921.

Molloy, James L. 'O Sun That Wakenest All'. Words: Alfred, Lord Tennyson, 1873. (British Library.)

Molloy, James L. 'Twice My Love Has Smiled on Me'. Words: Alfred, Lord Tennyson, 1873. (British Library.)

Momigny, Jerome et Piccini. *Le Chevalier de la Table rond, ou Roger et Naida*. Librettist: J.G.A Cuvelier. Première: Salle Jeux Gymnastiques, Paris, 17 June 1811. Published: Paris, Hocquet et Cie.

Momigny, Jerome. *Le Entree des Chevaliers Français dans Serica*. Librettist: J.G.A. Cuvelier. Première: Paris, 17 June 1811. Published: Paris, Hocquet et Cie.

Montgomery, William H. 'Too Late, Too Late'. Words: Alfred, Lord Tennyson. Published: London, Evelyn, Adams & MacKay.

Montgomery, William H. 'Turn Fortune, Turn Thy Wheel'. Words: Alfred, Lord Tennyson.

Moody Blues. 'Are You Sitting Comfortably?' in *On the Threshold of a Dream*. (Source: Keir Howell.)

Moorat, Joseph. 'Good King Arthur'. Words: Traditional. In *Thirty Old Time Nursery Songs*. New York, Thames and Hudson, 1980. Reprint of 1912 edition.

Morgana LeFay. 'Excalibur'. 1993. In *Knowing Just As I*. (Source: Keir Howell.)

Morlacchi, Enrico. *Bretagna*. Librettist: Giulio Coronati. Première: Teatro Adriano, Rome, 3 March 1907 (private). (Stieger, I, 189.)

Morris, Haydn. 'My Olwen'. 1950. (British Library.)

Moszkowski, Moritz. 'Isoldens Tod'. Published: Leipzig, C.F. Peters, 1914.

Mueller, J. Frederik. *Percival und Griseldis*. Librettist: Klesheim and Heitzing. Première: Zagreb, 19 February 1841. (Stieger, III, 937.)

Murray, Anthony Gregory. 'The Grail Prayer'. 1961. (British Library.)

Mycielski, Zygmunt. 'Lamento di Tristano'. (orchestral). (Slonimsky, *Twentieth Century*.)

Naylor, Edward Woodall. 'Arthur the King' (Cantata). Words: Alfred, Lord Tennyson. Published: London, Vincent, 1902. (British Library.)

Naylor, Edward Woodall. 'Follow the Gleam'. Words: Alfred, Lord Tennyson. Published: London, Educational Supply, 1910.

Nedellec, Patrick. 'Le Chevalier de Broceliande'. 1985. (Bellaing.)

Neilsen, Frederick Brooke. *King Arthur and the Knights of the Round Table*. Librettist: Bearle. Published: Philadelphia, PA, W.H. Boner, 1894.

Nelson, Paul. 'How Happy the Lover'. Words: John Dryden. Published: Carl Fischer, 1967.

Nestor, Larry. *Connecticut Yankee*. Librettist: Tim J. Kelly. Published: Denver, CO, Pioneer Drama Service, 1990.

Neumeier, John. *König Artus* (Ballet). 1982. (Lacy and Ashe, 273.)

Neupert, Fritz. *Lohengrins Ende*. Librettist: Wilhelm Hagen. Première: Kammerspiel, Nürnberg, 5 May 1918. (Stieger, II, 727.)

Newman, Lionel. 'Chimes of Avalon'. Librettist: Earl Carroll. 1948. (British Library.)

Newton, Ernest Richard. 'Green Isle of Avalon'. Words: F.E. Weatherly. 1919. (British Library.)

Newton, Ernest Richard. 'When Good King Arthur Ruled This Land'. Words: Traditional. Published: Boston, Crescendo.

Nichol, Henry Ernest. *The Holy Grail* (cantata). Words: C. Stern, 1906. (British Library.)

Nicholls, Frederick. 'Elaine's Song'. Words: Alfred, Lord Tennyson. Published: London, Lucas, Weber, Pitt & Wakefield, 1880.

Obradovic, Alexander. 'The Green Knight' (vocal). (Slonimsky, *Twentieth Century*.)

O'Brien, Eugene. 'Tristan's Lament'. (orchestral). (Slonimsky, *Twentieth Century*.)

Olivadoti, J. 'Avalon Nights'. Published: Chicago, Rubank, 1952.

Ollivier, Hector. 'Fantasien über Motive der Richard Wagnerschen Opern'. Published: Leipzig, C.F. Peters, 18__. [from *Lohengrin*].

Orth, L.E. 'King Arthur'. Words: Traditional. Published: Boston, MA, Oliver Ditson, 1901.

Ortone, Ernest W. 'Enid'. Published: Pro Arte, 1960.

Palmer, G. Molyneux. 'Sir Galahad' (Poem for Chorus and Orchestra). (Library of Congress.)

Papale, Henry. 'Follow the Gleam'. Words: Alfred, Lord Tennyson. Première: State Street Concert, Brooklyn, New York, 1972. Published: Cincinnati, OH, Westwood, 1967.

Papini, Guido. 'Elaine, the Lily Maid of Astolat'. Words: Alfred, Lord Tennyson. Published: n.p., B. Schott's Sohne, 1887.

Parker, Horatio. Librettist: Brian Hooker. Morven and the Grail. 1915. (Lacy, New Arthurian Encyclopedia, 338.)

Parker, Horatio W. Merlin and the Gleam (Cantata). Première: Boston, MA, 13 April 1915. (Library of Congress.)

Parry, C.H.H. 'Vivien'. Composed: 1873. Destroyed by composer 1873.

Parry, C.H.H. Guinevere. Librettist: Una Taylor. Never performed or published. (London, Royal College of Music.)

Parry, John. 'King Arthur's Maxim'. Words: Traditional. Published: London, Privately published, 1842.

Parry, Joseph. King Arthur. Librettist L.F. Merriam. Première, Cardiff, 1897. (Aberystwyth, Wales: National Library of Wales.)

Patusset, Alfred. Lohengrin à L'Alcazar. Librettist unknown. Première: Alcazar, Paris, 25 February 1885. (Tower, 383 and 823.)

Patusset, Alfred. Lohengrin à L'Eldorato. Premiere: Theatre L'Eldorato, 1856. (Tower, 384 and 823, also gives an alternate last name for the composer, 'Patnussex'.)

Pearsall, Robert Lucas. 'The River Spirit's Song' (a Madrigal for 4 Voices). Words: John Dryden. Published: London, Novello, 1887.

Pease, Alfred H. 'O Morning Star'. Words: Alfred, Lord Tennyson. Published: Chicago, 1873.

Peaslee, Richard. Sir Gawain and the Green Knight. Librettist: Kenneth Cavender. Première: Brooklyn, NY, 18 October 2001.

Pedrali, Patrick. 'Lancelot' (Piano and Voices). Words: Alain Lacaux. Published: London, Chappell, 1975.

Pendragon. 'Excalibur'. 15 September 1986. (Source: Keir Howell.)

Perducet, Gustave. Idylle au (du) Bretagne. Librettists: Roger Perducet et Babin de Fontenelle. Première: Salle Journal, Paris, 26 August 1906. (Stieger, II, 601.)

Pfitzner, Hans. Café Lohengrin. Librettist: Hans Pfitzner. Published: Avant Scene Opera.

Phillips, Madge. 'Lo! I Forgive Thee'. Words: Alfred, Lord Tennyson. Published: London, West and Co., 1914.

Phillips, Mrs. A.A. 'Elaine's Song'. Words: Alfred, Lord Tennyson, 1892.

Pijper, William. Merlijn. Librettist: S. Vestdijk. Première: Rotterdam, 7 June 1952. Published: Amsterdam, Holland, Donemus, n.d.

Plumpton, A. 'Sweet is True Love'. Words: Alfred, Lord Tennyson, 1866.

Polignac, Armande de. Morgane. (Slonimsky, 1425, and Stieger, II, 829.)

Porter, Timothy. Lancelot, or the Tale of the Grail. Librettist: Timothy Porter. Première: 1985.

Porter, Timothy. Sir Gawain and the Green Knight. Librettist: Timothy Porter. 1970.

Porter, Timothy. The Marvels of Merlin. Librettist: Timothy Porter. Première: Blockley, August 1981.

Porter, Timothy. Tristan and Essylt. Librettist: Timothy Porter. 1980.

Poston, Elizabeth. 'Good King Arthur'. Words: Traditional. Published: New York, Thomas Crowell Co., 1972. in The Baby's Song Book.

Pringer, H.T. *Guinevere, or Love Laughs at Law*. Librettist: Stanley Stevens. Première: Town Hall, Kilburn, 19 March 1890. (Lacy and Ashe, 268, Nicholl, V, 583.)
Priori, Massimo. *Lanval*. (oratorio) Words: Marie de France. Première: Barga, 1996.
Pugno, Raoul and Lippacher, C. *Viviane* (Ballet). Première: Théâtre Eden, Paris, 28 October 1886. Published: Paris, E. Gondinet, 1886.
Purcell, Henry (Arne, Thomas). *Arthur and Emmeline*. Libretto: John Kemble. Première: London. Published London, J. Jarvis, 1784.
Purcell, Henry. *King Arthur*. Librettist: John Dryden. Première: Dorset Gardens Theatre, London, 14 May 1691. Published: Many editions: the standard one is the Purcell Society edition, vol. XXVI.
Purcell, Henry. *Merlin or the British Enchanter*. Librettist: John Dryden, edited by Henry Giffard. Première: Edinburgh, 7 December 1750. Published: London, E. Curll.
Rae, Allan. *Wheel of Fortune*. (orchestral). (Slonimsky, *Twentieth Century*.)
Raff, Joachim. 'Lohengrin Fantaisie'. Published: New York, G. Schirmer, 1885. [from *Lohengrin*].
Raisen, Jacques. *Merlin Garcon*. Librettist: Jacques Raisen. Première: Théâtre Français, Paris, 7 October 1690. (Stieger, II, 805.)
Ramsey, S. et al. *Skyclad. The Wayward Sons of Mother Earth*. Words: M. Walkyier. 1991. (Source: Keir Howell.)
Rauchenecker. *Tristanderl und Sussholde*. Librettist: unknown. Première: Munich, 29 May 1865. Neither text nor music of this parody have survived. (Stieger, 547.)
Raymond, Friedrich. *Die Jungfrauen von Avallon*. Librettists: P. Frank and P. Herz. Première: Zentral-Theater, Dresden, 16 June 1929. (Stieger, III, 660.)
Raymond, Joseph. 'More Things are Wrought by Prayer'. Words: Christopher Crown. Published: Milwaukee, Whalen, 1956.
Redford, J.A.C. *Kid in King Arthur's Court*. (Sound Track).
Reed, Thomas German. *The Ancient Britons*. Librettist: G.A. Beckett. Première: St George's Hall, London, 1874. (Stieger, I, 76.)
Reinecke, Carl H.C. 'Acht Gesange Op. 103 No. 8'. Words: J. Meyer. Published: 1881.
Reinecke, Carl H.C. 'Herr Tristan'. (British Library.)
Reinecke, Carl H.C. 'King Arthur' in *Fifty Children's Songs*. Published: New York, G. Schirmer, 1901.
Reissman. *Gralspiel*. Première: Berlin, 1895.
Renner, Josel, Jr. 'Isolde in Vier Lieder'. Words: M.G. Conrad. Published: Leipzig, F.E.C. Leuchkart, n.d.
Reva e Napoleon, Antonio Paladino (a.k.a. Antonio Paladino Reva, Cayan Jorge Gadia y Napoleon, and Herbert Clarence Victor Wong). 'King Arthur and the Knights of the Round Table'. Words: Reva e Napoleon. Published: São Paulo, Musical Sonata, 1972.
Rice, Thomas. 'Sir Gawain and the Green Knight'. Published: New York, Seesaw Music, 1978.
Rich, Max. 'Drifting on the Avalon'. Published: 1930. (British Library.)
Richardson, Norman. 'Avalon: Diversions on an Original Theme'. 1971. Published: London, Boosey & Hawkes, 1971. (British Library.)
Richmond, W. 'It Chanced one Day that Enid Sang'. Words: Alfred, Lord Tennyson. Published: London, Weinppert, 1871.
Rimbault, Edward Francis. 'Sir Lancelot du Lac' (Ballad). Words: Traditional. Published: London, Novello, 1847.
Robert, Guy. *Roman de Tristan et Yseut*. Librettist: Medieval text from MS in Österreichische Nationalbibliothek, Vienna. Published: Arion, France, 1985.
Roberton, H.S. 'King Arthur'. Published: London, J. Curwen, 1911.

Roberts, W. Jarrett. 'The Inundation of Cantre'r Gwaelod'. Words: D.C. Harries, 1881.

Robrecht, Carl. 'Fata Morgana'. Published: London, Bosworth, 1936.

Rodgers, Richard. *A Connecticut Yankee in King Arthur's Court*. Librettist: Lorenz Hart. Première: Vanderbilt Theatre, New York, 3 November 1927. Published: London, Chappell, 1929.

Roff, Joseph. 'More Things are Wrought by Prayer'. Words: Alfred, Lord Tennyson. Published: New York, Fox, 1959.

Rogowsky, Ludomir Michel. 'Three Symphonic Poems'. (Lacy, *New Arthurian Encyclopedia*, 338.)

Rootham, C.B. 'The Lady of Shalott'. Words: Alfred, Lord Tennyson. 1909–10.

Ropartz, J. Guy. 'Le Chasse du Prince Arthur'. Published: Paris, A. Durand et Fils, 1913.

Rose, Vincent. 'Avalon'. Words: Al Jolson. Published: New York, Remick, 1920.

Roser, Frank. *Arthur*. Librettist unknown. Première: Josefstadt Theater, Vienna, 1814. (Stieger I, 110, lists it as a pantomime.)

Ross, Herbert. *Tristan* (Ballet). (Lacy and Ashe, 273.)

Roth, Uli Jon. *Prologue to the Symphonic Legends*. 1996. (Source: Keir Howell.)

Rousseau, M. Samuel. *Le Roi Arthur*. Librettist: Fernand Beissier. Published: Paris, Choudens, 1903.

Rowland, A.C. 'Turn Fortune, Turn'. Words: Alfred, Lord Tennyson. Published: London, Addison, Hollier & Lucas, 1861.

Roza, Miklos. *Knights of the Round Table*. (film score). (Slonimsky, *Twentieth Century*.)

Ruby, Harry. 'That Night in Avalon'. (British Library.)

Rudd, Colin, Nick Hill, Allen Moller, Chris Knowles, Anthony Grinnins, and Hugh MacKay. *Merlin's Arthur*. Librettists: collaborative. Recorded: Brenin Productions, 1995.

Rufer, Philippe. *Merlin*. Librettist: L.A. Hofman Lipzis. Première: Königliche Oper, Berlin, 28 February 1887. Published: Leipzig, Breitkopf and Hartel, 1887.

Rummel, Walter Morse. 'Sir Lancelot'. Words: Richard Aldington. Published: London, Augener, 1914.

Runnalls, Jana. 'Spirit of Avalon'. Recorded: Stroppy Cow Records, 1985.

Russell, Robert C. Kennedy. 'There's an Orchard Green in Avalon'. Words: F.E. Weatherly. 1914. (British Library.)

Ryberg, Jean B. 'Sir Lancelot'. Published: New York, Witmark, 1954.

Saariaho, Kaija. *Graal Theatre*. (orchestral). (Slonimsky, *Twentieth Century*.)

Sahr, Henrich von. 'Tristan: Acht Gesange'. Published: Leipzig, n.p., 1877.

Salaman, Charles. 'Late, Late, So Late'. Words: Alfred, Lord Tennyson. Published: London, SLW, 1886.

Saloman, Siegfried. *Bretagne*. Première: Stockholm, 26 May 1898. (Slonimsky, 1579–80.)

Sassone, ——. *Il Capitan galappo, e Merlina Serva Finta d'una Vedova*. Première: Teatro della Pallacorda, Rome, 1737. Published: Rome, G.B. de Caporali, n.d.

Schafer, R. Murray. 'Le Cri de Merlin'. Published: Toronto, Arcana, 1987.

Schep, Nick. 'The Grail' (for Piano and Harp). (Lacy and Ashe, 275.)

Schibler, Armin. *La Folie de Tristan*. Librettist: Armin Schibler. Première: Montreux, 1981. Published: Adliswil und Lottstetten, Switzerland, Kunzelmann, 1982.

Schnabel, Karl. *Griseldis und Percival*. Librettist: Karlo. Première: Stadttheater, Breslau, 5 June 1851. (Stieger, II, 551.)

Schoop, Paul. *Fata Morgana*. (orchestral). (Slominsky, *Twentieth Century*.)

Sciarrino, Salvatore. *Lohengrin*. Librettist: Salvatore Sciarrino. Première: Milan, 15 January 1983. Published: Milan, Ricordi, 1983.

Scott, Francis G. 'O Merlin in Your Crystal Cave'. Words: Edwin Muir. (Gooch, 585.)

Sealy, Frank L. 'Sir Galahad'. Words: Alfred, Lord Tennyson. Published: New York, G. Schirmer, 1903.

Sessions, Roger H. *Lancelot and Elaine*. Librettist: Unknown. Begun and abandoned when Sessions was quite young.

Severn, Edmund. *Lancelot and Elaine*. (orchestral). (Slonimsky, *Twentieth Century*.)

Shaw, Martin. *The Thorn of Avalon*. Librettist: Barclay Baron. Première: Crystal Palace, London, 6 June 1931. Published: London, Oxford University Press, 1931.

Shelley, Gladys. 'Arthur'. Published: 1977. (British Library.)

Sherman, Richard. *The Sword in the Stone*. Words: Robert Sherman. Published: Burbank, CA, Wonderland Music, 1962.

Sherwin, Manning. 'King Arthur Was a Gentleman' (film score). London, Gainsborough Films, 1942.

Shippen, Eugene Rodman. *The Consecration of Sir Galahad*. Librettist: Elizabeth Blount Shippen. Première: Boston, MA, 1 March 1923. Published: Boston, MA, Beacon Press, 1923.

Sibelius, Jean [Adapted]. *Camelot*: (Ballet). Book: Sebastian.

Sibelius, Jean. [Adapted]. *The Lady of Shalott*. (Ballet). Book: Frederick Ashton. Première: 12 November 1931.

Sieber, Ferdinand. 'Funf Gesänge: Herzeleid, Standchen, An Isolde'. Words: T. Ullrich. Published: 1883.

Silas, E. 'Enid's Song'. Words: Alfred, Lord Tennyson. Published: London, CKP, 1880.

Silcher, Friedrich. 'Lohengrin – A Legend'. Words: M. Louise Baum. Published: Boston, Ginn, 1927.

Simmons, Mike. *Dreams of Avalon*. (Source: Keir Howell.)

Singalee, Jean Baptiste. '*Lohengrin* Fantasie'. Published: Boston, Jean White, 1887. [from *Lohengrin*].

Skyclad. 'Cardboard City'. in *Prince of the Poverty Line*. 1994. (Source: Keir Howell.)

Skyclad. 'Declaration of Indifference'. in *A Burnt Offering for the Bone Idol*. 1992. (Source: Keir Howell.)

Skyclad. 'Wickedest Man in the World'. in *Jon Ah's Ark*. 1993. (Source: Keir Howell.)

Sluten, Jan. *Merlins Gebürt*. Librettist: Ruth Waldsbetter. Published: Basel, Switzerland, R. Geering, 1934.

Smart, Henry T. 'Sir Brian the Bold'. Words: W.H. Bellamy. Published: London, n.p., 1886.

Smieton, J.M. *King Arthur*. (Cantata). Published: London, Novello, 1893.

Smith, Eliseo. 'Four Songs from Idylls (Guinevere)'. Words: Alfred, Lord Tennyson. Published: London, n.p., 1864.

Smith, Eliseo. 'Late, Late, So Late'. Words: Alfred, Lord Tennyson. 1864.

Smith, Eliseo. 'Turn Fortune, Turn Thy Wheel'. Words: Alfred, Lord Tennyson. Published: London, Davison, 1864.

Soil Bleeds Black. *March of the Infidels*. 1997. (Source: Keir Howell.)

Soil Bleeds Black. *May the Blood of Many a Valiant Knight be Avenged*. 1997. (Source: Keir Howell.)

Soil Bleeds Black. *The Kingdom and Its Fey*. 1996. (Source: Keir Howell.)

Soil Bleeds Black. *The Maiden, the Minstrel, and the Magician*. 1998. (Source: Keir Howell.)

Somervell, Arthur. *Thomas the Rhymer*. Librettist: W.M. Dixon. Première: London, 1911. Published: London, Boosey, 1911.

Sonnehalb, Franklin. 'Romantic Lyrics for the Piano' (Op. 3, number 5, 'Lancelot and Elaine'). Published: New York, F.A. Mills, 1900.

Sowerby, Leo. *The Vision of Sir Launfal* (Cantata). Words: J.R. Lowell. Published: Boston, C C. Birchard, 1928.

Speer, Charlton. *Song of Love and Death*. Words: Alfred, Lord Tennyson. Published: London, 1897.

Spillane, D. *King Arthur, or the Days and Knights of the Round Table*. William Brough. Première: London, 26 December 1863. Text published in Thomas Lacy, *Lacy's Acting Edition of Plays, Drama, Farces, and Extravaganzas*, vol. 61. London, Thomas Hailes Lacy, n.d.

St. Claire, E. 'You Were My Love in Avalon'. 1927. (British Library.)

Stabler, Gerhard. 'Wirbelsäulenflote'. Published: Dortmund, Verlag Plane, 1984. [from Purcell's *King Arthur*].

Stacey, Alexander. 'The Merlin Polka' (for Pianoforte). Published: London, n.p., 1857.

Stanford, Charles Villiers. 'Merlin and the Gleam'. Words: Alfred, Lord Tennyson. Published: London, Stainer and Bell, n.d.

Stanynought, E. 'Sweet is True Love'. Words: Alfred, Lord Tennyson. Published: London, Lonsdale, 1860.

Steed, Albert. 'Guinevere'. Words: Alfred, Lord Tennyson. Published: London, Jewell, 1861.

Steed, Albert. 'Love and Death'. Words: Alfred, Lord Tennyson. Published: London, Jewell, 1861.

Steed, Albert. 'Turn Fortune Turn'. Words: Alfred, Lord Tennyson. Pubished: London, Jewell, 1861.

Steel, Christopher. 'Six From the Sixties: Fantasy on a Theme by Purcell'. Published: Borough Green, Novello, 1985. [from Purcell's *King Arthur*].

Steele, Herbert. 'Happy Arthur'. Published: London, West, 1914.

Steffens, Gustave. *Frau Lohengrin*. Librettists: E. Jacobson and L. Treptow. Première: Ernest Theater, Berlin, 21 December 1895. (Stieger, II, 485.)

Steggale, Reginald. 'Elaine' (Dramatic Scena). Words: Helen Schweitzer. (Royal Academy of Music.)

Stettenheim, Julius. *Lohengrin: Humoreske in 4 Gesangen*. Published: Berlin, 1859.

Stewart, Al. *Twenty Four Carrots*. 1980. (Source: Keir Howell.)

Stidston, Catherine. 'The Song of Love and Death'. Words: Alfred, Lord Tennyson. Published: Cincinnati: J. Church and Co., 1904.

Stiegler, Karl Von. '*Lohengrin*-Fantasie'. Published: Munich, H. Pizka. [from *Lohengrin*].

Stiegler, Karl von. '*Tristan und Isolde* Fantasie'. Published: Munich, H. Piska, 1891. [from *Tristan und Isolde*].

Stites, Kevin. *Adventures with Young King Arthur*. Librettist: David Lewman. Published: Dramatic Publishing, 1995.

Stivall, Alan. 'Broceliande' in *Reflets*. 1970. (Source: Keir Howell.)

Stivall, Alan. *The Mist of Avalon*. 1991. (Source: Keir Howell.)

Stolz, Edward. *Falsche Lohengrin von die bestrafte Zauberring*. Librettist: J. Boehm. Première: Thalia Theater, Vienna, September 15 or 18, 1858. (Stieger, II, 422.)

Stone, David. 'Funf Gedichte No. 5: Träume'. Published: London, Boosey and Hawkes, 1972. [from *Tristan und Isolde*].

Stonehenge. *Tales of Old Britain*. 1997. (Source: Keir Howell.)

Straus, Oskar. *Die Prinzessin von Dragant*. Librettist: Johann Nestroy. Première: Hof-Operntheater, Vienna, 13 November 1912.

Street, Tison. *Montsalvat*. (orchestral). (Slonimsky, *Twentieth Century*.)

184   JEROME V. REEL

Strohl, Aimee-Rita. *La Forêt de Broceliande*. Words: Charles Grandmougin. 1887. (Bellaing.)

Strong, George T. 'King Arthur'. Published: Geneva, Henn, 1922.

Stuppner, Hubert. 'Tristan: Ein Deutsches Nirwana'. Words: T. Box Zelenski. Published: Munich, Edition Modern, 1978.

Sturges, Perry MacKay. 'Avalon Waltz'. Published: Perry MacKay Sturges, 1948.

Suckling, Norman. *A Vision of Avalon*. Composed in 1928.

Sullivan, Arthur. 'Guinevere'. Words: L.H. Lewin. Published: London, J.B. Cramer, 1873.

Sullivan, Arthur. *King Arthur*. Incidental music to play by J. Comyns Carr. Première: Lyceum Theatre, London, 2 January 1895. Published: (Drama) London, Macmillan, 1895. Arranged for concert performance by W. Bendall, 1903.

Suppe, Franz von. *Lohengelb, oder Die Jungfrau vom Dragant*. Librettist: M.A. Grandjean e Costa. Première: Vienna, 28 November 1870. Published: Vienna, n.p., 1871.

Sussmayer, F.X. *Idris und Zenida*. Librettist: C.L. Giesecke. Première: Freihaustheater, Vienna, 11 May 1795. (Stieger, II, 601.)

Sutherland, Iain. 'Sadie and Her Magic Mr. Galahad'. 1968. (British Library.)

Sweeting, E.T. 'King Arthur' (Part Song). Words: Traditional. Published: London, Leonard, Gould and Bolter, 1949.

Sykes, H.H. 'King Arthur Ruled the Land'. Words: Traditional. Published: London, E. Arnold, 1929.

Taft, Linwood. *Galahad: A Pageant of the Holy Grail*. Published: Barnes and Noble, 1924.

Talbot, Howard with Herman Finck. *Vivien*. Librettist: Unknown. Première: England: Prince of Wales Theatre, Birmingham, UK, December 1915.

Tanner, David. 'Excalibur; Overture for Band'. Published: Melville, New York, Belwin-Mills, 1980.

Tate, Phyllis. 'The Lady of Shalott'. Words: Alfred, Lord Tennyson. Published: Oxford University Press, 1956.

Tesh, John. 'Avalon'. Published: Port Chester, New York, Cherry Lane Music, 1997.

Thiessen, Heinz. *Merlin*. Librettist: Carl Immermann. Première: Volkstheater, Berlin, October 1918.

Thomas, Andrew. 'Merlin'. Published: Newton Center, Margun, 1989.

Thomas, Vincent. *Enid*. Incidental music to a play by Ernest Rhys. Première: Court Theatre, London, 24 November 1908. Published: London, Boosey and Co., 1913.

Thomas, Vincent. *Gwenevere*. Incidental music to a play by Ernest Rhys. Première: Coronet Theatre, London, 13 November 1905. Published: London, Boosey and Co., 1906.

Thomas, Vincent. *The Quest of the Holy Grail*. Incidental music to a play by Ernest Rhys. Première: Court Theatre, London, 7 March 1908. Published as *Masque of the Holy Grail*, London, Boosey and Co., 1908.

Thomas, Vincent. 'Nimue's Dance from *Quest of the Grail*'. Première: Glastonbury, 21 August 1914.

Thomas-Mifune, Werner. 'Fragment of *Parsifal*'. Published: Adleswil/Zurich. Edition Kunzelmann, 1988. [from *Parsifal*].

Titl, Emil. *Tristan*. Librettist: Weiten. Première: Burgtheater, Vienna, 19 November 1859. (Stieger, III, 1232.)

Torrent, C. *La Bretonne*. Librettist: Prunier. Première: 4 February 1898. (Stieger, I, 189.)

Tournemire, Charles. *Legend de Tristan*. (Slonimsky, *Twentieth Century*.)

Mayhew, Ralph. 'Good King Arthur'. Words: Traditional. Published: New York, Harper-Columbia, 1919.

Treharne, Bryceson. 'Olwen'. Words: H.E. Lewis. 1898. (British Library.)

Treharne, Bryceson. 'The Romance of Owain'. Words: (English) L. Henry; (Welsh) T. Gwynn Jones, Published: Llangollen, 1940. (British Library.)

Treharne, Bryceson. 'Montserrat in *Five Songs Composed for Baritone and Piano*'. Words: Arthur Symons. Published: New York, G. Shirmer, 1917.

Treharne, Bryceson. 'The Ravens of Owain'. Words: Leigh Vaughan Henry. Published: Rowlands, 1931.

Treharne, Bryceson. 'The Return of Arthur' in *Ten Dramatic and Descriptive Songs*. Published: New York, Composers' Music Corporation, n.d.

Trento, Vittorio. 'Canto Funebre alla Tomba di Perceval'. Words: C. Carovita. Published: London, n.p., 1912.

Tritsch, Jacques. *Perceval: ou, le destrier paladin, gardien d'honneur et de vertu*. Librettist: Leon Chancerel. Published: Paris, Le Hutte, c.1945.

True, Lyle C. 'Vivienne: A Caprice'. Published: San Francisco, CA, Sherman, Clay & Co., 1903.

Tutt, David. *The Bells of Lyonesse*. Librettist: Peter Scupham. Première: 1888. Published: Cambridge, Cambridge University Press, 1888.

Urswick, Christopher. 'The Wheel of Fortune'. Words: Alfred, Lord Tennyson. Published: London, Novello, 1902.

Vance, John. 'Swan Song' in *Junior Laurel Songs*. Published: Boston, C.C. Birchard & Co., 1916.

Various. *Youth's Quest for the Holy Grail*. Librettist: E. Harvey Herring. Première: Philadelphia, 1933. Published: Milwaukee, Morehouse, 1933.

Vaughan Williams, Ralph (adapted from). *Im Reich von Konig Artus, oder: Der Weg nach Avelon*. (Ballet). Book: Pierre Wyss. Première: Wiesbaden, 27 October 1987.

Ventadorr, Bernart de. 'The Testament of Tristan'. Recorded: Hyperion.

Veremans, Renaat. *Lanceloot en Sanderien*. Librettist: J. Diels. Première: Royal Flemish Opera, Antwerp, 13 September 1968. (Antwerp: Archief en museum voor het Vlaamse culturleven.)

Vernon, W. Carlile. *Merry Mr. Merlin; or Good King Arthur*. Librettist: E.H. Patterson and H. Grattan.

Vives, Amadeo. *Arthus*. Librettist: Trullot y Plana. Première: Teatro Novedades, Barcelona, 1895. (Slonimsky, 1971.)

Vogrich, Max W.K. *König Arthur*. Librettist: Max W.K. Vogrich. Première: Leipzig, 26 November 1893. Published: New York, G. Schirmer, 1893.

Voorn, Joop. 'Perceval et Blanchefleur'. (vocal). (Slonimsky, *Twentieth Century*.)

Wade, J.A. 'Too Late'. Words: Alfred, Lord Tennyson. 1878.

Wagner, Joseph. 'Merlin and Sir Boss'. Published: New York, Seesaw Music, 1978.

Wagner, Richard. *Lohengrin*. Librettist: Richard Wagner. Première: Grand Ducal Theatre, Weimar, 28 August 1850. Published: Leipzig, Breitkopf und Härtel, 1852.

Wagner, Richard. *Parsifal*. Librettist: Richard Wagner. Première: Festspielhaus, Bayreuth, 26 April 1882. Published: Mainz, B. Schotts Söhne, 1883.

Wagner, Richard. *Tristan und Isolde*. Librettist: Richard Wagner. Première: Royal Court and National Theatre, Munich, 10 June 1865. Published: Leipzig, Breitkopf und Härtel, 1860.

Wakeman, Rick. *Myths and Legends of King Arthur and the Knights of the Round Table*. Librettist: Rick Wakeman. Published: London, Rondor Music, 1974.

Wandersleb, A. *Lanval*. Librettist: L.B. Wolfe. Première: Gotha, 1852 (concert version). (Tower, 371 and 874.)

Warlock, Peter. *Valses Rêves d'Isolde* (Piano). Preface by Fred Tomlinson, 1976. (British Library.)

Warren, Elinor Remick. *The Passing of King Arthur*. Librettist: Alfred, Lord Tennyson. Première: Los Angeles, CA, 1940. Published: New York, Novello, 1939.

Weir, A.E. 'King Arthur'. Words: Traditional. Published: New York, Mumil.

Weisman, Ben. 'This is Living'. 1962. (British Library.) [from *Kid Galahad*].

Welcher, Dan. 'The Visions of Merlin' (Suite). Published: Bryn Mawr, PA, Theodore Presser, 1980. Première: Sunriver, OR, 23 August 1980.

Wells, Jack. 'When Roses Bloom in Avalon'. Words: Alfred Bryan. 1914. (British Library.)

White, David. 'Elegy and Exaltation'. Published: Southern Music Co., 1991.

Whitehead, Gillian. *Tristan and Isolt*. Librettists: M. Hill and M. Crowthers. Première: British Broadcasting Corporation, April 1980. Published: Wellington, NZ, Price Milbourne Music, 1977.

Whithorne, Emerson. 'Fata Morgana'. Published: New York, Cos Cob, 1930.

Whittaker, W.G. 'Come Follow Me'. Words: John Dryden. Published: London, Oxford University Press, 1928.

Wickede, F. von and Morena, C. *Fantasie: Parsifal*. Published: Mainz, B. Schotts Söhne, 1914.

Wigan, Arthur Cleveland. 'Elaine: When Thou Art Gay Forget Me' (Canzonet). Published: Dover, n.p., 1860.

Wilcock, F.S. 'In the Days of Good King Arthur'. 1928. (British Library.)

Willan, Healey. 'Elaine's Song'. Words: Alfred, Lord Tennyson. 1902.

Williams, Charles 'Dream of Olwen'. (Piano; also vocal versions). Published: London, Wright, 1947, 1949.

Williams, John. *Indiana Jones and the Last Crusade*. (Film score). 1989.

Williams, Joseph (a.k.a. Florian Pascal). *Cymbia, or the Magic Thimble*. Text: Harry Paulton. Première: Royal Strand Theatre, London, 24 March 1883. Published: London, Joseph Williams, n.d.

Williams, Julius P. *Guinevere*. Librettist: Anita Rosenau. Rosenau did two other Arthur libretti as part of a proposed trilogy.

Williams, W.S. Gwynn 'The Flower Maiden' (from *Two Celtic Songs*). Words: Ernest Rhys. Published: London, CR, 1930.

Williams, W.S. Gwynn. 'Arthur yn Cyfodi' ("Arthur is Arising"). Words: Silyn Roberts. 1924 (Lacy, *New Arthurian Encyclopedia*, 338.)

Williams, W.S. Gwynn. 'Morning Light' (from *Two Celtic Songs*). Words: Ernest Rhys. Published: London, 1924.

Williams, W.S. Gwynn. 'Ymadawiad Arthur' ("The Passing of Arthur"). Composed, 1935. (Lacy, *New Arthurian Encyclopedia*, 338.)

Wingate, M. *When Abbots Ruled at Avalon*. 1923.

Winn, W. *O Morning Star that Smilest*. Words: Alfred, Lord Tennyson. Published: London, 1873.

Woeltge, Louise. *Sweet is True Love*. Words: Alfred, Lord Tennyson. Published: Stanford, Connecticut: Klock, 1903.

Woestijne, David van de. *Graal 68 ou L'Impromptu de Gand*. Librettist unknown. Première: Ghent, 1968. (Grove, XX, 471.)

Wohl, Yehuda. *Fata Morgana*. (orchestral). (Slonimsky, *Twentieth Century*.)

Wood, Charles. *Fortune and Her Wheel*. Words: Alfred, Lord Tennyson. Published: London, Boosey and Hawkes, 1927.

Woodgate, Leslie. 'Merlin'. Words: M. Collins. Published: London, Stainer and Bell, 1924.

Wright, Denis S.S. *Glastonbury Overture.* Published: London, W. Paxton, 1953.

Wright, Denis S.S. *Tintagel: Symphonic Suite for Brass Band.* Published: London, R. Smith, 1956.

Wright, Julian. 'Ode to Olwen'. 1938. (British Library.)

Zaerr, Laura. *The Harper in the Hall.* Published: Rosewood Music, 1998.

Zumsteeg, J.R. *Die Pfauenfest.* Librettist: Friedrich A.C. Werthes. Première: Hoftheater, Stuttgart, 24 February 1801.

Zylstra, Dick W. *A Computer Whiz at King Arthur's Court.* Librettist: M.S. Zylstra. Première: 1990. Published: Louisville, Aran.

[Anonymous.] 'Am Bròn Binn' ("The Sweet Sorrow"). Celtic Traditional. Published: Linda Gowans (Lacy, *New Arthurian Encyclopedia*, 338.)

[Anonymous.] 'Arta Ef A Dhe' ("He Shall Come Again"). Celtic Traditional.

[Anonymous.] 'Laoidh am Amadain Mhóir' ("Lay of the Great Fool"). Traditional. (Lacy, *New Arthurian Encyclopedia*, 338.) See Linda Gowans, *Gaelic Arthurian Literature* on the Camelot Project website for books giving tunes for this.

[Anonymous.] 'Oh Say Not That Arthur'. (British Library).

[Anonymous.] *A Mask of King Arthur's Knights.* 1539. (Lacy, *New Arthurian Encyclopedia*, 315.)

[Anonymous.] *Jack the Giant Killer and Tom Thumb; or Harlequin King Arthur.* Librettist Frank W. Green. Première: Royal Surrey Theatre, London, 1 November 1876.

[Anonymous.] *Jack the Giant Killer; or the Knights of the Round Table.* Première: Royal Surrey Theatre, London, April 1846.

[Anonymous.] *King Arthur.* Librettist: Arthur Earle and E.H. Sim. Première: James Street Theatre, London, 16 May 1895.

[Anonymous.] *King Arthur: A Pantomine Adventure in Camelot.* Librettist: Paul Reakes. Published: New York, S. French, 1997.

[Anonymous.] *Le Laquais d'Arthur.* Librettist unknown. (L'Opera Archives AJ13/1049.)

[Anonymous.] *Merlin in Love; or Youth Against Magic.* Librettist: Aaron Hill. Published: London, T. Lowds, 1760.

[Anonymous.] *Merlin; or The Enchanter of Stonehenge.* Première: Sadler's Wells, London 13 May 1767. Published: London, Watts, 1734.

[Anonymous.] *Merlin's Cave; or Harlequin's Masquerade.* Première: Royal Amphitheatre, London, 11 April 1814.

[Anonymous.] *Noble Acts Newly Found of Arthur of the Round Table.* Librettist: Thomas Deloney. Harvard, MA: Houghton Library.

[Anonymous.] *Os Encantos de Merlin.* Librettist Unknown. Première: Casa De Theatro Publicio Da Montaria, Lisbon, 1741. Published: Lisbon, S.T. Ferrevia, 1741.

[Anonymous.] *Prince Henry's Barriers.* Librettist: Ben Jonson. Première: London, 1610.

[Anonymous.] *Princely Pleasures.* Librettist: George Gascoigne. Première: 1576.

[Anonymous.] *Taliesen.* Librettist: Richard Hovey. Published: Boston, MA, Small, Maynard and Co., 1899.

[Anonymous.] *The Birth of Galahad.* Librettist: Richard Hovey. Published: Boston, Small, Maynard and Co., 1900.

[Anonymous.] *The Dragon-King.* Librettist: John Fitzgerald Pennie. Published: London, Maunder.

[Anonymous.] *The Island of the Mighty.* (Ballet-drama). Book: John Arden and Margaret Darcy. 1972.

[Anonymous.] *The Marriage of Guinevere*. Librettist: Richard Hovey. Published: Boston, MA, Small, Maynard and Co., 1900.

[Anonymous.] *The Marriage of Sir Gawaine*. Librettist: John Seally. Text published in *European Magazine*, 1782.

[Anonymous.] *The Quest of Merlin*. Librettist: Richard Hovey. Published: Boston, MA, Small, Maynard and Co., 1898.

[Anonymous.] *Ye Seconde Parte of Ye Tragycall Hysttorie of Thomas Thumb*. Première: English Opera, London, 12 June 1840. London, British Library.

[Various]. *The Vision of Sir Launfal: A Pageant*. Librettist: D. Clark, D. and G. Unverzagt. Première: 1928. Published: New York, Barnes, 1928.

List of Abbreviations

Archives de l'Opéra de Paris: Inventaire sommaire. Paris, France: Bibliothèque Nationale, 1988.

Avery, Emmett, et al. *The London Stage: A Critical Introduction*. Carbondale, Illinois: Southern Illinois University Press, 1968.

Bellaing, Vefa De. *Dictionnaire des Compositeurs de Music en Bretagne*. Nantes: Quest Editions, n.d.

Clement, Felix and Pierre Larousse. *Dictionnaire des Opéras*. Paris, France: Grand Dictionnaire Universel, n.d.

Fiske, Roger. *English Theatre Music in the Eighteenth Century*. New York: Oxford University Press, 1986.

Ganzl, Kurt. *The British Musical Theatre*. Oxford, England: Oxford University Press, 1986. Two volumes.

Gillis, Don and Barre Hill. *List of American Operas Compiled for the American Opera Workshop of the National Music Camp*. Interlocken Press, 1959.

Gooch, Bryan N.S. and Thatcher, David S. *Musical Settings of Early and Mid-Victorian Literature*. New York: Garland, 1979.

Grove Sadie, Stanley, ed. *The New Grove Dictionary of Music and Musicians*. London, England: Macmillan Ltd., 1980. Twenty volumes.

Howell, Keir. *Arthurian Music List*. www.geocities.com/sunsetstrip/palladium/7195/arthur/arthur.html

Lacy, Norris J. et al. *The New Arthurian Encyclopedia*. New York: Garland, 1996.

Lacy, Norris J. and Geoffrey Ashe. *The Arthurian Handbook*. New York: Garland, 1988.

Nicoll, Allardyce. *The History of English Drama, 1660–1900*. Cambridge, England: Cambridge University Press, 1959 and following. Six volumes.

Northouse, Cameron. *Twentieth Century Opera in England and the United States*. New York: G.K. Hall, 1976.

Parsons, Charles H. Mellen: *Opera Reference Index*. Lewiston, NY, Edwin Mellen Press, 1986. 4 volumes.

Slonimsky, Nicholas. *Baker's Biographical Dictionary of Musicians*. 8th Edition; New York: Schirmer Books, 1992.

Slonimsky, Nicholas. *Baker's Biographical Dictionary of the Twentieth Century Classical Musicians*. (ed. Laura Kuhn). New York: Schirmer Books, 1997.

Stieger, Franz. *Opernlexicon: Titel-Katalog*. Tutzing: Verlegt bei Hans Schneider, 1975. Three volumes.

Tower, John. *Dictionary Catalogue of Operas and Operettas*. New York: Da Capo, 1967.

Index

(a) Major Arthurian characters

Anfortas, 27, 32, 33
Arthur, 4, 12, 13, 14, 15, 16, 17, 18, 21, 39, 40,
   41, 46, 47, 57, 58, 74, 75, 76, 77, 78, 79, 80,
   81, 83, 84, 87, 88, 89, 93, 96, 97, 98, 99, 102,
   128, 146, 151, 152, 153, 154, 155, 157

Elaine, 4, 100, 103

Galahad, 98, 99, 103, 147
Gareth, 39, 40, 46
Gawain, 7, 100, 128, 129, 132, 133, 136
Guinevere, 3, 4, 39, 40, 41, 46, 47, 48, 58,
   68, 72, 73, 75, 77, 78, 79, 80, 81, 82, 84,
   85, 86, 96, 97, 98, 99, 100, 152, 153, 154,
   155
Gurnemanz, 32, 33

Igraine, 96
Iseult (Isolde), 1, 5, 6, 24, 28, 30, 104, 113

Klingsor, 33, 34
Kundry, 28, 33

Lancelot, 4, 39, 40, 41, 46, 47, 48, 58, 72, 74,
   75, 77, 78, 79, 80, 81, 82, 83, 84, 85, 86,
   87, 97, 98, 99, 100, 152, 153, 154, 155

Mark, 2, 28, 75
Merlin, 2, 4, 6, 15, 16, 20, 21, 57, 58, 66, 84,
   96, 97, 113, 157
Mordred, 39, 40, 46, 47, 73, 77, 78, 80, 84, 85,
   87, 98, 100, 154
Morgan le Fay, 128, 129, 132, 146, 154

Parsifal, 3, 27, 31, 33, 34

Tristan, 1, 2, 3, 6, 24, 27, 28, 29, 30, 31, 104,
   105, 108, 111, 111, 113

Uther, 96

Vivian (Nimue, Nivian, Viviane) 4, 57, 58,
   59, 66, 96, 97, 113

(b) Musical works discussed

Albéniz, Isaac: Merlin, 3, 51, 53, 56, 57, 58,
   59, 60

Bax, Arnold: Tintagel, 4
Birtwistle, Harrison: Sir Gawain and the Green
   Knight, 7, 27–144
Boughton, Rutland: Arthur of Britain cycle, 5,
   92
Boughton, Rutland: Galahad, 98, 99, 102
Boughton, Rutland: The Death of Arthur
   (Avalon), 93, 98, 99, 102
Boughton, Rutland: The Holy Grail (Galahad),
   95
Boughton, Rutland: The Lily Maid, 94, 95, 98,
   102
Boughton, Rutland: The Queen of Cornwall, 5,
   95, 104
Boughton, Rutland: The Round Table, 94,
   101
Boughton, Rutland: Uther and Igraine (The
   Birth of Arthur), 93, 94, 96, 101
Britten, Benjamin: King Arthur (incidental
   music), 5

Britten, Benjamin: The Sword in the Stone
   (incidental music), 5
Bruns, George: The Sword in the Stone
   (incidental music), 157

Chausson, Ernest: Le roi Arthus, 4, 61–89
Chausson, Ernest: Viviane, 4, 65

Elgar, Sir Edward: King Arthur (incidental
   music), 4, 5

Innes, Neil: Monty Python and the Holy Grail
   (incidental music), 158

Lamento di Tristano, 1
Lerner, Alan Jay and Loewe, Frederick:
   Camelot, 7, 152–156
Lyrics in Prose Tristan manuscript, 1, 2

Martin, Frank: Le vin herbé, 6
Messiaen, Olivier: Cinq Rechants, 108, 111, 113
Messiaen, Olivier: Harawi, 107, 111, 113

Messiaen, Olivier: *Tristan et Yseult* (incidental music), 107
Messiaen, Olivier: *Turangalila Symphonie*, 105, 109, 110, 111, 112, 113, 114–125

Parry, Hubert: *Guenever*, 3, 35, 39, 39–44, 46
Purcell, Henry: *King Arthur*, 2, 9, 12, 13, 14, 15, 16, 17, 18, 19, 20, 21

Quest for Camelot, 159

Rodgers, Richard and Hart, Lorenz: *A Connecticut Yankee at King Arthur's Court*, 145–151

Sachs, Hans: *meisterlieder*, 2
Sullivan, Sir Arthur: *King Arthur* (incidental music), 3, 4

Vives, Amadeu: *Artus*, 54

Wagner, Richard: *Lohengrin*, 2, 24, 25
Wagner, Richard: *Parsifal*, 3, 23, 24, 25, 27, 28, 31, 32, 33, 34, 37
Wagner, Richard: *Tristan und Isolde*, 3, 23, 24, 26, 27, 28, 29, 30, 31, 34, 35, 67, 71, 79, 114

ARTHURIAN STUDIES

    I ASPECTS OF MALORY, edited by Toshiyuki Takamiya and Derek Brewer
   II THE ALLITERATIVE MORTE ARTHURE: A Reassessment of the Poem, edited by Karl Heinz Göller
  III THE ARTHURIAN BIBLIOGRAPHY, I: Author Listing, edited by C. E. Pickford and R. W. Last
   IV THE CHARACTER OF KING ARTHUR IN MEDIEVAL LITERATURE, Rosemary Morris
    V PERCEVAL: The Story of the Grail, by Chrétien de Troyes, translated by Nigel Bryant
   VI THE ARTHURIAN BIBLIOGRAPHY, II: Subject Index, edited by C. E. Pickford and R. W. Last
  VII THE LEGEND OF ARTHUR IN THE MIDDLE AGES, edited by P. B. Grout, R. A. Lodge, C. E. Pickford and E. K. C. Varty
 VIII THE ROMANCE OF YDER, edited and translated by Alison Adams
   IX THE RETURN OF KING ARTHUR, Beverly Taylor and Elisabeth Brewer
    X ARTHUR'S KINGDOM OF ADVENTURE: The World of Malory's Morte Darthur, Muriel Whitaker
   XI KNIGHTHOOD IN THE MORTE DARTHUR, Beverly Kennedy
  XII LE ROMAN DE TRISTAN EN PROSE, tome I, edited by Renée L. Curtis
 XIII LE ROMAN DE TRISTAN EN PROSE, tome II, edited by Renée L. Curtis
  XIV LE ROMAN DE TRISTAN EN PROSE, tome III, edited by Renée L. Curtis
   XV LOVE'S MASKS: Identity, Intertextuality, and Meaning in the Old French Tristan Poems, Merritt R. Blakeslee
  XVI THE CHANGING FACE OF ARTHURIAN ROMANCE: Essays on Arthurian Prose Romances in memory of Cedric E. Pickford, edited by Alison Adams, Armel H. Diverres, Karen Stern and Kenneth Varty
 XVII REWARDS AND PUNISHMENTS IN THE ARTHURIAN ROMANCES AND LYRIC POETRY OF MEDIEVAL FRANCE: Essays presented to Kenneth Varty on the occasion of his sixtieth birthday, edited by Peter V. Davies and Angus J. Kennedy
XVIII CEI AND THE ARTHURIAN LEGEND, Linda Gowans
  XIX LAƷAMON'S BRUT: The Poem and its Sources, Françoise H. M. Le Saux
   XX READING THE MORTE DARTHUR, Terence McCarthy, reprinted as AN INTRODUCTION TO MALORY
  XXI CAMELOT REGAINED: The Arthurian Revival and Tennyson, 1800–1849, Roger Simpson
 XXII THE LEGENDS OF KING ARTHUR IN ART, Muriel Whitaker

XXIII GOTTFRIED VON STRASSBURG AND THE MEDIEVAL TRISTAN LEGEND: Papers from an Anglo-North American symposium, *edited with an introduction by Adrian Stevens and Roy Wisbey*

XXIV ARTHURIAN POETS: CHARLES WILLIAMS, *edited and introduced by David Llewellyn Dodds*

XXV AN INDEX OF THEMES AND MOTIFS IN TWELFTH-CENTURY FRENCH ARTHURIAN POETRY, *E. H. Ruck*

XXVI CHRÉTIEN DE TROYES AND THE GERMAN MIDDLE AGES: Papers from an international symposium, *edited with an introduction by Martin H. Jones and Roy Wisbey*

XXVII SIR GAWAIN AND THE GREEN KNIGHT: Sources and Analogues, *compiled by Elisabeth Brewer*

XXVIII CLIGÉS by Chrétien de Troyes, *edited by Stewart Gregory and Claude Luttrell*

XXIX THE LIFE AND TIMES OF SIR THOMAS MALORY, *P. J. C. Field*

XXX T. H. WHITE'S *THE ONCE AND FUTURE KING, Elisabeth Brewer*

XXXI ARTHURIAN BIBLIOGRAPHY, III: 1978–1992, Author Listing and Subject Index, *compiled by Caroline Palmer*

XXXII ARTHURIAN POETS: JOHN MASEFIELD, *edited and introduced by David Llewellyn Dodds*

XXXIII THE TEXT AND TRADITION OF LAƷAMON'S *BRUT, edited by Françoise Le Saux*

XXXIV CHIVALRY IN TWELFTH-CENTURY GERMANY: The Works of Hartmann von Aue, *W. H. Jackson*

XXXV THE TWO VERSIONS OF MALORY'S *MORTE DARTHUR*: Multiple Negation and the Editing of the Text, *Ingrid Tieken-Boon van Ostade*

XXXVI RECONSTRUCTING CAMELOT: French Romantic Medievalism and the Arthurian Tradition, *Michael Glencross*

XXXVII A COMPANION TO MALORY, *edited by Elizabeth Archibald and A. S. G. Edwards*

XXXVIII A COMPANION TO THE *GAWAIN*-POET, *edited by Derek Brewer and Jonathan Gibson*

XXXIX MALORY'S BOOK OF ARMS: The Narrative of Combat in *Le Morte Darthur, Andrew Lynch*

XL MALORY: TEXTS AND SOURCES, *P. J. C. Field*

XLI KING ARTHUR IN AMERICA, *Alan Lupack and Barbara Tepa Lupack*

XLII THE SOCIAL AND LITERARY CONTEXTS OF MALORY'S *MORTE DARTHUR, edited by D. Thomas Hanks Jr*

XLIII THE GENESIS OF NARRATIVE IN MALORY'S *MORTE DARTHUR, Elizabeth Edwards*

XLIV GLASTONBURY ABBEY AND THE ARTHURIAN TRADITION, *edited by James P. Carley*

XLV THE KNIGHT WITHOUT THE SWORD: A Social Landscape of Malorian Chivalry, *Hyonjin Kim*

XLVI   ULRICH VON ZATZIKHOVEN'S *LANZELET*: Narrative Style and Entertainment, *Nicola McLelland*

XLVII   THE MALORY DEBATE: Essays on the Texts of *Le Morte Darthur*, *edited by Bonnie Wheeler, Robert L. Kindrick and Michael N. Salda*

XLVIII MERLIN AND THE GRAIL: *Joseph of Arimathea, Merlin, Perceval*: The Trilogy of Arthurian romances attributed to Robert de Boron, *translated by Nigel Bryant*

XLIX   ARTHURIAN BIBLIOGRAPHY IV: 1993–1998, Author Listing and Subject Index, *compiled by Elaine Barber*

L   DIU CRÔNE AND THE MEDIEVAL ARTHURIAN CYCLE, *Neil Thomas*

LI   NEW DIRECTIONS IN ARTHURIAN STUDIES, *edited by Alan Lupack*